SPORTS STARS

SERIES 2

SPORTS STARS
SERIES 2

volume 2
l–z

Edited by
Michael A. Paré

AN IMPRINT OF GALE

SPORTS STARS, SERIES 2

Edited by *Michael A. Paré*

Staff

Julie L. Carnagie, *U·X·L Assistant Developmental Editor*
Carol DeKane Nagel, *U·X·L Managing Editor*
Thomas L. Romig, *U·X·L Publisher*

Margaret A. Chamberlain, *Permissions Associate (Pictures)*
The Graphix Group, *Typesetting*

Shanna P. Heilveil, *Production Assistant*
Evi Seoud, *Assistant Production Manager*
Mary Beth Trimper, *Production Director*

Cynthia Baldwin, *Product Design Manager*
Michelle Dimercurio, *Art Director*

Paré, Michael A.
    Sports stars II / Michael A. Paré.
        p.   cm.
    Includes bibliographical references and index.
    Contents: v. 1. A-K — v. 2. L-Z.
    Summary: Contains sixty biographical sketches of popular athletes active in a variety of sports.
    ISBN 0-7876-0867-X (set). — ISBN 0-7876-0868-8 (v. 1). — ISBN 0-7876-0869-6 (v. 2)
        1. Athletes—Biography—Juvenile literature.   [1. Athletes.]
I. Title.
GV697.A1P325   1996
796' .092' 2—dc20
[B]

96-10646
CIP
AC

Cover photographs (clockwise from top left): Mary Pierce, Grant Hill, Drew Bledsoe and Gail Devers, reproduced by permission of AP/Wide World Photos.

∞™ This book is printed on acid-free paper that meets the minimum requirements of American National Standard for Information Sciences—Permanence Paper for Printed Library Materials, ANSI Z39.48-1984.

Printed in the United States of America

Contents

Biographical Listings
VOLUME 1: A-K

Biographical Listings
VOLUME 2: L-Z

Athletes by Sport

Italic numerals indicate series.

BASKETBALL

BICYCLE RACING

BOXING

FIGURE SKATING

FOOTBALL

GOLF

GYMNASTICS

HOCKEY

HORSE RACING

SKIING

SOCCER

Reader's Guide

Sports Stars, Series 2, presents biographies of sixty amateur and professional athletes, including Grant Hill, Michael Irvin, and Michelle Kwan, as well as two sports teams, the Colorado Silver Bullets and the *Mighty Mary* yachting team. Besides offering biographies of baseball, basketball, and football sports figures, *Sports Stars,* Series 2, provides increased coverage of athletes in a greater variety of sports, such as swimming, gymnastics, and yachting, and features biographies of women, including Sheryl Swoopes, Manon Rheaume, and Picabo Street, who have broken the sex barrier to participate in the male-dominated sports of basketball, hockey, and skiing.

Athletes profiled in *Sports Stars,* Series 2, meet one or more of the following criteria. The featured athletes are:

- Currently active in amateur or professional sports

- Considered top performers in their fields

- Role models who have overcome physical obstacles or societal constraints to reach the top of their professions.

Format

The sixty profiles of *Sports Stars,* Series 2, are arranged alphabetically over two volumes. Each biography opens with the birth date and place of the individual as well as a "Scoreboard" box listing the athlete's top awards. Every essay contains a "Growing Up" section focusing on the early life and motivations of the individual or team and a "Superstar" section highlighting the featured athlete's career. The profiles also contain portraits and often additional action shots of the individual or group. A "Where to Write" section listing an address and a list of sources for further reading conclude each profile. Additionally, sidebars containing interesting details about the individuals are sprinkled throughout the text.

Additional Features

Sports Stars, Series 2, includes a listing by sport of all the athletes featured in Series 1 and Series 2 as well as a cumulative name and subject index covering athletes found in both series.

Acknowledgments

The author would like to thank the U·X·L staff, especially Julie Carnagie, for her hard work and patience in helping finish *Sports Stars,* Series 2. Special thanks also to Daniel Power, who provided invaluable assistance in determining who would be profiled in *Sports Stars.* Finally, the author would like to thank his wife, Ellen, who made innumerable sacrifices so this project could be completed on time, and his daughter, Chloe, who will be a star in whatever she decides to do when she grows up.

Comments and Suggestions

We welcome your comments on this work as well as your suggestions for individuals to be featured in future editions of *Sports Stars.* Please write: Editor, *Sports Stars,* U·X·L, 835 Penobscot Bldg., Detroit, Michigan 48226-4094; call toll-free: 800-877-4253; or fax toll-free: 800-414-5043.

Photo Credits

The photographs featured in *Sports Stars,* Series 2, were received from the following sources:

AP/Wide World Photos: pp. 1, 11, 17, 21, 26, 32, 41, 48, 50, 59, 64, 67, 71, 73, 80, 88, 92, 97, 100, 109, 116, 124, 126, 133, 146, 148, 159, 163, 166, 189, 201, 203, 210, 217, 219, 227, 233, 235, 281, 283, 287, 290, 316, 318, 322, 325, 331, 333, 342, 348, 351, 359, 361, 369, 381, 389, 398, 401, 413, 415, 422, 425, 445, 450, 459, 462, 477, 484, 486, 493, 495, 504, 506, 512, 515, 524, 528, 536, 538; **Photograph by Scott Olson. Reuter/Archive Photos:** p. 9; **Reuters/ Bettmann:** pp. 24, 56, 245, 442, 452, 522; **Photograph by Gary Hershorn. Reuter/Archive Photos:** pp. 35, 182, 212; **UPI/Bettmann:** p. 82; **Photograph by Peter Jones. Reuter/Archive Photos:** p. 107; **Photograph by Tami L. Chappell. Reuter/Archive Photos:** p. 114; **Photograph by Jeff Christensen. Reuter/Archive Photos:** p. 136; **Photograph by Tony Quinn. Courtesy of ALLSPORT Photography USA Inc.:** p. 141; **Photograph by Rebecca Cook. Reuter/Archive Photos:** p. 159; **Reuters/Bettmann Newsphotos:** p. 174; **Photograph by Wolfgang Rattay.**

Reuter/Archive Photos: p. 183; **Photograph by Blake Sell. Reuter/Archive Photos:** p. 191; **Photograph by Fred Prouser. Reuter/Archive Photos:** p. 243; **Photograph by Brent Smith. Reuter/Archive Photos:** p. 307; **Photograph by Ray Stubblebine. Reuter/ Archive Photos:** p. 314; **Photograph by Masaharu Hatano. Reuter/ Archive Photos:** p. 340; **Photograph by Sue Ogrocki. Reuter/Archive Photos:** p. 371; **Photograph by Jack Dabaghian. Reuter/Archive Photos:** p. 379; **Courtesy of the Milwaukee Bucks:** p. 406; **UPI/Corbis-Bettmann:** p. 433, 435; **Courtesy of Texas Tech Sports Information. Used with permission:** p. 468; **Courtesy of Texas Tech University. Used with permission:** p. 470; **Photograph by: Susumu Takahashi. Reuters/Archive Photos:** p. 475; **Bettmann Newsphotos:** p. 531.

Alexi Lalas

1970—

At one point in his career Alexi Lalas considered giving up soccer. He had been unable to earn a position on a professional team in Europe and did not know what he was going to do with the rest of his life. Just when things seemed their worst, Lalas got an invitation to try out for the U.S. national team. The invitation cut short a possible career as a rock guitarist, but Lalas was back where he wanted to be—on the soccer field. During the 1994 World Cup tournament, held in the United States for the first time, Lalas became a star.

Growing Up

KICKING AROUND IN GREECE. Panayotis Alexander Lalas was born June 1, 1970, in Royal Oak, Michigan, a suburb of Detroit. His father, Demetrius, is a mechanical engineer and meteorologist, and his mother, Ann Woodworth, is a publisher. Lalas was six when his parents divorced, and he moved

"Through my career people have said there's no way you can play on the Olympic team, there's no way you can play on the National team, there's no way you can play in the World Cup.... But you know, here I am."—Alexi Lalas

with his father to Athens, Greece. It was in Greece that Lalas first became interested in soccer. Four years later he returned to Michigan to live with his mother and younger brother, Greg.

TWO-SPORT STAR. During the summer, Lalas played soccer on a local team that traveled around the state. In the winter he played what is really his favorite sport: hockey. Lalas attended Cranbrook Kingswood High School, a prestigious prep school. He led the school's hockey team to a state championship and was named Michigan Player of the Year in soccer. Despite his athletic success, only one college offered Lalas an athletic scholarship. That college was Rutgers University in New Jersey.

BEST IN THE LAND. Lalas continued to play both hockey and soccer at Rutgers. He led the varsity hockey team in scoring in 1988 and was the captain of the soccer team his last three seasons. After his sophomore season, Lalas decided to give up hockey and concentrate solely on soccer. He led Rutgers to the Final Four of the National Collegiate Athletic Association (NCAA) Soccer Tournament in 1989 and 1990. Lalas won the Hermann Award, awarded to the best college soccer player in the United States, after his senior season in 1991.

It was no surprise that the U.S. national team recruited Lalas after his graduation. He played on the gold medal-winning U.S. team at the Pan American Games in Cuba in 1991 and was a member of the 1992 U.S. Olympic team. One week before the Olympics began, however, Lalas broke his left foot. He played despite his injury, but his play was limited.

DOWN BUT NOT OUT. Looking for a career as a professional soccer player, Lalas went to Europe because there were no professional teams in the United States. He tried out with the Arsenals, an elite British team, but did not make the squad. "I

was sitting in a hotel room in London, all alone doing nothing," he recalled in the *New York Times Magazine*. "I had no team. If you're not an established international player, coming from the United States you have no credentials; you just sort of bum around and try to find someone to pick you up."

GUITAR HERO? Lalas returned to the United States and tried to figure out what to do. He thought about devoting more time to his rock band, the Gypsies. Lalas became interested in music as a child, learning how to play the piano, singing in choirs and barbershop quartets, and taking an interest in writing. He taught himself the guitar in college, and his group played at small clubs in New Jersey and New York City. The group also released a 12-song CD, *Woodlands,* on Alexi Lalas Records. Unfortunately, the record did not sell very well.

During the 1994 World Cup Lalas (center) slides past Bolivia's Jaaime Moreno.

BARBER OR BUST. Before the Gypsies headed out on the road, the U.S. national team called and offered Lalas a tryout. He impressed U.S. national team coach Bora Milutinovic, but Milutinovic had one requirement before he would let Lalas practice with the team—that Lalas cut his long hair. "It was a test," Lalas admitted in the *Detroit Free Press*. "Here I was, a 22-year-old punk, and Bora wanted to see how serious I was about soccer. For me to cut my hair was a big deal. I was really mad. But I wanted to play so badly." Lalas still had not made the team, but at least he had a chance if he improved. He soon grew back his long hair and trademark goatee beard and scored a big goal in a historic victory over England in 1993.

Superstar

WORLD CUP WONDER. The United States hosted the World Cup, the international soccer championship tournament, for the first time in 1994. The U.S. team had been steadily improving, but no one seriously believed they would be contenders against the best teams in the world. Lalas was now a starter, a standout defender and one of the team's highest scorers. When the upstart Americans defeated the powerful Colombian team, 2-1, Lalas became a star. He appeared on the *Tonight Show* and ABC's *Wide World of Sports*. Lalas also had an inch of his beard trimmed by David Letterman. "Whatever happens," Phil Hersh of the *Chicago Tribune* wrote, "Lalas will remain one for the books, a classic example of the instant stardom that can come to someone whose story is a little different."

The U.S. team advanced to the second, single-elimination round of the tournament. There they faced the powerful team from Brazil. The last time the United States had defeated Brazil in international competition was in 1930, and that was also the last time the Americans had even scored against the Brazilian team. "If we lose, nobody cares," Lalas told *Sports Illustrated*. "That is what we are supposed to do. But if Brazil loses. . . ."

The U.S. team did lose, 1-0, to the eventual champions, but Lalas had proved himself. He was the sole American representative on the World Cup All-Tournament team. "The spotlight of the World Cup has brought out the best in Lalas, both as a celebrity and player," Phil Hersh explained in the *Chicago Tribune.* "He has flinched from neither the demands of constant attention nor those of playing against some of the world's best attackers." Lalas was one of only five U.S. players to play every minute of every game in the World Cup.

"The whole summer is a blur," Lalas explained in *Sports Illustrated* after the World Cup. "The World Cup is a blur. I can't remember any of the particular things that happened. All I know is that I was having a blast, and it still hasn't stopped."

TURNS PRO. Lalas returned to Europe after the World Cup, but this time teams were fighting for his services. He eventually signed with Padua in Italy. "Now it is up to me to show I can play at this level," Lalas explained in *Newsweek.* Lalas, the first American to ever play in what is arguably the best professional league in the world, became an instant star in Italy. "There were all these fans," he told *Soccer America,* "with banners and singers and scarves, the whole bit. In the middle of the questions, they started a 'Lalas' cheer." His success in soccer has surprised even himself. "I never expected any of this," he said in *Sports Illustrated.* "I never set out to play professional soccer as a kid, much less play over here [in Italy]. I never had the dreams. That's why this is so crazy. I never would've thought of this in a million years." Lalas scored three goals during his first season in Italy, including two game winners.

OFF THE FIELD. Lalas and his girlfriend, Jill McNeal, currently live in Italy during soccer season. He is taking Italian language lessons so that he can better talk with his teammates. Lalas earned his bachelor's degree in English in 1991. He owns 12 guitars and sang the national anthem before a U.S.

national team match in 1994. Someday, he says, he hopes to return to the United States and play in an American professional soccer league. Lalas still competes for the United States in international competitions.

Hard work paid off for Lalas, who realizes he does not have the natural ability of many other players. "There are definitely guys on this team who have more skill in their pinky than I'll ever have in my whole life," he admitted in the *San Bernardino Sun*. "The key is to recognize your abilities and not overextend yourself." Lalas also has something to say to the people who have doubted him in the past. "Through my career," Lalas explained to the Reuters news agency, "people have said there's no way you can play on the Olympic team, there's no way you can play on the National team, there's no way you can play in the World Cup and have success. But you know, here I am."

Sources

Chicago Tribune, July 3, 1994; August 14, 1994.
Detroit Free Press, December 4, 1993; June 16, 1994; June 28, 1994.
Detroit News, March 27, 1994.
Los Angeles Times, November 8, 1993.
Newsweek, June 20, 1994; October 10, 1994.
New York Times Magazine, March 13, 1994.
People, June 6, 1994.
Soccer America, August 15, 1994.
Sports Illustrated, January 31, 1994; July 4, 1994; July 11, 1994; September 26, 1994.
Sports Illustrated for Kids, June 1995.
USA Today, July 24, 1994.
Additional information provided by U.S. Soccer Federation.

WHERE TO WRITE:
U.S. SOCCER FEDERATION,
1801-1811 S. PRAIRIE AVE.,
CHICAGO, IL 60616.

Rebecca Lobo

1973—

Every team starts the season undefeated, but very few finish without a loss. Only nine major college basketball teams, men's and women's, have ever finished the season without a loss. One of those teams is the 1994-95 Connecticut Lady Huskies, who won the National Collegiate Athletic Association (NCAA) Women's Championship with a 35-0 record. The main reason for their success was senior center Rebecca Lobo, voted the 1995 Women's Collegiate Player of the Year. Lobo overcame her mother's illness to become the player *Sports Illustrated* called "the post with the most."

Growing Up

FAMILY TREES. Rebecca Lobo was born October 16, 1973, in Hartford, Connecticut. Lobo's parents, Dennis and Ruth Ann, are school administrators. She got her height (six feet, four inches) from her parents. Lobo's mom is five feet eleven inches tall, and her father is six feet five inches. Her brother,

"I try to live my life the right way, like my parents taught me. If a kid wants to make you a role model, you're a role model."
—Rebecca Lobo

Jason, stands six feet ten inches and played basketball at Dartmouth. Lobo's sister, Rachel, is an assistant basketball coach at Salem State in Massachusetts. Lobo and her brother and sister played all sorts of sports together. "One of my favorite images of Rebecca is her in the homemade catcher's outfit she put together out of paper, with a football helmet on her head, with me pitching and Rachel swinging," Jason Lobo recalled in *Sports Illustrated*. Her parents call Lobo "Becca" for short.

Lobo gives credit to her parents for her determination. "In third grade, I was taking tap-dance lessons, and about six weeks before the recital I wanted to quit," Lobo told *People*. "My mom said, 'No, you're going to stay with it.' Well, I did it, and I was bad, too! But my parents never let their kids walk away from something because it was too hard."

Lobo's parents also taught their daughter about honesty. One time Lobo took an eraser she wanted from a neighbor, Mrs. Lukasik. "I told Rebecca that the eraser wasn't hers, and she had to return it," Mrs. Lobo recalled in the *New York Times*. "And I watched as she walked, sobbing, to Mrs. Lukasik's house. It broke my heart to see it, but I think it helped her understand right from wrong. And to think about other people."

LEARNS THE GAME. Lobo learned to play basketball in her family's backyard. "She's always been a gutsy player," Jason Lobo explained in *People*. Lobo joined her first team in fourth grade. She always had to play on boys' teams because there were no teams for girls. "Once I showed them I could play, they were great about it," Lobo recounted in *People*.

NO PONYTAILS. When Lobo was growing up, there were no role models for girls who wanted to play basketball. "It's not like on a Saturday or a Sunday you could turn a television on and see women's basketball," Lobo remembered in the *New York Times*. "So I didn't know a whole lot about it. I watched the boys play, but I couldn't picture myself there because no one on the court had a ponytail. No one was a female." Lobo never gave up her dream of playing professional basketball. She once even sent Boston Celtics president Red Auerbach a note saying she was going to be the first woman to play for the Celtics.

Lobo showed her talent in her first high school game. She scored 32 points for Southwick-Tolland Regional High. Lobo went on to become the leading scorer in Massachusetts high school history, in men's or women's play. She scored 2,710 points in her career. Lobo also proved herself an all-star in the classroom, graduating as her class salutatorian. She also played field hockey, ran track, and played softball.

FIELD HAND. When she was a teenager, Lobo worked five summers in the tobacco fields of Southwick, Massachusetts. She picked the tobacco and tied up the plants. Lobo did the hard work to help build her physical endurance and determination. "I would come home, my hamstrings [leg muscles] all tight, and just soak in the tub," Lobo recalled in *People*.

CHOOSES CONNECTICUT. More than 100 universities recruited Lobo. She chose the University of Connecticut, only 90 minutes from home. Her mom helped her make the decision, grilling college coaches who came to visit about why her daughter should attend their schools.

Lobo was a solid starter for the Huskies her first two seasons, averaging 14.3 and 16.7 points per game. But Lady Huskies coach Geno Auriemma felt she was not living up to her potential. He wanted her to be tougher and told her, according to *Sports Illustrated,* "We're at a crossroads. I can't reach you. If you want to leave, fine. Or you stay here, and I'll leave." Lobo listened, and made the effort to improve.

"I'LL TAKE CARE OF THIS." Lobo faced hard times in December 1993. She learned that her mom had breast cancer. "I had just played the best week of basketball of my life," Lobo

recalled in *People,* "and I met my mom in the bleachers after a game. She told me, and I started to cry. But Mom didn't. She said, 'You take care of your thing on the court. I'll take care of this.'"

Doctors removed a lump from Mrs. Lobo's breast, but then discovered that the cancer had spread. She had to have surgery to remove her breast. Mrs. Lobo then needed months of chemotherapy, a procedure using radiation to kill any remaining cancer. Chemotherapy has some bad side effects, as Lobo told *Sports Illustrated for Kids:* "After that came a hard moment for me—my mom came to a game wearing a wig. Chemotherapy had made her hair fall out. It hit me for the first time that she was very sick."

NUMBER ONE FAN. Despite her health problems, Lobo's mom continued to attend her daughter's games. Doctors told her not to go because of the large crowds at the games. "Some of the doctors said, 'We don't think you should be in crowds,'" Mrs. Lobo recalled in the *New York Times,* "and I said, 'Yeah, right.'" Lobo remembers talking to her mom about the problem. "When she said it to me [that she wanted to continue to come to the games] the first time, it hit me," Lobo told the same newspaper. "She said it was kind of like her therapy, to come here [to the games]. She gets all wrapped up in the games, the officiating. She loves it. It was kind of her way to escape thinking about it [her illness], but she was the one going through it."

Lobo wanted to help her mom, but there was not much she could do. "You have a helpless feeling," Lobo confessed in the *New York Times.* "What can you really do? It's not like I could have gone home and taken care of her, because she didn't really need to be taken care of." Mrs. Lobo is cancer-free now but has to have checkups every three months. "Scoring points means nothing compared to what she went through," Lobo con-

◀ *Lobo goes up for a shot during the 1994 NCAA Women's Final Four championship in Minneapolis.*

fessed in *People*. "I was scared, but it made me think my family means more to me than anything."

Superstar

TOUGH TICKET. By Lobo's junior season Connecticut Lady Huskies' tickets were hard to come by. Lobo had her best season so far as a junior. She averaged 19.2 points and 11.2 rebounds a game. Connecticut finished the season 30-3. The NCAA tournament invited the Lady Huskies, and they lost in the quarterfinals to the eventual champions, the University of North Carolina. "We had a chance to win," Lobo told the *Sporting News*. "It was really a dream season for us, we wanted to win every day so that any way our season ended would have been bad."

"LOBOCOP." Lobo earned the name "LoboCop" from Connecticut fans. The Lady Huskies averaged close to 8,000 fans every game. Teenage girls in the stands began wearing their hair in Lobo's trademark French braid and gave flowers to her mom to pass along to their favorite player. Lobo realized that she was a role model for many young children. "I first realized that I had become a role model when I was in college," Lobo explained in *Sports Illustrated for Kids*. "I try to live my life the right way, like my parents taught me. If a kid wants to make you a role model, you're a role model. You have to be aware of that when you make decisions."

PERFECTION. Lobo developed into an all-around player in her senior season. Teams tried to double-team her, but Lobo learned to pass to her teammates. "Rebecca understands what to do if they double-team her, if they do try to take her out of the game," Auriemma explained to the *New York Times*. Auriemma also said his star player's only weakness was that Lobo was too willing to pass the ball. He said he wanted her to be more selfish and shoot more.

The 1994-95 season was a dream come true for Lobo and the Lady Huskies. Connecticut firmly established themselves as the number one team in the country on January 16, 1995, when they defeated then number one-ranked Tennessee, 77-66. The team stayed on the floor at the University of Connecticut's Gampel Pavilion after the game listening to the crowd sing Aretha Franklin's "Respect." "I could never imagine this day would happen: 8,000 people singing 'Respect,' even though most of them don't know the words," Lobo told *Time*. Later in the season, Lobo's parents took the floor with her during Senior Night. The crowd gave Lobo, and her mom, a standing ovation.

PLAYER OF THE YEAR. Lobo finished the season averaging 17.3 points, 10.1 rebounds, and 3.5 blocks per game. Because Connecticut beat their opponents by an average of 35 points per game, Lobo only played 28 minutes of the 40-minute games. She became a two-time basketball and academic All-American, only the second player to achieve this rare double feat. Lobo made the dean's list every semester at Connecticut. She also won every player of the year award given to women collegiate players for the 1994-95 season.

The end of her career at Connecticut made Lobo sad. "Right now everything's going so great, I'm not ready for it to end," Lobo admitted in *People*. "I just want it to end on a good note." Lobo made the most of her last few weeks in college, staying an hour after games to autograph basketballs for fans. She also answered numerous letters from young girls who looked at her as their role model. Many also wrote her with their personal stories of dealing with mothers who had breast cancer. "I try to answer every letter I get," Lobo says.

BOOMING BUSINESS

The 1995 season brought new respect to women's college basketball. Attendance grew from 1.3 million in the 1983-84 season to 3.6 million in 1994-95. "I liken the game to a beautiful flower that is only now coming into bloom," said sportswriter Mel Greenberg in *Time*. Experts also began to recognize that in many ways women's basketball is superior to the men's game. "It's more of a team sport," Tennessee coach Pat Summitt told *Time*. "You can watch the strategy evolve over the course of a game." Women players, because there is less opportunity to make a living playing basketball, have a much better graduation rate than their male counterparts. It is also much easier to get an autograph from one of the stars of the women's teams. And if you want to see dunks, Charlotte Smith of the University of North Carolina became the first women's player in history to throw one down during the 1995 season. Lobo has advice for anyone who thinks women's basketball is boring. "If you still think it's [women's basketball] boring, then I say, 'Go home,' because someone else can use your ticket," Lobo told the *Sporting News*.

STILL PERFECT. Connecticut won the Big East championship game over Seton Hall. The win improved Connecticut's record to 29-0, leaving them as the only Division I school, in men's or women's basketball, to be undefeated at the end of the 1994-95 regular season. Connecticut entered the 1995 NCAA Women's Basketball Tournament as the favorite, although they did not believe they were getting the recognition they deserved. The Lady Huskies remained undefeated by beating Maine and Louisiana Tech in the East Regional, earning themselves a spot in the Final Four. Connecticut defeated Stanford in the national semifinals. They were now in the championship game, where they would face a rematch with their archrival, Tennessee.

CHAMPIONSHIP GAME. Lobo's parents did not talk to their daughter before the final game. "We rarely do talk with her beforehand," her mom told the *New York Times*. "But we can guess how she's feeling: anxious." The game was a classic. Lobo picked up three first-half fouls and was forced to sit out the last 11 minutes and 58 seconds of the opening 20 minutes. "It's a helpless feeling knowing you can't go back in," Lobo admitted in the *New York Times*. Connecticut trailed 38-32 at the half. Their dream seemed to be slipping away.

Lobo picked up her fourth foul midway through the second half. One more and she would be out of the biggest game of her life. Her teammates, however, picked up the slack. Then Lobo exploded, scoring eight of the Huskies' next 11 points. "There comes a time when you just have to play," Lobo explained in the *Sporting News*. "I wasn't going to go out of the last game playing tentatively [scared to pick up another foul]." With 28.9 seconds left, Lobo stood at the free throw line facing the biggest shots of her life. Connecticut led 65-62. Lobo was shooting a one-on-one. If she made the first shot, she would get a second. If she missed, Tennessee was still in the game. Lobo made both free throws and her teammates mobbed her.

NATIONAL CHAMPIONS. Connecticut won the game and the national championship, 70-64. The Lady Huskies accomplished something only eight other Division I (major college) basketball teams and only one women's team had ever done: finish the season undefeated. Lobo finished the game with 17 points, 14 in the second half, and the media covering the game named her the Most Valuable Player (MVP) of the Final Four. She and her teammates cut down the nets, a traditional ritual for winning teams. "This is just a picture perfect way for someone to end their career," Lobo exclaimed in the *Sporting News.* "We're undefeated, we're national champions and I did it with the people I love."

COMPLETE PACKAGE. Lobo has the unique ability to play an all-around game. She is one of the all-time leaders in NCAA history in shot blocking, can score inside and outside, is an aggressive rebounder, and is one of the leaders on her team in assists. Lobo's real strength is her intensity. Opponents know that she will never back down. Lobo is also an outstanding leader. "She keeps the rest of the team loose and doesn't let any of the pressure get to her," Auriemma told *People.* Lobo's talent made her the player her teammates looked up to. "My team knows I can make a big play if we need one," Lobo explained in *People.* Lobo can best be described as a complete player. "What is she great at?" Auriemma asked in *Sports Illustrated.* "I can't say one thing. But the sum of all the parts is unreal."

OLYMPIC DREAM. Lobo looks forward to playing for the United States on the 1996 Olympic women's basketball team. She wants to help the team win on their home turf in Atlanta, Georgia. "That'll be a dream come true if I make [the national team]," Lobo told the *New York Times.*

After that, Lobo has to decide whether to continue her basketball career. She is considering playing in Europe, where

UNBLEMISHED

The Connecticut Lady Huskies became only the ninth Division I (major college) team in NCAA history to finish their season undefeated. The nine teams, the year they were undefeated, and their record for the season are give below.

	Women	
Year	**Team**	**Record**
1966	Texas	34-0
1995	Connecticut	35-0

	Men	
Year	**Team**	**Record**
1956	San Francisco	29-0
1957	North Carolina	32-0
1964	UCLA	30-0
1967	UCLA	30-0
1972	UCLA	30-0
1973	UCLA	30-0
1976	Indiana	32-0

women players can make six-figure salaries, because there are no women's professional basketball teams in the United States. "I don't know if it's definitely unfair," Lobo explained in the *New York Times*. "But it's a little frustrating. I've also always known that I wouldn't be playing in the NBA."

OFF THE COURT. Lobo is single and lives in Southwick, Massachusetts. After her basketball career is over, Lobo is considering a career in sports broadcasting. She visited ESPN, located near the Connecticut campus, and appeared on ESPN2. Despite a 3.65 grade point average in political science, Lobo told *People* that she does not want to be a politician. "Half of the people hate you, and I don't want that," she said. "Besides, I don't lie well enough to be a politician."

Lobo plays the saxophone. She applied for a Rhodes scholarship to attend the prestigious Oxford University in England. Lobo is a huge fan of rocker Bruce Springsteen, and her basketball idol is David Robinson. She has not had time for boyfriends because she has been so busy with basketball and her school work. The attention she has received amazes Lobo, so much so that she asked in the *New York Times*, "Don't these people realize I'm pretty boring?"

Sources

New York Times, March 6, 1995; April 3, 1995; April 28, 1995.
People, March 20, 1995.
Sporting News, February 6, 1995; April 3, 1995; April 10, 1995.
Sports Illustrated, March 20, 1995.
Sports Illustrated for Kids, June 1995; August 1995; September 1995.
Time, March 27, 1995.
Additional information provided by the University of Connecticut and USA Basketball.

WHERE TO WRITE:
C/O USA BASKETBALL,
5465 MARK DABLING BLVD.,
COLORADO SPRINGS, CO 80918.

Mighty Mary

For 144 years the America's Cup has been the most prestigious award in the sport of yachting. Usually, however, the competitors have been rich yacht club members, and until recently only three women had ever been members of an America's Cup sailing crew. That all changed in 1995. The crew of the ship *Mighty Mary* broke down barriers with every race they sailed in the 1995 America's Cup competition. The all-female team proved that women could do anything on a ship that a man can do and that through hard work and determination dreams can come true.

"Don't limit yourself—go for everything you can."—Courteney Becker-Dey, member of the Mighty Mary crew

Getting Started

AMERICA3. On March 9, 1994, Bill Koch, the man who had successfully defended the 1992 America's Cup for the United States, announced that he would support an all-female crew on his boat, *America3* (America Cubed) in the 1995 America's Cup. Koch had made a fortune estimated at more than

$600 million in the petroleum and chemical industries and offered $5 million and his experience and technology to the women's team.

Koch had skippered *America3* to a 4-1 victory over Il Moro di Venzia from Italy in the finals of the 1992 America's Cup. His competitors claimed he had bought the Cup in 1992, because he could spend a great deal of money to design the fastest boat. Koch disagreed. "You have to have a certain amount of money just to get in the game," he explained in the *Boston Globe* "But you can't buy the Cup. You have to win it."

WHY WOMEN? Koch admitted that part of the reason for supporting an all-female crew was to attract publicity to the America's Cup. "We did a big survey of corporations to find out America's perception [thinking] of the Cup," Koch stated in *Motor Boating and Sailing.* "We found out that the majority of the public perceived it as a rich man's sport sailed out on the backwaters of a snooty yacht club." Team captain Kimo Worthington added in *Time* magazine: "The sport needed a shot in the arm. It's boring to watch the same old guys going at it. The women make it interesting."

Koch, however, wanted to win and had confidence that he could put together the right crew. "If we can find the right combination of women with strength, the attitude and sailing talent—and put that together with superior technology—we can win," Koch confided in *Women's Sports and Fitness* magazine. He added in *Motor Boating and Sailing:* "It fits in with my philosophy that you don't have to be a star to win. You just have to have the right attitude."

BREAKING BARRIERS. For years yacht owners prevented women from racing in the America's Cup because they did not have sailing experience. The problem was that women could not get experience unless someone gave them a chance. Experts also argued that women did not have the strength necessary to lift the heavy sails and carry out the other split-second maneuvers needed to successfully win an important yachting race. Some men even argued that women on ships brought bad luck.

Koch set out to prove the experts wrong. He ran a trial for an all-women crew in 1992 with a boat called *Kanza*. He learned that with minor adjustments, such as placing equipment lower so that shorter women could reach it, an all-female crew could be just as successful as an all-male team. Brute strength, according to Koch, would not be a problem. "Only 2 percent of the race is about strength," he explained in *People* magazine. "This race is about teamwork, tactics, and a fast boat. The women have all three."

AMERICA'S CUP

The America's Cup is the most prestigious yacht race in the world. Queen Victoria of England donated the trophy as the prize for an international race in 1851, making the competition 144 years old in 1995. The first race took place in 1851, and the U.S. ship *America* defeated 14 British ships in a race around the Isle of Wight. American ships won the event in every competition after that until 1983. In that year Australia won the Cup, defeating Dennis Conner and his ship, *Liberty,* four races to three. Conner won back the Cup in 1987, and Bill Koch successfully defended the trophy in 1992.

PICKS CREW. In 1994 Koch and his coaches picked the crew for *America3* from 687 applicants. Women from across the United States called the number (800)WOMENA3 to apply. Koch picked the team for teamwork, attitude, and sailing ability. The media called the team the Cubens, after *America3* (cubed). Of the final 28 team members—16 of which make up the crew each race—selected on May 22, 1994, two had won Olympic sailing medals, three were former Yachtswomen of the Year, one was an aerospace engineer, another a world-class weight lifter, and yet another a professional bodybuilder.

After the crew was selected, they had only nine months to prepare to race. The women worked hard, going through a 13-hour schedule every day that included calisthenics, strength training, and sailing. "We're the underdogs, so we have to work 110 percent harder," helmsman Dawn Riley told *Time* magazine. To be successful, an America's Cup crew must work with precise teamwork because one mistake can

THE LAST TIME

The last time a woman had raced in the America's Cup finals was 1934. That year Harold S. Vanderbilt and his wife, Gertie, defeated T. O. M. Sopwith and his wife, Phyllis Brodie Gordon Sopwith. The wives held stopwatches for their husbands but did not actually sail themselves. Another woman, Hope Goddard Iselin, sailed in 1895, 1899, and 1903.

cost valuable time. Sailing can also be dangerous. One team member, Hannah Swett, had the tip of her little finger torn off when a piece of rope wrapped around it.

PUBLICITY STUNT? Many experts and racing fans looked at the *America3* crew as a publicity stunt and did not give them credit for their sailing ability. "These boats aren't all that difficult to sail," J. J. Isler remarked in *Women's Sports and Fitness*. "On one of the first days we sailed them, it was embarrassing. We went out to do a demonstration for the press, and the people watching seemed to be holding their breath. We did one tack—a basic turn—and they all started clapping. What did they expect, that just because we're women we wouldn't be able to handle an America's Cup boat?"

SKIPPER. Isler earned a spot as one of the *America3* skippers. Twice she had earned Rolex Yachtswoman of the Year honors, and she held a world ranking of eighteenth among men and women skippers in match (one-on-one) racing. Isler began sailing when her father gave her a boat at age four. She went on to become the first woman captain of the Yale University sailing team and won a bronze medal at the 1992 Summer Olympics in Barcelona, Spain. Sailing for the America's Cup excited Isler. "I never thought it would happen," she admitted in *People* magazine. "This gives us a chance to finally see if we can beat the guys."

SIREN SAILS. Shelly Beattie, best known as Siren on the television show *American Gladiators,* made the team as a grinder. The grinders are responsible for turning the winches that raise the 1,000-pound sails. They must be extremely strong, and Beattie is a weight lifter. She won the U.S. bodybuilding championship in 1992 and is a former Ms. Olympia finalist.

Beattie was also different from the rest of the crew because she is 90 percent deaf. She had to communicate with her teammates with hand signals and through an interpreter. "I didn't want them to treat me as if I'm handicapped," Beattie said in *Sports Illustrated*. Beattie loved her new sport. "You can't imagine how beautiful it is," she told *People* magazine. "I'll definitely continue to sail when this is over. There's such a sense of freedom out there on the water."

TROUBLESHOOTER. Dawn Riley captained the coed sailing team at Michigan State University. In 1989-90 she sailed with an all-women crew on the boat *Maiden* in the Whitbread Round-the-World race (they finished third) and she captained the all-women crew of the ship *Heineken* in the same race in 1993-94. In 1992 she was a backup navigator for Koch and the only female sailor in the America's Cup competition.

Riley's job on *America3* was crew boss, the person responsible for taking care of any problems aboard the boat as they came up. "We need Dawn to help out all over the boat; everyone else has only been doing this for nine months," team captain Kimo Worthington told *Sports Illustrated*. The chance to sail in the America's Cup was a dream come true for Riley. She stated in *People* magazine, "It's what I do. It's who I am. This whole thing is the opportunity of a lifetime."

GETTING FEET WET. The *America3* team got its first taste of international competition in the America's Cup Class World Championships in November 1994, on the same waters near San Diego, California, where the America's Cup races were scheduled to be held. They finished second in the competition against the best sailors in the world. The Australian team, led by John Bertrand, the first skipper from outside the United States to win the America's Cup (in 1983), won the event. "We showed them they better take us seriously," Isler exclaimed in *Time* magazine.

Their performance in the world championships gave the team confidence. "There were a lot of doubters on the outside and even a little corner of everyone's mind on the inside that said, 'Can we do this?'" Anna Seaton-Huntington, an Olympic rowing medalist, admitted in *Newsweek*. "Now I really believe we're going to win."

THE MAN TO BEAT. More impressive, the women's team defeated Dennis Conner and his *Stars and Stripes* boat in three of the championship's four races. Conner had the most experience in the America's Cup of any skipper in history. He won his first Cup in 1974 on the boat *Courageous.* In 1983 he became the first American skipper to lose the Cup, as Australia defeated his *Liberty* crew, four races to three. Four years later he traveled to Australia and won the Cup back, the first skipper to win the Cup back after losing it. Conner successfully defended the America's Cup in 1988 against New Zealand, but he lost to Koch in 1992 before the finals. A win in the 1995 defender trials would make Conner the first skipper to sail in five Cup finals.

Superstar

WINS FIRST. The races began in January. Three U.S. teams competed in a round-robin tournament to decide who would defend the Cup for the United States. Besides *America3* and Conner's *Stars and Stripes,* the PACT 95 team and their boat, *Young America,* skippered by Olympic sailing gold medalist Kevin Mahaney, also were in contention. Eight teams from outside the United States also battled to earn the right to challenge the U.S. team. Two teams each came from Australia, France, and New Zealand; Japan and Spain also provided teams.

Koch gave his crew a pep talk before the races began. "It'll be tough," Koch warned the team on the last day of tryouts, according to *Women's Sports and Fitness.* "Because you're women, you will have to work harder and fight longer. People will pry into your personal lives and call you animals. But if you really want to win, you will. And I think, as women, you really want to win."

On January 13, *America3* defeated Conner and *Stars and Stripes* in the first race of the defender selection series by one minute and nine seconds. "We're thrilled to win today," helmsman Leslie Egnot told the *San Diego Union-Tribune.* "But we realize there is a long way to go." The performance impressed Conner, as he told in the *San Diego Union-Tribune:* "The women are doing a great job. They are tough. It's not like there are major differences out there."

MIGHTY MARY. After their initial success, however, the crew of the *America3* then lost eight of the next nine races, falling behind both *Stars and Stripes* and *Young America*. In the first four rounds of trials, *America3* had a 5-16 record. The women, however, sailed the oldest boat in the fleet in these early rounds. "I was encouraged that we had some good, close races with our old boat," Isler told the *San Diego Union-Tribune*. "When we get our new boat, we'll be able to [win]. I think it is truly within our grasp to beat these guys."

In February the team received their new boat, *Mighty Mary,* named after Koch's mother. The new boat cost $3 million and was much faster than the *America3*. Because the America's Cup scoring system awards more points for races won later in the competition, the crew still had a chance to catch up. "We can win this," Riley stated in *Sports Illustrated*. "Once we get our new boat, we'll be rocket-fast." Koch contributed some funds to purchasing the new boat, but Chevrolet, Hewlett-Packard, the Lifetime cable television channel, American Express, Gillette, and *Glamour* magazine also sponsored the team.

GETTING BETTER. The early rounds of the competition also gave the crew much-needed experience. "It's disheartening to be beaten, but we've come a long way," Egnot confided to the *San Diego Union-Tribune*. "Our boat-handling is as good if not better in some aspects than the men's. But we've had more practice, too. In the long run, we'll get ahead of them and beat them consistently."

The team's early performance pleased Koch. "[This] might sound strange," he confessed in the *San Diego Union-Tribune*. "But it is better to have our losses now. You learn more from your losses than from your wins. This team is just learning how to sail in these light and sloppy conditions. And it's doing a good job."

MAN ON BOARD. Even after the delivery of *Mighty Mary,* the team continued to trail the other two U.S. boats. The crew realized that they did not have enough experience to win the competition without some help. They asked Koch to add David Dellenbaugh, who had led *America3* to victory in 1992, to the crew. "The idea came from the women," Koch insisted.

Though many people, including the team's sponsors, opposed the change, claiming that it removed the unique "women only" quality of the team, Koch added Dellenbaugh to the crew. The women on the team, who wanted most of all to win, supported the move. "When this quest is over, we want to be able to look back on it with no regrets and say we did everything we could to try and win," Stephanie Maxwell-Pierson explained in *Motor Boat and Sailing*.

BAD DEAL. At the end of the preliminary races, *Stars and Stripes* and *Mighty Mary* had the same number of points. They would have to sail one race to decide which boat would face *Young America* in the defender finals. Before the race took place, however, the leaders of the three U.S. racing teams got together and decided to let all three teams enter the finals, claiming that it would be unfair to have one race decide so important an event.

Koch, however, did not tell the *Mighty Mary* crew about the deal. The women voted overwhelmingly the night before to support a negotiated deal, but he told them before the one-race showdown that the negotiations were off. On April 4 *Mighty Mary* defeated *Stars and Stripes* by five minutes and fifty-nine seconds. As the crew heard the finish gun, they believed they had eliminated Conner and were part of a two-team defender final. "Before we went into the race, we thought there was no deal left," Egnot told the *San Diego Union-Tribune*. "We went in thinking do or die. When we finished, I've never seen such happy people. We excelled today under the highest of pressure. It was a real disappointment when we heard."

BLOWS LEAD. After another series of races, the competition to defend the America's Cup again came down to one race, *Mighty Mary* against *Stars and Stripes*. *Mighty Mary* got off to a huge lead, sailing beautifully in light winds. The crew gradually built up the lead from two and one-half minutes to four minutes, or 42 boat lengths, heading into the last part of the race. They decided to go the left side of the course, while Conner went right. "If we get ourselves out of this one, it's gonna be a miracle comeback," Conner told a crewmate, according to the *San Diego Union Tribune.*

Conner and his helmsman, Paul Cayard, who steered Italy's challenger in a losing effort against Koch in 1992, then got a lucky break. *Mighty Mary* hit dead air with little wind. "A well-deserved miracle," Conner called it, according to the Reuters news service. Conner's boat not only caught up with but passed *Mighty Mary,* winning the race by 52 seconds. *Stars and Stripes* made up five minutes in three short miles, the biggest comeback in the history of the America's Cup. "Is that the race of all time or is that the race of all time?" Cayard exclaimed as his boat crossed the finish line first. A win by *Mighty Mary* would have eliminated *Stars and Stripes* from the competition. *Mighty Mary* and *Young America* would have had a one-race sail-off to decide who would defend the Cup.

EXPERIENCE WINS OUT. Conner won six races in the defender finals, just enough to win. In the end *Mighty Mary* lost, but not without a battle. The difference came down to experience, but the team proved they had the determination and strength to win. "*Stars and Stripes* had the best team," Koch admitted in the *San Diego Union-Tribune.* "They have the weakest of the three boats, but the best team."

THE FINALS. Conner had the home water advantage in the America's Cup Finals but did not have a very fast boat. Because of this he rented *Young America* from his old competitors. Conner tried to rent *Mighty Mary,* but the crew objected to the idea. "If we gave him our boat, some of the women told me they'd knock holes in it first," Koch explained in *Sports Illustrated.* (Conner's crew had repeatedly yelled obscene insults at the crew of *Mighty Mary* during the competition.)

Conner faced Team New Zealand, representing the Royal New Zealand Yacht Squadron, and their boat, *Black Magic,* in the finals. Peter Blake led the New Zealand team, which had 32 world titles among its crew and went 42-1 in the Challenger competition. "To take the America's Cup back to my country is the best present I could ever give my country," Blake said, according to the Reuters news agency. The finals, a best-of-nine series, were held in May. The New Zealand team swept Conner five races to none.

IMPORTANT LESSON. Despite their loss in the finals, the crew of the *Mighty Mary* taught women and men an important lesson, as Courtney Becker-Dey explained in *Motor Boating and Sailing:* "Don't limit yourself—go for everything you can."

Sources

Boston Globe, July 26, 1994.
Motor Boating and Sailing, May 1995; June 1995; December 1995.
Newsweek, January 16, 1995.
People, February 20, 1995.
San Diego Union-Tribune, November 5, 1994; January 14, 1995; January 22, 1995; April 5, 1995; April 27, 1995.
Sports Illustrated, January 23, 1995; February 20, 1995; May 22, 1995; March 20, 1995.
Time, January 16, 1995; May 15, 1995.
U.S. News and World Report, October 31, 1994.
Women's Sports and Fitness, January/February, 1995.
Additional information provided by Reuters news wire, May 5, 1995.

WHERE TO WRITE:
C/O U.S. YACHT RACING UNION,
P.O. BOX 209,
NEWPORT, RI 02840.

Reggie Miller

1965—

The three-point shot is one of the most exciting plays in basketball. No one in the National Basketball Association (NBA) shoots the three-point shot better than Reggie Miller of the Indiana Pacers. An NBA All-Star and member of the "Dream Team II," which won the World Basketball Championships in 1994, Miller is not even the best basketball player in his family. Despite living in the shadow of his famous basketball-playing sister, Cheryl, and being born with a serious disability, Miller has established himself as one of the best players in the NBA.

Growing Up

TOUGH LOVE. Reginald Wayne Miller was born August 24, 1965, in Riverside, California. His parents met at a jazz club where his dad was playing saxophone. Miller's father, Saul, was an air force officer, and his mother, Carrie, was a housewife. Mr. Miller stressed discipline with all of his five chil-

"People who told him he couldn't play—when they were getting out of bed in the morning Reggie had been shooting for two or three hours."

—Cheryl Miller, Reggie Miller's sister

dren. "It's a tight family," Miller explained in the *Sporting News*. "Everyone had their chores. We all had to eat together every meal. Mom cooked, we helped, while we waited for dad to come home from work. I was so scared of my parents that if I did anything wrong, my conscience would kill me. But I'm glad I had the upbringing I did. I was very lucky."

"YES, HE WILL." When Miller was born, there was no reason to believe he would become a pro basketball star. There was serious question about whether he would ever walk. Miller was born with hip and feet problems and a chest cavity that had not closed. Doctors told his mother that Miller would never walk correctly and would never play sports. "Yes, he will," she corrected the doctors. "I say he will." Miller wore braces on his legs until he was four, but did learn to walk at a normal age.

"I remember I was always in the house with my mom," Miller recalled in the *Sporting News*. "I was in the kitchen with her, a real momma's boy. She'd always say, 'You'll be out there soon, honey. You just got to get your legs stronger.' She was so optimistic. My parents never told me anything negative. They told me, 'You will walk. You will run. You will play basketball.'"

SUPERSTAR SISTER. Despite his talent, Miller may be only the second-best basketball player in his family. His sister, Cheryl, was a member of the gold medal-winning 1984 U.S. Olympic women's basketball team. That same year she was the Women's Collegiate Player of the Year at the University of Southern California (USC). Now the coach of the women's basketball team at USC, she is one of the greatest female players of all time. "That poor boy has spent most of his basketball days playing second fiddle to his sister," Miller's dad told the *Akron Beacon Journal*.

"Overcoming my sister's shadow has been the biggest obstacle in my life," Miller confessed in the *Sporting News*. "I'll always be known as Cheryl Miller's little brother." Even today, NBA fans chant "Cheryl, Cheryl" when Miller takes the court. His sister also forced Miller to learn to shoot from outside. "You didn't want your sister slapping your best stuff into the flowers," Miller admitted in *Esquire*. The Millers would often trick other kids in two-on-two games. The Millers' opponents were surprised when they found out the sweet, innocent-looking girl was actually the best player on the court.

Miller used his sister as an inspiration. He had reached six feet seven inches tall by the time he entered Riverside Poly High, but he weighed just 155 pounds. Many coaches believed he was too skinny to play college basketball. "Reggie never argued with anyone about it, he just worked," Cheryl Miller recounted in the *Los Angeles Times*. "People who told him he couldn't play—when they were getting out of bed in the morning, Reggie had been shooting for two or three hours. And when they went to bed, he was still shooting." It took some time for Miller to develop his deadly jump shot. "I can remember my shot in sixth and seventh grade—a one-handed push shot that started down by my hip," Miller told *Sports Illustrated*. "It wasn't until my sophomore year in high school that I got a real jump shot."

BRUIN BOMBER. Miller received a scholarship in 1983 to attend the University of California-Los Angeles (UCLA), a collegiate basketball powerhouse. He starred for UCLA, finishing his career with 2,095 points—second in UCLA history only to the legendary Kareem Abdul-Jabbar. Miller refined his game during the summer. He played with Los Angeles Lakers stars Earvin "Magic" Johnson and Michael Cooper. "Magic and Coop taught me so much about the pro game," Miller recalled in *The State* (Columbia, South Carolina). "I

OH, SIS!

In an interview with the *Saint Paul Pioneer Press*, Cheryl Miller recalled an incident in 1982 in which her brother, then a star at Riverside Poly High, came home bragging about scoring 39 points that night. "He said, 'Everything I put up went in,'" Cheryl said. "He was smirking. Then I told him I had played that day, too. So he asked, 'How many did you get today, Cheryl?' I said, 'A hundred and five.' Reggie just went sheet-white."

played with them almost every day for three summers, and it was an education. Part of my game is the result of Magic's influence and another part of it is Coop's influence. Because of them, I knew what to expect from the NBA."

PACER PICK. Professional scouts rated Miller as an outstanding prospect, although he was still very thin. "People were always telling me I couldn't make it in the NBA because I was too skinny and not physical enough," Miller recalled in the *Sporting News*. The Indiana Pacers selected Miller with the eleventh pick in the first round of the 1987 NBA Draft. Pacers fans booed the selection, wanting the team to pick Indiana University star Steve Alford instead. Miller soon won them over. He started immediately and averaged ten points per game as a rookie. Miller lifted his average to 16 points per game in his second season (1988-89).

Miller raised his game to another level in 1990. He averaged 24.6 points per game and appeared in his first NBA All-Star Game. He also kept working on his game. Instead of relying only on his jump shot, he learned to take the ball to the basket and draw fouls. Miller averaged 20 points or more for the next three seasons and became the Pacers' all-time leading scorer in 1993. Despite his thin frame, Miller started 345 consecutive games in one stretch. He proved to be an expert at making the jump shot, a lost art in the NBA. "These days you don't go to the playground to shoot your J [jump shot]," Miller explained to *Sports Illustrated*. "You go to try to dunk on someone's head. I did that, too, but I always brought my jump shot with me."

Superstar

TIRED OF LOSING. The Pacers remained a mediocre team despite Miller. Indiana had talent, including Rik Smits, Chuck Person, and Detlef Schrempf, but never reached their potential. Before the 1993-1994 season the team hired Larry Brown to coach. Brown had coached several NBA teams and had led the University of Kansas Jayhawks to a National Collegiate

Athletic Association (NCAA) championship. Brown thus brought a history of success to the team, and Miller decided he had to become the team leader. "To tell the truth, I'm sick and tired of losing," Miller admitted to the *Fort Wayne News-Sentinel*. "It's time for me to lead by example." When the Pacers traded both Person and Schrempf, Miller was Indiana's undisputed main man. "I knew I was going out there by myself, so I was the one that was going to have to sacrifice points," Miller said at the time. "There was no way I could be selfish."

Miller averaged more than 20 points again during the 1993-94 season, but the team still struggled, finishing third in the NBA Central Division. Surprisingly, the Pacers beat the Orlando Magic three straight games in the first round of the play-offs. They then disposed of the Atlanta Hawks, the team with the best record in the Eastern Conference. Miller averaged 22 points in the first two rounds of the play-offs, leading the Pacers. He was in the NBA Eastern Conference Finals for the first time in his career.

Indiana faced the Atlantic Division champion New York Knicks. For the first time Miller would be in the spotlight. "Reggie Miller had waited too long for this forum to continue to let it slip away," wrote John Smallwood of the *Philadelphia Daily News*. "Trapped in obscurity with the rest of the Indiana Pacers, Miller had been itching for seven seasons to play in a national spotlight."

TOO QUIET. Indiana dropped two of the first three games to the Knicks. Miller was slumping and, surprisingly, quiet. Miller received a call from his sister before Game Four. "She told me that I wasn't being Reggie Miller," Miller revealed in the *Philadelphia Daily News*. "Being quiet was my decision. I tried to be a model citizen, but it didn't work. I'm not a nice guy, and I was playing too nice. I was trying to be a model citizen for my teammates and they were the ones telling me to go back to being the jerk. When I'm quiet and just going through the motions, it's not the same. I think I involve my teammates, the fans and the opposing fans more when I'm a little bit more free and open and having a good time."

Miller went back to his old style, and the Pacers came roaring back. He scored 31 points in Game Four—including 11 in the final five minutes—and Indiana evened the series at two games apiece. Miller then had his best game ever in Game Five. He exploded for 39 points, including a remarkable 25 in the fourth quarter, 15 of those coming on five consecutive three-point shots. Film director Spike Lee, a Knicks fan, who earlier in the game accused Miller of "choking" by putting his hands over his throat, inspired the fourth-quarter outburst. "I don't remember a lot that happened that night," Miller recalled in the *Sporting News*. "I saw the whole floor from above. I saw players cutting before they cut. I knew things were going to happen before they happened."

The Pacers eventually lost the series in seven games, but Miller had arrived as a superstar. "People look at me now like, 'Where did he come from all of a sudden?'" Miller explained in the *Orlando Sentinel*. "But, hey, I've been here all along. It's just that when you play in a small market like Indianapolis, and you're not on national television, people never recognize you. But I'm used to that. In some ways, I've been playing in shadows my entire life." Cheryl Miller told the *Sporting News* that "taking the Knicks to Game 7 really boosted his confidence. Now he knows he's a superstar."

DREAM TEAMER. In July 1994 Miller was named one of the three captains chosen for the "Dream Team II" squad, which represented the United States at the World Basketball Championships in Toronto, Ontario, Canada. Miller was the star of the U.S. team. He averaged 17.1 points per game as the U.S. team swept through the much weaker competition. Miller scored a tournament team high 31 points against Australia.

BEST SEASON. The Pacers entered the 1994-95 season as a favorite to win the NBA title. Miller was elected as a starter in the 1995 All-Star Game, and the Pacers won the NBA Central Division. Miller averaged 19.6 points per game during the regular season and 25.5 points per game during the play-offs, including a play-off-career-high tying 39 points in a first-round series game against the Atlanta Hawks. After their win over the Hawks, the Pacers once again faced the Knicks in the play-offs, this time in the Eastern Conference semifinals.

KNOCKS OFF KNICKS. Miller almost single-handedly won Game One of the series, scoring the Pacers' last eight points in the space of 8.9 seconds. In Game Six, Miller scored 15 points in the fourth quarter, almost pulling the game out for Indiana. The Pacers had led the series 3-1, but New York would not quit, forcing a final and deciding game. In Game Seven, Knicks center Patrick Ewing missed a short jump shot with only seconds remaining, giving the Pacers the game, 97-95, and the series. Miller scored 29 points in the victory.

Indiana then faced the Orlando Magic in the Eastern Conference Finals. Shaquille O'Neal and **Anfernee Hardaway** (see entry) led the Magic, the team with the best record in the Eastern Conference during the regular season. Orlando got off to a 2-0 lead in the series, but Indiana came back, tying the series at 2-2 and then 3-3 with clutch victories. The series went seven games, with the deciding contest being played in Orlando. The home court was the difference, as the home team won every game in the series. The Magic won the right to play in the NBA Finals with a 105-81 victory.

The loss disappointed Miller, especially since he scored only 12 points in Game Seven. He took the blame for the defeat. "I take the burden for this loss," Miller told the *New York Times*. "I feel bad for the guys because I didn't play particularly well. They [his teammates] should have nothing to put their heads down about. This was definitely Reggie Miller blowing it for them." Although Miller did not

TRASH-TALKING

Trash-talking, or excessive bragging and celebrating, is now widespread throughout professional sports. Some people think it should be banned, while others believe that players are only expressing themselves. Miller, one of the prime trash-talkers in the NBA, says it all began in junior high school. "Look at me," he told the *Sporting News*. "I'm so skinny. I was always getting knocked down. But I would never show the other kids they hurt me. I'd get up and say, 'Is that your best shot? Come on, hit me harder.' I think trash talking jacks [fires] me up. It gives me security. I know I'm not the best. I don't resent being booed or when they yell, 'Cheryl, Cheryl.' It motivates me when they yell at me. I just could never play the game without talking." Trash-talking does not seem to affect Miller's game, but it has made him the player most hated by opponents and an easy target for the boos of opposing-team fans. "When it comes to getting under people's skin, nobody can touch him," Knicks guard Derek Harper stated in the *Sporting News*.

Miller moves the ball up court.

win his NBA title, he will get a chance to win an Olympic gold medal in 1996 when he once again represents the United States as a member of the "Dream Team III" squad in Atlanta, Georgia.

OFF THE COURT. Miller is married and lives with his wife Marita in Riverside, California. His basketball idol is "Magic" Johnson, because Johnson always made his teammates better. Miller's favorite movies are *Sixteen Candles, Pretty in Pink,* and *Some Kind of Wonderful.* He graduated in 1987 from UCLA with a bachelor's degree in history. Miller is superstitious and goes through the same routine before every game.

Miller says he hopes to become a radio talk show host when he is finished with basketball. He is now the host of a weekly television show for teenagers in Indianapolis. The show's focus is not basketball, but such issues as homelessness, drug abuse, and teen pregnancy. "Every topic that's on the show is not because someone else picked it," Miller explained to the *Gary Post-Tribune*. "It's because I picked it because I want to know." Miller also runs a basketball camp, supports the United Negro College Fund, and visits children in hospitals. "I understand what it's like for a kid to be trapped inside behind four walls," he explained to *Sporting News*.

Despite his trash-talking, Miller has not let his success go to his head; as he said in an interview in the *Sporting News*, "I'm lucky to be here."

Sources

Akron Beacon Journal, June 3, 1994; June 7, 1994.
Columbia State (South Carolina), February 6, 1990; June 5, 1994.
Dallas Morning News, June 21, 1987.
Esquire, December 1994.
Fort Wayne News-Sentinel, July 9, 1992.
Gary Post-Tribune (Indiana), March 31, 1991.
Lexington Herald-Leader, December 27, 1987.
New York Daily News, May 10, 1994; May 27, 1994; May 30, 1994; June 6, 1994.
New York Times, August 12, 1994; May 22, 1995; May 26, 1995; May 30, 1995; June 1, 1995; June 5, 1995.
Orlando Sentinel, August 8, 1994.
Philadelphia Daily News, May 31, 1994.
Sport, May 1995.
Sporting News, November 22, 1993; December 26, 1994.
Sports Illustrated, May 13, 1991; May 4, 1992; May 30, 1994; November 7, 1994; May 15, 1995; June 5, 1995.
Additional information provided by Indiana Pacers.

WHERE TO WRITE:
INDIANAPOLIS PACERS, MARKET SQUARE ARENA,
200 E. MARKET ST.,
INDIANAPOLIS, IN 46204.

Dominique Moceanu

1981—

"I want people to remember me for being happy and for my smile."
—Dominique Moceanu

Dominique Moceanu has gymnastics in her genes. Her parents, both gymnasts themselves, started training their daughter at age three. By the time Moceanu turned ten years old, she was training with the legendary gymnastics coach Bela Karolyi, whose former students include Olympic champions Nadia Comaneci and Mary Lou Retton. Moceanu earned the title of best U.S. gymnast when she won the all-around championship at the 1995 U.S. Gymnastics Championships. Her goal now is to win a gold medal at the 1996 Summer Olympics in Atlanta, Georgia.

Growing Up

GYMNASTIC GENES. Dominique Moceanu (Mo-che-ah-new) was born September 30, 1981, in Hollywood, California. She grew up in Florida with her parents and sister. Both of Moceanu's parents are from Romania and both were gymnasts. Her father, Dumitru, defected to the United States from the Communist country of Romania in 1979, and her mother, Camelia, left a year later. Dumitru Moceanu had been a member of the Romanian junior gymnastics team and worked as a car salesperson in the United States. Mrs. Moceanu worked at a beauty salon.

CALL TO KAROLYI. Moceanu's parents hung her from a clothesline when she was only an infant to test her grip. She started in gymnastics when she was three. Her father called Bela Karolyi, a famous gymnastics coach who also originally lived in Romania, and offered to move his family near Karolyi's gym in Houston if he would coach his daughter. "I told them, 'Let her grow up a little first,'" Karolyi recalled in *Newsweek*. "'Don't make any major family sacrifice.'" Moceanu began training at a local club but dreamed of some day working with Karolyi.

When Moceanu was nine years old her dream came true. Her family moved to Houston and Karolyi began to coach the young gymnast. "Her gymnastics weren't very good, but there was something sparkling in her face," legendary gymnast Nadia Comaneci told *Newsweek*. "She was jumping and smiling and she had the biggest eyes."

JUNIOR CHAMP. At age ten, Moceanu qualified for the U.S. junior national team—the youngest athlete ever to make the team. She finished second in the balance beam and fifth in the all-around competition in the junior division of the 1992 U.S. Gymnastics Championships. In 1994 Moceanu reached the top of U.S. junior gymnastics, winning the all-around competition, floor exercise, and vault, and finishing third in both the balance beam and uneven parallel bars in the junior division at the U.S. Gymnastics Championships. By age 13 she was ready to move up to the senior division.

Superstar

SENIOR SUCCESS. In her first senior competition, Moceanu won the vault, finished second in the all-around, and took third in the balance beam and floor exercise at the American Classic/Pan American Games Trials. She then took center stage at the U.S. Gymnastics Championships in August 1995. In a stunning performance, Moceanu won the gold medal in the all-around competition, defeating Shannon Miller and the previous year's winner, **Dominique Dawes** (see entry). With her victory Moceanu became the youngest ever national champion at only 13 years of age. "Everyone's making such a big deal," Moceanu stated in *Newsweek*. "But I'm trying not to pay any attention."

Moceanu came back the next day and won a silver medal in the floor exercise and a bronze medal in the vault. She fell in both the balance beam and uneven parallel bars competitions, knocking her out of medal contention in those events. Moceanu did not let her mistakes discourage her. "It's more fun in the seniors," Moceanu said in *Sports Illustrated*. "I liked it."

WORLD COMPETITION. Moceanu followed up her success at the national championships by winning a silver medal in the balance beam at the 1995 World Gymnastics Championships in Sabae, Japan. She was the only U.S. gymnast to win an individual medal and helped the U.S. squad win a bronze medal in the team competition. Moceanu finished fifth in the all-around competition and seventh in the floor exercise. This performance was very impressive for her first time competing in the world championships.

WHY SO GOOD? Moceanu wins over fans and judges with her outgoing personality. Karolyi encourages his young gymnast to let her happiness show. "We need to see the human emotion on the floor, not just the stunts," Karolyi said in *Newsweek*.

◀ *During the 1995 World Team Trials in Austin, Texas, Moceanu leaps through the air.*

NADIA COMANECI

Moceanu bears a striking resemblance to another great gymnast: Nadia Comaneci. Also trained by Karolyi, Comaneci was only 14 when she took the 1976 Summer Olympics in Montreal, Quebec, Canada, by storm, winning three gold medals. She also was the first gymnast to ever score a perfect 10 in Olympic competition. "Wow! We do look so much alike," Moceanu recalled in *Newsweek*, referring to seeing Comaneci for the first time on television. "The look, the style is frighteningly similar," Karolyi told the same magazine. Moceanu tries to look as much like Comaneci as possible, wearing her hair in a ponytail just like her more famous forerunner. "Nadia is always helping me and encouraging me," Moceanu told *Sports Illustrated for Kids.*

Comaneci advises Moceanu but says their styles are very different. At the 1976 Olympics, Comaneci was very intense and determined. Moceanu is very open and fun-loving. "I grew up in a different system and was taught to keep everything inside," Comaneci explained in *Newsweek*. "She takes all her feelings outside. That's the American way."

"She's [Moceanu] like a little bird on a wire, all the time fluttering and chirping and always playing to the crowd."

Karolyi compares Moceanu's personality to another of his famous champions, Mary Lou Retton of the United States. "She's an outgoing kid, like Mary Lou," Karolyi told *Sports Illustrated*. "She's not a hidden personality. She can laugh one minute and cry the next—an open book. This is a good kind to coach." In fact, sometimes Moceanu has to stop smiling to concentrate on her routines. "I want people to remember me for being happy and for my smile," Moceanu explained in *Sports Illustrated*.

LEARNS FROM BEST. Moceanu works out for seven hours every day at Karolyi's gym in Houston. There she trains with former world all-around champions Kim Zmeskal of the United States and Svetlana Boguinskaia from Russia. Moceanu tries to learn from other gymnasts. "Svetlana's so sharp on her movements, so elegant and expressive," Moceanu said in *Sports Illustrated*. "Kim's so powerful, and I try to take that with me to the vault." Moceanu impresses her more experienced friends. "In a couple of years she could be the best in the world," Boguinskaia declared in *Sports Illustrated*.

OUT OF THE GYM. Moceanu lives in Houston, Texas. When not competing, she likes to swim, read, shop, and play with her computer. Moceanu also enjoys country music. She attends Northland Christian School and someday would like to work in sports medicine. Karolyi also trains Moceanu's younger sister.

Karolyi worries that Moceanu may have raised expectations of her performances too high. "I don't want to create an early sensation," Karolyi admitted in *Newsweek*. "I've seen the ones who peaked too early or got in a situation where pressure turned into a destructive element." Moceanu ruined Karolyi's plans to surprise everyone at the 1996 Summer Olympics in Atlanta. "I wanted to win anyway," Moceanu told *Newsweek* after the U.S. Gymnastics Championships. "So I went out and did my very best." Karolyi hopes Moceanu's youth works to her advantage. "This is a good age," Karolyi told *Sports Illustrated*. "At 13, they don't get psycho yet over the pressure."

Sources

Newsweek, October 2, 1995.
Sports Illustrated, May 8, 1995.
Sports Illustrated for Kids, December 1995.
Additional information provided by USA Gymnastics.

WHERE TO WRITE:
C/O USA GYMNASTICS,
PAN AMERICAN PLAZA, STE. 300, 201 S. CAPITAL AVE.,
INDIANAPOLIS, IN 46225.

BELA KAROLYI

Bela Karolyi became famous by making the Romanian women's gymnastic team the best in the world. His most famous pupil was Nadia Comaneci, who won three gold medals at the 1976 Summer Olympics. He defected from Romania and came to the United States, where he has trained some of the best female American gymnasts in history. Among his pupils in the United States are Mary Lou Retton, the only American to ever win an Olympic all-around gold medal (1984), and Kim Zmeskal, the first American to ever win an all-around competition at the World Gymnastics Championships (1991).

Alonzo Mourning

1970—

"I consider myself one of the tough guys in the game."—Alonzo Mourning

Life as a center in the National Basketball Association (NBA) is tough. One of the toughest in the game is Alonzo Mourning of the Miami Heat. During his three NBA seasons Mourning has developed into one of the game's dominant big men, as his selection to the "Dream Team II" squad, which won the World Basketball Championship in 1994, shows. He also helped make the Charlotte Hornets one of the NBA's elite teams and hopes to do the same for his new team, the Miami Heat. A tough guy on the court, he is a gentle giant in real life, serving as a spokesperson against child abuse.

Growing Up

ROUGH START. Alonzo Mourning Jr. was born February 8, 1970, in Chesapeake, Virginia. He lived with his natural parents, Alonzo Sr. and Julia, until he was 12 years old. His parents then divorced. "My parents were getting a divorce," Mourning recalled in *Sports Illustrated for Kids*. "I wasn't mad at them, but I wasn't comfortable at home. Divorce is hard to understand when you're a kid."

His parents sent Mourning to a foster home run by an amazing woman named Fannie Threet. There Mourning joined a large family of Threet's foster and natural children. In all, Threet had two children of her own and helped raise 49 others. "My foster mother gave me the love I needed not just to work hard at basketball, but also to be a caring human being," Mourning told the *Sporting News*. "I am lucky to have had people such as her in my life." Threet helped Mourning keep his priorities straight. "She never went to my games, but she would drop everything to help me work on my school assignments," Mourning explained in *Sports Illustrated for Kids*. "Fannie made me see how important an education is. I love my real mom and dad dearly, but Fannie guided me every step of the way. Her message was always: You can do it."

"ZO." Basketball helped Mourning deal with his problems, although he was not always a star. His friends gave him the nickname "Zo" in junior high. "I started playing basketball, and I was real clumsy and awkward," Mourning recalled in *Sport* magazine. "Instead of calling me Alonzo, a lot of my friends just called me Zo for short. The name kind of traveled. The more people heard it, the more people called me Zo."

Mourning soon got over his clumsiness on the court. At age 16 he attended the prestigious Five Star Basketball Camp, where he competed with other high school players from across the nation. Five Star coach Frank Marino described Mourning in the *Washington Post* as "the big man who will take you to the places that you want to go." Soon college recruiters became interested in Mourning.

Mourning led his Indian River High School team to a state championship as a junior. He averaged 21.8 points, 11 rebounds, and 9.6 blocked shots per game. College recruiters began calling the Threet home at all hours of the day and night trying to convince him to attend their schools. Mourning was soon forced to ask his high school coach, Bill Lassiter, to help him handle the calls. Mourning narrowed his choices to five colleges: the Universities of Maryland and Virginia, Georgetown University, Syracuse University, and Georgia Tech. He visited all these schools during his senior year.

GEORGETOWN BOUND. Eventually Mourning chose Georgetown University, in Washington, D.C. This was a tough decision for Mourning, mainly because he worried about how tough Hoyas coach John Thompson was on his players. Thompson improved his chances by inviting Mourning to try out for the 1988 U.S. Olympic basketball team, which Thompson was coaching. Mourning was the only high school player trying out for an Olympic spot. "Trying out for the Olympics and playing against all that talent while being the youngest player out there really molded me to the point where I was ready," Mourning explained in the *Washington Post.* "I was comfortable in the college atmosphere I was in [at the tryouts], so I didn't really have to all of a sudden adjust to it. Just by playing against that talent, I learned. So, when different situations happened to me in college, I was pretty much comfortable with them because I had been through them already."

Mourning arrived at Georgetown University in the fall of 1988, and many people already considered him a superstar. He quickly became Georgetown's starting center, and in his freshman year the Hoyas won the Big East Tournament. Georgetown lost in the regional final of the National Collegiate Athletic Association (NCAA) Basketball Tournament to Duke University, but the future looked bright for Mourning.

LEARNING PROCESS. Soon Mourning found out he had a lot to learn. His sophomore season had barely begun when the police asked him to explain his relationship with Rayful Edmond III, a drug dealer now serving a life sentence for sell-

Mourning (right) tips in a rebound ▶
during a game against the Washington Bullets.

ing crack cocaine. During his junior season Mourning was in competition for his job with Dikembe Mutombo, now of the Denver Nuggets. Mutombo, a senior seven feet two inches tall, shared time with six feet ten inches tall Mourning at center to start the season. Soon, however, Thompson decided to use his "Twin Towers" at the same time. Unfortunately, Mourning then injured his foot, sustaining the first serious injury of his career.

STAYS IN SCHOOL. Mourning considered entering the NBA Draft after his junior year but decided to stay at Georgetown for one last season. He decided to stay at Georgetown mainly because he realized that he needed more time to mature, both as a player and as a person. In the summer between his junior and senior seasons Mourning practiced with Mutombo and former Hoya Patrick Ewing. Thompson credited Mourning for the decision to stay in school and told the *Washington Post* that his star center "had sense enough to recognize the need to be in a school setting and that he needed guidance."

Mourning blossomed as a dominating star in his senior year. He averaged 21.3 points, 10.7 rebounds, and 5.0 blocked shots per game. Big East experts named Mourning Big East Conference Most Valuable Player (MVP), Defensive Player of the Year, and MVP of the Big East Tournament. Mourning finished his career as only the second Georgetown player—Ewing being the first—to score more than 2,000 points (2,001) and grab more than 1,000 rebounds (1,032) in his career. He finished second in Georgetown history in blocked shots (453), third in rebounding, and fourth in scoring. Mourning was a finalist for the prestigious Naismith and Wooden Awards. Only one college player—Shaquille O'Neal—earned more awards than Mourning in 1992.

Superstar

HORNET PICK. Mourning was the second pick overall in the first round of the 1992 NBA Draft; he was chosen by the Charlotte Hornets. People compared Mourning right from the start to the number one pick overall, O'Neal. With O'Neal's "power, size and brute strength against Mourning's quickness, agility and hostility," remarked Pat Williams of the Orlando Magic in *Sports Illustrated,* "I think people see a reincarnation of Wilt Chamberlain and Bill Russell. The far bigger player [O'Neal], the true Goliath, being combated by the smaller, more agile, maybe more athletic center [Mourning]. For 15 years that was the greatest matchup in sports. I think people will see that again."

Mourning refused to compare himself to O'Neal. "The media has basically been trying to make it out to be a Shaquille-Alonzo battle," he told *Sport* magazine. "We're not the only two guys in the league. They were trying to make us out to be fighters. They wanted us to box or something. I never wanted to get involved in that type of stuff, because I thought it was unnecessary and it only catered to the media. They're trying to create some type of duel between us for the rest of our careers. If anything, we should be worried about all those other guys we gotta play against night in and night out. I don't go to the game thinking, 'I gotta score more points than Shaquille tonight.'"

FIRST-YEAR FLASH. Mourning had a fine rookie season, scoring 21.0 points per game and grabbing 10.3 rebounds per contest. He was a unanimous choice for the NBA All-Rookie team and finished second to O'Neal in the balloting for Rookie of the Year honors. Mourning also led the Hornets in play-off scoring (23.8 points per game), rebounding (9.9 per game), blocks (3.44 per game), and minutes (40.8 per game). More important, Mourning teamed up with Larry Johnson and Muggsy Bogues to lead the Hornets to their first ever play-off series victory, a first-round defeat of the Boston Celtics.

CHAMBERLAIN VS. RUSSELL

Wilt Chamberlain, who played with the Philadelphia Warriors and the Los Angeles Lakers, and Bill Russell of the Boston Celtics participated in one of the great rivalries in the history of sports. Chamberlain was a giant, more than seven feet tall at a time when that was rare in the NBA. He averaged 30.1 points per game (second all-time), grabbed 23,924 rebounds (first all-time), and scored 31,419 points (second all-time). Chamberlain once scored 100 points in a single game. Russell was a shorter man, six feet nine inches tall, but he used his quickness and aggressive defensive style to frustrate much taller opponents. Russell averaged 15.1 points per game and pulled down 21,620 rebounds (second all-time) for an amazing average of 22.5 boards per game. Most important, Russell's Celtics teams won 11 NBA championships, while Chamberlain's teams won only two.

ALL-STAR. Optimism was running high before the 1993-94 season. Mourning did not disappoint, leading the team once again in scoring (21.5 points per game), rebounding (10.2 per game), and blocked shots (3.13 per game). Eastern Conference coaches named Mourning to the NBA All-Star Game for the first time, but an injury kept him from playing. Unfortunately, Mourning missed 22 games, and an injury also sidelined Larry Johnson. The Hornets finished 41-41, missing the play-offs.

DREAM TEAMER. In 1994 U.S. basketball officials honored Mourning by naming him to the "Dream Team II" squad, which represented the United States at the World Basketball Championships in Toronto, Ontario, Canada. Despite this recognition, Mourning has gained a reputation for being mean on the court. He offers no apologies. "I look at the game as a business," he confessed in *Sport* magazine. "It's fun to me, but at the same time, I'm out there in a businesslike manner. I understand the things I have to do to go out and try to help the ballclub win. I go out there with my game face on every [time]. I try to let my actions filter out amongst my teammates so they can get a feel, an understanding of where I'm coming from. I consider myself one of the tough guys in the game."

BEST SEASON. Mourning and Johnson were back and healthy for the 1994-95 season, and the Hornets had their best year ever. Mourning again was the team leader in scoring (21.3 points per game), rebounding (9.9 per game), and blocks (2.92 per game). He was named to the NBA All-Star team for a second time, and this time played. Charlotte reached the play-offs for the second time in their history and played the Chicago Bulls in the first round, a team rejuvenated by the return of Michael Jordan. Mourning was a force in the series, averaging 22 points and 13.3 rebounds per game. It was not enough; the Bulls eliminated the Hornets in four games.

TURNING UP THE HEAT. The Hornets shocked the basketball world by trading Mourning and two other players to the

IN THE PAINT

Mourning is one of 24 NBA centers and forwards who generate donations through their scoring, rebounding, and shot blocking to help prevent child abuse. The program's name is "In the Paint" and Mourning acts as the team's captain. He told the *Sporting News* about his work for abused children: "I can relate to what the kids at Thompson Children's Home, a home for abused children in Charlotte, NC, go through every day. As I was growing up in a foster home, I had some of the same fears. So, whenever I visit Thompson's, I make sure to remind them that they are not alone in their struggle. I like to let them know that people care. Just to see them smile, after all they've been through, makes me feel good. Some days, instead of me lifting their spirits, they lift mine. I want them [abused children] to know they are not limited—they can work hard and accomplish their dreams."

Miami Heat for Glen Rice and two other players before the beginning of the 1995-96 season. The Hornets traded Mourning because management could not agree on a contract with their big center and was afraid he might leave after the season as a free agent. Miami hired championship coach Pat Riley during the off-season, and the Heat believe Mourning is the player around which they can build a championship contender. "He is considered a franchise player, well beyond an impact player," Riley said after the trade.

OFF THE COURT. Mourning lives in Chesapeake, Virginia. He is active in the NBA's Healthy Families America program. He is also active in many local charities and assisted in putting up basketball nets in underprivileged Charlotte neighborhoods. In 1994 Mourning traveled to South Africa to do clinics and visit schools. He received his college degree in sociology. Mourning is a spokesperson for Nike, signing a $16 million contract in 1992. With hard work, the sky is the limit for the young star. "I really can't predict how far I'm going to develop," Mourning admitted to the *New York Times*. "I think my attitude is great toward learning, and I want to learn. If I keep growing, maturing, and learning, there's no telling how good I can get."

Sources

Detroit Free Press, November 4, 1995.

Jet, November 30, 1992.

New York Times, March 13, 1989.

Sport, February 1994; December 1994.

Sporting News, August 31, 1992; May 2, 1994.

Sports Illustrated, March 20, 1989; March 2, 1992; October 26, 1992; October 11, 1993; November 8, 1993.

Sports Illustrated for Kids, October 1993.

Washington Post, February 8, 1988; January 7, 1989; March 7, 1992.

Additional information provided by Charlotte Hornets.

WHERE TO WRITE:
C/O MIAMI HEAT,
MIAMI ARENA,
MIAMI, FL 33136.

Cam Neely

1965—

Many people believe that athletes today are spoiled and will not play with injuries. In some cases that may be true. Boston Bruins forward Cam Neely, however, is not one of those players. In 1991 he suffered a severe knee injury that almost ended his career. Over two years Neely steadily worked his knee back into shape, and in the 1993-94 season he became only the third player in National Hockey League (NHL) history to score 50 goals in fewer than 50 games. Today, he is one of the best power forwards in the NHL and an inspiration to all athletes who want to work hard to succeed.

"There's nobody out here who can handle him."
—Florida Panthers scout Paul Henry

Growing Up

CLOSE FAMILY. Cameron Michael Neely was born June 6, 1965, in Comox, British Columbia, Canada. He grew up in nearby Maple Ridge. Neely's father, Mike, had retired from the Canadian Air Force and worked in real estate; his mother's name was Marlene. His family was very close. He and his brother, Scott, played games all day. Neely was friends with Larry Walker, who went on to star with the major league baseball Montreal Expos and the Colorado Rockies.

Neely's father was his role model. "My father never complained about anything," Neely recalled in *Sports Illustrated.* "He was one of those fathers. He didn't push you, but he told you things."

WINS CHAMPIONSHIP. Neely loved playing hockey and soon became a star. When he was 16, he led the Portland, Oregon, junior team of the Western Hockey League (WHL) to a championship. Neely scored 56 goals, dished out 64 assists, and finished with 120 points in only 72 games. He had nine goals and 11 assists in 14 play-off games and scored a hat trick (three goals) in the Winter Hawks' 8-3 Memorial Cup championship win over Oshawa.

CANUCKS' CHOICE. The Vancouver Canucks selected Neely with the ninth overall pick in the first round of the 1983 NHL Draft. He got his first chance to play in the NHL in the 1983-84 season, when he played 56 games with the Canucks. Neely scored 16 goals and had 15 assists. He spent the next two seasons in Vancouver but saw only limited action, scoring 21 goals in 1984-85 and 14 goals in 1985-86. The lack of ice time bothered Neely, but the Canucks played close to his hometown and his family could easily come to games.

THE BEST. In the spring of 1986 Vancouver traded Neely and a number one draft pick to the Bruins for center Barry Pederson. The trade turned his career around. In his first five seasons with Boston, Neely established himself as one of the best power forwards in the game. (A power forward is a player known for his offensive skills, strength, and checking ability.) He scored 35 or more goals each season and became only the second Bruin to score more than 50 goals in consecutive seasons—55 in 1989-

90 and 51 in 1990-91. In his first five seasons with Boston, Neely scored 221 goals. "If he's not the best power forward in the game, he's number two," former teammate Glen Wesley stated in the *Sporting News*. "Every time he's out on the ice he's going to be creating chances and banging guys."

TRAGIC NEWS. While his professional career improved, Neely received bad news in his personal life in 1986. Doctors diagnosed both of his parents with cancer. Marlene Neely died in 1987. "It was emotional, all kinds of emotions at once," Neely recalled in *Sports Illustrated*. "I was in Vancouver for three years, and they weren't using me very much, so my career wasn't going anywhere, but my personal life was wonderful. Everyone could come to the games all the time, and everyone was healthy. I go 3,000 miles across the country, and my career takes off, but my personal life falls apart. It teaches you an awful lot about your priorities, about what really counts."

CAREER THREATENED. On May 11, 1991, Neely's career almost ended. The Bruins were playing the Pittsburgh Penguins in the Wales Conference Finals, one step from the Stanley Cup Finals. During Game Six, Neely collided with Pittsburgh defenseman Ulf Samuelsson. "I went to hit him, and he ducked," Neely explained in *Sports Illustrated*. "His knee was bent, and my thigh hit his knee." The collision injured the muscles in Neely's left thigh and knee.

The injury caused a disease called myositis ossificans, which turned part of Neely's left thigh muscle into bone. Doctors told him the only way for his injury to heal was through rest. The rehabilitation process was frustrating for Neely, as it has been for other players with similar injuries. "It isn't like a broken leg or broken arm, where someone can tell you, 'You're going to be in a cast for X number of months, it's going to take X number of weeks to get your strength back, and then you're going to be healed,'" former Bruin Gord Kluzak, forced into retirement by a similar injury, explained to the *Sporting News*. "Those injuries are easy. It's the ones where the doctors are uncertain as to whether or not you'll even play again, they have no time frame to work under, there's no real progression, oftentimes, of how well you're getting better. Those kinds of injuries are very difficult to deal with emotionally."

MORE PROBLEMS. Neely tried to come back in January 1992. He scored nine goals in nine games, but soon his knee began to hurt again. Neely thought a minor problem caused the pain, but soon found out that he had cartilage damage in his knee. Doctors told him he would need knee surgery. "That was the shock," Neely admitted in *Sports Illustrated*. "I went to sleep thinking 10 days, and I woke up, and the first thing the doctor said was, 'Your season's over and I'm worried about your career.' Just like that."

For months Neely worked to get his knee back into shape. "There have been moments when I thought that it was all over for Cam," Bruins assistant general manager Mike Milbury explained to *Sports Illustrated*. "But he kept fighting back." Bruins conditioning coach Mike Boyle worked with Neely, using exercises that strengthened the muscles around his knee without putting too much pressure on the injury. "Cam's knee is not a situation where one good whack, one trip on a crack in the ice, will do it so much damage," Boyle told the same magazine. "The worry is overuse. More than anything, Cam's knee needs rest."

Superstar

COMEBACK I. It took nearly two years for Neely to return from his leg injury. In March 1993 he played in a game against the Minnesota North Stars (now the Dallas Stars). The crowd at Boston Garden cheered every time he took the ice. With only 4:51 gone in the game, Neely slapped a rebound past Minnesota goalie Jon Casey. The fans threw hats, shoes, and a stuffed Bruins doll onto the ice, and Neely acknowledged their cheers by pumping his left arm. Later in the game he delivered a tough check to Dave Gagner of the North Stars.

Before the game with the North Stars, Neely promised not to back down from checking because of the injury. "I don't plan on playing any differently than I ever have," Neely explained in *Sports Illustrated*. "I have to play physical to play well." Neely's return made his teammates happy. "I think I was more nervous than he was," Bruins center Adam Oates admitted in the same magazine. "He played great." Trying not to overdo it, Neely played only 13 of the Bruins' 24 remaining games. He scored 11 goals and had seven assists.

FAST 50. Neely started fast during the 1993-94 season, earning his second NHL All-Star Game berth. By the All-Star break he had 32 goals in 28 games, second best in the league, and a league-leading eight game-winning goals. Neely finished the season with 50 goals in only 49 games. Only two other players, Wayne Gretzky and Mario Lemieux, have ever scored 50 goals in fewer than 50 games. (Gretzky turned the trick in 1982-83 and 1983-84 and Lemieux did it in 1988-89.) Neely led the NHL with 13 game-winning goals. In honor of his hard work, hockey writers awarded him the Masterton Trophy, given annually to "the NHL player who exemplifies the qualities of perseverance, sportsmanship, and dedication to hockey."

Boston coaches worked hard to make sure Neely did not reinjure himself. They did not make their superstar practice and sat him out of games to let his knee rest. Neely did not like missing games. "I get too nervous to watch a whole game [on television]," Neely confessed to *Sports Illustrated*. "It's hard to explain. I guess I want to be out there so bad. If we have a power play, I'll watch the whole thing. Then I have to look somewhere else. It's easier for me not to look than to look."

ANOTHER INJURY. Unfortunately, on March 19, 1994, Neely injured his right knee when he collided with Ken Daneyko of the New Jersey Devils. The injury forced him to miss the rest of the season and the play-offs. The new injury almost convinced Neely to retire. An afternoon at a in-line skating rink after the season, however, made him decide to continue. "Anytime you come back from something a lot of people don't expect you to, it's a great feeling," Neely told the *Sporting News* during the Bruins' training camp before the 1994-95 season. "That day on Rollerblades, I proved to myself that the knee would be just fine. I couldn't wait to get back on the ice."

DAD DIES. During the 1993-94 season Mike Neely died of cancer. Before he died, Mike Neely spent time with both his sons and had fun. "It's the same thing as before," Neely told *Sports Illustrated*. "When my career wasn't going right, my personal life was going right. Now that my career is going right, my personal life isn't going right. I not only lose my father, I lose my best friend. [You] think about him, think about things you want to tell him about. I'm lucky, I guess, to be around a team, to have all these people around me, to be involved."

The death of his parents put his hockey career into perspective. "If I couldn't play hockey again, it wouldn't be the worst thing in the world," Neely admitted in the *Sporting News*. "It would be disappointing, but it wouldn't even come close to what happened with my parents. [The injury] wasn't the best thing in the world, but it didn't come close to comparing to what my mom and dad went through. So, yeah, that probably helped in the rehab process; just realizing if I can't play again, so what? I can still do something else."

COMEBACK II. The 1995 season almost never started. The NHL owners locked the players out until they agreed to a contract. The disagreement involved issues such as players' salaries and free agency. The lockout finally ended in January 1995 when the two sides reached an agreement. The lockout caused the NHL to shorten the regular season to only 48 games. The shortened schedule called for most teams to play every other night for most of the season.

Commentators wondered how playing so many games without rest would affect Neely. The lockout, however, had helped him get his knees in shape. "I knew I'd play more than I did last year," Neely explained in the *Sporting News,* "but with the lockout my knee has had time to heal even more, and I think I've got more strength. I don't really want to say, 'Yeah, I can play almost every game.' I'm just taking it as it comes, and I'm very optimistic."

Neely returned to form and played like the player he had been before his injury. He scored 27 goals (ninth in the NHL) and added 14 assists. Neely led the NHL in power-play goals with 16. More important, he played 42 of the Bruins' 48 games. "We're seeing the real Cam Neely," Bruins coach Brian Sutter stated in the *Sporting News*. "He's on the ice every day for practice, skating better than he's ever skated, playing hard, and playing physical. We've got him killing penalties, playing all aspects of the game."

WHY SO GOOD? Neely is one of the strongest players in the NHL. He is so strong that opposing teams have a hard time moving him out from in front of their nets. "He's so strong nobody can move him out of there, and if he gets his stick on it [the puck] he's going to put it in," NHL scout Don McKenney explained in the *Sporting News*. Florida Panthers scout Paul Henry added in the same magazine: "There's nobody out here who can handle him. He's always been outstanding, but now he's dominating."

Because of his injuries, Neely probably will never be able to play every game again. "I guess I'm day-to-day for the rest of my career," he confessed to *Sports Illustrated*. "I guess that's my philosophy. You think about it, and it's not a bad philosophy for any athlete to have. Isn't every athlete just one play away from the end of his career? Couldn't any game be his last game?"

Despite his injuries, Neely has reestablished himself as one of the best power forwards in the NHL. "I think he's the [perfect] hockey player," Bruins general manager Harry Sinden told *Sports Illustrated*. "I know you have Wayne Gretzky and Mario Lemieux, and I'm not saying I wouldn't take them first in a draft, but Cam does more things, things that they don't do. He hits. He works the corners. I don't say there aren't other guys who do that, but Cam does it as well as anybody."

OFF THE ICE. Neely is single and lives in Winchester, Massachusetts, a suburb of Boston. He established the Cam Neely Foundation, which supports cancer patients and their families at the New England Medical Center. Plans are under way to open the Cam Neely House, a place where cancer patients and their families can stay during treatment.

As for the future, Neely knows his career could end any time. "There's a lot of things that I want to do," Neely explained in the *Sporting News.* "I want to play all the games, but I also want to be able to walk when I'm done playing. As much as I love playing, I'll have a lot of years after I'm playing this game to do things, too. I'm not going to sacrifice myself to play one more game. But if I can play, I'll play."

Sources

Sporting News, September 5, 1994; March 13, 1995.
Sports Illustrated, March 8, 1993; January 31, 1994.
Village Voice, March 15, 1994.
Additional information provided by Boston Bruins.

 WHERE TO WRITE:
C/O BOSTON BRUINS,
150 CAUSEWAY ST.,
BOSTON, MA 02114.

Hideo Nomo

1968—

People often call baseball the great American pastime. Although invented in the United States, many countries throughout the world play baseball. Baseball is a very popular sport in Japan, but before 1995 only one Japanese player, Masonori Murakami, had ever appeared in an American major league game. That was before Hideo Nomo signed to play with the Los Angeles Dodgers. An All-Star in Japan, "The Tornado" took the National League by storm. Nomo earned the right to be the starting pitcher in the 1995 All-Star Game and won Rookie of the Year honors. Along the way his skill and unusual pitching motion helped make him one of the most popular players in the major leagues.

Growing Up

SUPERMAN. Hideo (He-DAY-o) Nomo was born August 31, 1968, in Osaka, Japan. Nomo is the oldest son of Shizuo and Kayoko Nomo. His father is a postal worker in Osaka.

Nomo's first name means "a superman" in Japanese.

DREAMS OF MAJOR LEAGUES. Nomo grew up playing baseball. "I can't remember a day when we didn't play baseball," Nomo recalled in *Sports Illustrated for Kids*. He dreamed of playing in the United States when he was a child. Nomo developed his trademark pitching windup at Seijyo Kogyo High School, from which he graduated in 1986. He claims he does not know how he began throwing the way he does. "I just want to pitch," he told *People*. "Every part came naturally. Even I don't know how it formed." In 1988 Nomo led the Japanese baseball team to the Olympic gold medal in Seoul, South Korea.

MVP. Nomo joined the Kintetsu Buffaloes of the Japanese Pacific League in 1990. He was an instant sensation, winning both the Rookie of the Year and Most Valuable Player (MVP) Awards his first season. Nomo finished the season 18-8 with a league-leading 2.91 earned run average (ERA). He also struck out 287 batters in 235 innings and pitched 22 complete games in 29 starts. Nomo realized his dream of pitching against American major leaguers when he was 1-1 against a major league All-Star team traveling through Japan.

"TATSUMAKI." His rookie season began a streak of dominance for Nomo in Japan. His career record was 78-46 with 1,204 strikeouts (10.3 every nine innings), and a 3.15 ERA. Nomo led the Japanese major leagues in wins and strikeouts each of his first four seasons, all for a poor team. He won the Sawamura Award, the Japanese equivalent of the Cy Young Award, given to the league's best pitcher. Nomo's trademark delivery earned him the nickname "Tatsumaki" or "The Tornado."

Nomo's success began to attract the attention of American major league scouts. Nomo, who wanted to play in the United States, retired from the Kintetsu Buffaloes in order to

be free from his contract. "I had to go," Nomo explained in *People*. "My wife understands. She agreed with what I wanted to do."

DODGER IMPORT. Nomo injured his arm during the 1994 season, limiting him to only 114 innings. He had always pitched a lot of innings during his career in Japan, putting strain on his arm. Many American major league teams lost interest in him, thinking his arm injury would still bother him. One team that did not back away was the Los Angeles Dodgers. The Dodgers liked what they saw of Nomo in a seven-minute workout. The Dodgers also have a long history of promoting international baseball. In the 1980s Los Angeles had great success with Fernando Valenzuela of Mexico, the last pitcher to create the excitement Nomo would cause. Valenzuela had a delivery much like Nomo's. He would look out to the outfield before delivering the ball to the plate, a move that worried batters.

Nomo signed with the Dodgers in February 1995. "I am closer to realizing my dream," Nomo told the *Sporting News*. "I would hope a lot of fans will come out and watch me perform. I will not disappoint." He received a bonus of more than $2 million. "He has the type of ability that we believe is at a major league level," Dodgers president Fred Claire told the *Sporting News*. "He carries with that a dream to play at the major league level. I think he has the ability to be a starting pitcher this year."

Nomo became the first Japanese major leaguer to move to the American major leagues. "This is very, very big news in our country," Hiroto Shibata, a Japanese reporter, explained in the *Sporting News*. "I know it's not a big story in the United States, maybe because they don't know him, but he's a star in Japan."

STORM WARNINGS. A players' strike that threatened to cancel the 1995 season delayed Nomo's first pitches. He went to the Dodgers spring training camp but pitched only against minor

◀ *Nomo winds up to deliver his pitch in the 1995 All-Star Game.*

MASONORI MURAKAMI

Masonori Murakami was the only Japanese player before Nomo to play in the American major leagues. He was a left-handed pitcher who played for the San Francisco Giants during the 1964 and 1965 seasons. Murakami was 5-1 with a 3.43 ERA in 89 innings over two seasons. He returned to Japan following the 1965 season under pressure from his parents and his former Japanese team, the Nankai Hawks. Murakami injured his arm soon after his return and his career was over. He told the *Sporting News* that Nomo's success "brought back a lot of fond memories for me."

league players. Nomo finally took the mound in an exhibition game against the New York Yankees after the settlement of the strike. He shut the Yankees down. "I don't want to see that guy again in my life—he got me all confused," Luis Polonia of the Yankees told *People*. "Thank God he's in the National League so I don't have to worry about him."

When Nomo joined the Dodgers, he became only the second Japanese player to play in the American major leagues. In his first game in the majors, Nomo held the hard-hitting San Francisco Giants to one hit in five shutout innings. A large group of reporters was on hand from Japan. "This was a very, very big start," Japanese reporter Isao Shibata discussed in the *Sporting News*. "How he performs shows how far Japanese baseball has come. By him being successful, it will open the door to Japanese people. Who knows, maybe now there will be a second Nomo or a third Nomo."

Superstar

NOMOMANIA. Nomo soon became the hottest ticket in baseball. Many fans, still angry about the strike, refused to come to games. That changed when Nomo pitched. Season attendance records were set throughout the league wherever he pitched. Supporters chanted his name and unfurled Japanese flags in the stands at Dodger Stadium. Fans also bought Nomo caps, T-shirts, jerseys, pins, and pennants. Asian fans, who never before had an Asian star to cheer for, came to games in record numbers. "Nomo is universally loved by all Asians," Ray Kim Suzuki, a Japanese/Korean American fan told *People*. "He's our pride." Japanese tourists arrived at Dodgers Stadium by the busload.

ALL-STAR. Coming up to the All-Star game, Greg Maddux of the Atlanta Braves was the likely starter for the National League. Unfortunately for Maddux, an injury prevented him from pitching. That opened the door for National League manager Bobby Cox of the Atlanta Braves to name Nomo as the team's starting pitcher. Nomo came into the game averaging almost 12 strikeouts per game and led the league with 119 strikeouts. In one stretch he struck out 50 batters in four games and struck out 14 in one contest. Nomo became the first Japanese player to play in the All-Star game. More than 15 million people watched the game in Japan.

Nomo did not disappoint his growing number of fans in the game. He struck out Kenny Lofton of the Cleveland Indians on a wicked forkball to start the game. He then struck out Edgar Martinez of the Seattle Mariners and **Albert Belle** (see entry) of the Cleveland Indians in the second inning. Nomo pitched two innings, struck out three, and gave up only one hit against the best hitters in the American League.

CULTURE SHOCK. The pressure of Nomomania was hard on the new pitcher. "Think about what he's doing," teammate Tom Candiotti explained in the *Sporting News*. "He's out here with all these Japanese news people chasing after him, he can't speak the [English] language, he's trying to become part of the team, he's representing an entire country, everyone's counting on him." Huge video screens in downtown Tokyo carried Nomo's games, often causing traffic jams. He understood the interest of American fans. "The Americans' interest in me is because I am from Japan," Nomo told *Sports Illustrated*. "Now I'd like to let them know I can compete on this level."

His manager, Tommy Lasorda, learned to communicate with his new star. "You don't have to speak English to be a genius," Lasorda told *Esquire*. "The first word I taught him was *great*. I told him, 'When people ask you how you're doing, Hideo, you just say, "Great."' Which happens to be the truth."

UNHITTABLE. Nomo throws only two pitches, a fastball and a forkball. "It's tough being a two-pitch pitcher in this league, but he's done it so far," Dodgers catcher **Mike Piazza** (see entry)

THE TORNADO

Nomo confuses hitters with his unusual windup. Gordon Verrell described his windup in the *Sporting News:* "At the top of his delivery, his arms extend high above his head. His back is arched. Then he suddenly coils, his back turned toward the plate, his left foot pointing toward second base, his eyes directed away from the batter." Dodgers manager Tommy Lasorda decided not to tinker with success. "I told them [his coaches], 'Don't touch a thing with this kid's motion or his delivery,'" Lasorda explained in *Esquire.* "'The batter doesn't know what he's doing out there, but he does.'"

told the *Sporting News.* His forkball is his strikeout pitch. "It's so good, a lot of times you know it's coming, and you still can't hit it," Mets shortstop Jose Vizcaino confessed in the *Sporting News.* Six-time National League batting champion **Tony Gwynn** (see entry) of the San Diego Padres told the *Sporting News* that it is a "miracle to even get the bat on the ball."

Nomo ran into some tough times in August, caused mainly by a stiff elbow. He went 1-3 with a 6.20 ERA. Everyone has slumps, Piazza told the *Sporting News.* "Nomo's been so outstanding for so long that he can't slip up without it being a federal case," Piazza said. "One thing we all go through is a slump."

TOP ROOKIE. Nomo regained his form and finished the season strong. His 1995 record was 13-6, with a 2.54 ERA and a National League-leading 236 strikeouts in 191 innings. Nomo was a leading candidate for the National League Rookie of the Year Award. Some people said he should not be considered a rookie because he had pitched in the Japanese major leagues, but the rules said he qualified. Nomo won the award, beating out third baseman Chipper Jones of the Atlanta Braves. In another first, Nomo became the first Japanese player to win this prestigious award.

The Dodgers won the National League West division title, beating out the Colorado Rockies. Their play-off run ended quickly, however, as they were swept in three straight games by the Cincinnati Reds in the first round. Nomo signed a new contract with the Dodgers following the 1995 season, so "The Tornado" will be blowing away batters in the United States in the future.

OFF THE FIELD. Nomo lives with his wife, Kikuko, and son, Takahiro. Nomo still knows only limited English, but he understands baseball in any language. "He understands what I'm trying to say to him on the mound," Piazza told *Sports Illustrated for Kids*. "Baseball is an international language."

Sources

Detroit News, November 10, 1995.
Economist, May 27, 1995.
Esquire, September 1995.
People, July 17, 1995.
Sporting News, February 27, 1995; May 15, 1995; July 17, 1995.
Sports Illustrated, February 6, 1995; May 15, 1995; July 5, 1995; August 21, 1995; September 11, 1995.
Sports Illustrated for Kids, September 1995; October 1995.
Additional information provided by Los Angeles Dodgers.

WHERE TO WRITE:
C/O LOS ANGELES DODGERS,
1000 ELYSIAN PARK AVE.,
LOS ANGELES, CA 90012.

Greg Norman

1955—

"I've always believed that things happen in life for a reason."
—Greg Norman

Greg Norman is the top-ranked golfer in the world. He has won 68 tournaments in his career and more money than any golfer in history. In 1986 and 1993, Norman won the British Open, one of the four major championships of golf. His career has been successful by any standard, but golf fans know him best for the tournaments he did not win. Seven times Norman has finished second in major tournaments, the most times any golfer has been a runner-up. The Player of the Year in 1995, Norman says he hopes fans remember him as a great golfer and not as one of the unluckiest athletes in sports history.

Growing Up

SCRAWNY LAD. Gregory John Norman was born February 10, 1955, in Mount Isa, Queensland, Australia. He grew up in the nearby towns of Townsville and Brisbane. Norman's father, Merv, worked as a mining engineer and later as the general manager of a mining company. Growing up, Norman wanted to be a pilot in the Australian Air Force. "I wanted to fly F-16s," he recalled in *Maclean's*.

Norman excelled at sports as a youngster. "I was scrawny when I was about 12 or 13," he recalled in the *New York Times*. "Then I began doing lots of surfing and swimming and football. I had a very good physical-education teacher at school who was a specialist in developing lower-back and leg muscles. I got on machines and weights there. The swimming and surfing helped upper-body muscles." Norman ran track and played rugby, Australian rules football, cricket, and squash.

LEARNS FROM MOM. Norman did not take up the game of golf until he was 16. One day he was acting as caddy for his mother, Toini. When she took a break, Norman borrowed her clubs and tried playing. He discovered that he had natural ability for the game. Norman started working with Charlie Erp, a golf teaching professional at the Royal Queensland Golf Club, who encouraged him to hit the ball as hard and as far as he could and not worry about whether it went straight.

LEARNS FROM BEST. Soon Norman began working on his accuracy and improved so that he could consistently play par golf. He also learned from the best—Jack Nicklaus. Norman read the books *Golf My Way* and *55 Ways to Lower Your Golf Score,* both written by the legendary golfer. He sneaked the books into Aspley High School and read them while he was supposed to be reading his textbooks. "Jack Nicklaus has always been my idol," Norman confided in the *New York Times*. "I studied his game and I studied his approach to the game, but I did not try to pattern my style after him."

IN TRAINING. After graduating from high school, Norman worked briefly unloading trucks. The work, though hard, helped build up his strength. He then entered a golf apprenticeship (training) program. In Australia, unlike in the United States, players must serve a three-year apprenticeship before turning professional. "People think I'm a natural golfer," Norman explained in *Sports Illustrated*. "They have no idea of what went into it."

Norman worked first at a golf shop in Sydney, running the shop during the day and picking up golf balls on the driving range. After work, he continued to practice. Golf officials, however, would not let him play in a national tournament until his apprenticeship had ended, even though he dominated amateur tournaments in his local area. His father tried to talk his son out of playing golf professionally, encouraging him to take over the family mining company. "My father's good at everything he does, except golf," Norman told *Maclean's*.

Frustrated, Norman returned home to work with Charlie Erp. He made $28 a week but earned more than that by gambling during rounds of golf. Because he could not afford to lose any money, Norman developed the ability to concentrate during these matches. "I guess you learn to play under pressure when you've got to sink a putt for $800 that you don't have," Norman stated in *People* magazine. He added in *Time* magazine: "The gambling gave me a killer instinct."

TURNS PRO. Twice Norman won the Queensland Trainees Championship and finally earned a three-month pass to play on the Australian professional tour in 1976. He finished fourth, third, and thirteenth in his first three tournaments and then won the West Lakes Classic by five strokes over established professionals. Norman got a big thrill when he played with his idol, Nicklaus, at the Australian Open. He did not play well because he was so nervous, but Nicklaus still told him he was good enough to play on the American tour.

Over the next several years Norman played in Japan and England. He did not return to Australia, because golf officials there would have required him to finish his apprenticeship. "I was learning," he later recalled about this period. "I was

Hitting out of a sand trap, Norman makes a birdie during the 1995 Masters.

changing my swing. It was too upright. It took me about five years, but I still won at least one tournament every season."

During the next few years Norman won 19 tournaments in Asia, Australia, and Europe. He first made news in the United States when he finished fourth in the 1981 Masters tournament. He played with his idol, Nicklaus, in the third round and was in the hunt for the title well into the final round. "I had a chance to win until the tenth hole of the final round, when I got a double bogey six," Norman recounted in

THE GREAT WHITE SHARK

Some people believe Norman got his nickname, "the Great White Shark," because he chewed up his competition on the golf course. He explained in the *New York Times,* however, how the name actually came about: "I did a lot of fishing on the Barrier Reef and the edge of the continental shelf 100 miles northeast of Brisbane. When you pull the fish up, the sharks eat the fish before you get them boated. So I became irritated and had a rifle in my boat and would shoot the sharks to save my catch. That's where 'the Shark' comes from."

In 1990 Norman got into a shark cage under water and attracted sharks with raw meat. "Everybody seemed to think it was dangerous," Norman stated in *Esquire.* "Really isn't, unless the shark ends up on top of the cage and starts thrashing around. Then you've got a bit of trouble, of course, because it can break the line connecting you to the boat." Norman once caught a 1,100-pound shark.

the *New York Times.* "That took the wind out of my sails."

JOINS TOUR. In 1983 Norman played in nine tournaments sponsored by the Professional Golfers Association (PGA) and earned the right to play on the U.S. tour. He won his first tournament in the United States at the 1984 Kemper Open. Two weeks after that he made a miraculous comeback at the U.S. Open. He caught the leader, Fuzzy Zoeller, by sinking a 40-foot putt on the eighteenth hole and forced a one-round play-off. Norman waved a white surrender towel as he walked down the final fairway after losing the play-off by eight strokes.

Norman finished 1984 by beating his one-time hero, Nicklaus, to win the Canadian Open. He placed in the top-ten in six of 16 tournaments he entered and won $286,724, sixth best on the tour. Norman also became a crowd favorite, talking and joking with fans. "If I'm enjoying golf, I want others to enjoy it as well," Norman told the *New York Times.*

GRAND-SLAMMED. Norman proved himself the best golfer in the world in 1986. He threatened to win golf's Grand Slam—the Masters, the PGA Championship, and the British and U.S. Opens—in one year. No golfer had ever accomplished this feat, but Norman came close to being the first. He won the British Open and led in the final round of the other three majors.

Norman birdied four holes to tie with Nicklaus at the Masters. He needed only a par on the eighteenth hole to force a play-off with his idol, but he hit a wild four-iron shot in the crowd and cost himself a chance at the title. Norman missed the shot because he wanted to win the tournament on the last hole, not settle for a play-off. "I guess what makes me the maddest is that everybody remembers my bogey at the last [hole] and not the four birdies to get there," Norman stated in *Sports Illustrated*.

Superstar

BIG WIN. Norman achieved his greatest victory so far by winning the 1986 British Open (the British Open is the oldest golf tournament in the world). The victory came at the Ailsa Course in Turnberry, Scotland, a difficult challenge. He won the tournament against the best golfers in the world by shooting an even par 280. That score was good for a five-stroke win over Gordon Brand of England. In one round, Norman scored a 63, a score equaled by only nine golfers in major tournament history.

Bob Tway defeated Norman at the PGA Championship with a miraculous 25-foot shot from a sand trap; the ball went in for a birdie after Norman had lost a four-stroke lead during the final round. This was the first time a player had ever sunk the winning shot on the last hole of a major championship from off the green. Norman ended up losing three Grand Slam tournaments by a total of nine strokes.

ANOTHER TOUGH LOSS. Norman came close to another major win in 1987, losing in a play-off to Larry Mize at the Masters. Again an amazing shot defeated him, as Mize chipped in a 140-foot shot from off the green. The ball took a perfect bounce off the fringe area around the green and rolled into the cup. "I didn't think Larry would get down in two from there, and I was right," Norman joked in *Sports Illustrated*. "He got down in one."

Despite kidding around about his misfortune, the defeats started to bother Norman. "I admit there've been times when I've gotten hurt," Norman admitted in *Sports Illustrated*. "The time Larry Mize chipped in to beat me in the Masters, for instance. I went out and sat on the beach at three o'clock in the morning and cried. When that happened, right on top of Bob Tway beating me in the PGA by holing that shot from the bunker on the final hole, I was kind of, Ohhhh, what have I done wrong? I sat down in front of my house in North Palm Beach and just listened to the surf come in."

Norman suffered a wrist injury during the 1988 U.S. Open that sidelined him for seven and one-half weeks. Despite the injury, he had seven top-ten finishes that year and won his first tournament in two years, the MCI Heritage Classic. Norman gave the trophy after that victory to a young leukemia patient, Jamie Hutton, whom he had invited to accompany him on the course.

NOT AGAIN! Bad luck continued to haunt Norman in 1989. At the Masters tournament he needed only a par on the final hole to force a play-off with Nick Faldo, but he bogeyed. "I may not show it, but I'm incredibly disappointed, incredibly down," Norman admitted in *Sports Illustrated* after the tournament.

Then, at the British Open, Norman shot a final-round 64 to come back from seven shots down to earn a spot in a three-way, four-hole play-off. "This is the greatest round I've ever played," Norman told *Sports Illustrated*. He then birdied the first two holes of the play-off, but American Mark Calcavecchia stayed right with him. Finally, Calcavecchia birdied the last hole of the play-off to defeat Norman. "Sometimes you play bad golf and win," Norman explained in *Esquire*. "Sometimes you play great golf and lose. Because of the way things ended up, people forgot what I had created that day. I had painted this beautiful picture and I didn't win."

MOST POPULAR. Norman continued to play well in 1989 and 1990, both years winning the Vardon Trophy, given annually to the player with the lowest-scoring average on the tour. He continued to play tournaments in countries around the world and made millions of dollars in endorsements. Norman's good looks, cheerful personality, and exciting game thrilled fans all over the world.

ATTITUDE ADJUSTMENT. In 1991 Norman realized he needed to change his game and his life. He had not won a tournament in 18 months and finished fifty-third on the money list, his worst showing since his first year on the PGA tour in 1984. He injured his hip and had to drop out of the U.S. Open after 27 holes. Norman also lost his confidence. "I had to look myself in the mirror and ask, 'Do you want to do the work to get back on top again?'" Norman admitted in *Golf* magazine. "It would have been easy to walk away, but that would have been quitting and I've never thought of myself as a quitter. I knew climbing back up the mountain wouldn't be easy and it wouldn't happen fast. But I knew I wanted to do it. I missed Sunday afternoons. I missed that feeling of being in the hunt. Even if you don't win, being there feels so great. I wanted that back again. But I knew it would be hard. I also knew if I did it, it would be the best feeling I've had in golf. That's what makes failure so great. You can't really appreciate success—I mean really appreciate it—until you've failed."

Norman started to work with coach Butch Harmon. "He had stopped being Greg Norman," Harmon explained in *Golf* magazine. "The Greg Norman that was the world's best player, was beautiful to watch. No complicated thoughts, just get up there and hit the ball."

Norman worked hard to get back on top. He trained and watched what he ate, losing 15 pounds and doing exercises that strengthened his hip. He also tried to eliminate distractions, like business deals through his Great White Shark Enterprises, that took his mind off his game. "I still know what's going on, but I also know my primary job every day is to play golf," Norman confided in *Golf* magazine.

BREAKS SLUMP. Norman finally won a tournament after a 30-month drought in 1992, at the Canadian Open. He defeated Bruce Lietzke in a play-off. "I'm so glad I won the Canadian Open in a playoff," Norman exclaimed in *Maclean's*. "That did more for me than winning by three or four shots. What that told me was that I could play tough shots under a lot of pressure."

FINALLY FIRST. In 1993 Norman had his greatest victory. He shot a remarkable 64 in the final round of the British Open at Royal St. George's to beat one of the best fields in golf history and win his second major tournament. "Everything was perfect," Norman explained in *Golf* magazine. "My swing was good and my concentration was perfect. It's the first time I can remember going around a golf course and not mishitting a shot." His final-round score was the best ever by a British Open champion, and his four-round total of 267 also broke the record for lowest score in the Open.

"This makes me feel so good," Norman told in *Sports Illustrated* after the tournament. "For myself, my friends, my family. They've seen what I've gone through, and they see what I want to achieve. I did that today." Norman said he hoped that the victory would make people forget all the close losses in the past. "The disappointments I've had are still there," Norman confessed in the *Sporting News*. "The relief was that I kept on working at it. I worked harder than I did when I was 22. The relief comes because I proved I can do it."

TIES RECORD. Norman threatened to win a second major tournament at the 1993 PGA Championship. He tied with Paul Azinger and again faced a sudden death play-off. He lost the tournament when he bogeyed the second hole. "I've turned my career around just when some people thought it was over," a disappointed Norman told in the *Sporting News*. "I'm going to leave here with positive feelings."

The loss meant that Norman had lost play-offs in every major championship—the Masters (1987), the PGA Championship (1993), and the British (1989) and U.S. (1984) Opens. Only one other golfer—Craig Wood, who lost all four championships in play-offs in the 1930s—can match Norman's feat. "At least I've been there," Norman told *Golf* magazine. Norman finished in the top ten a total of 12 times in 15 PGA events in 1993.

Norman started hot in 1994, shooting a remarkable 24-under par to win the Players Championships. He finished the year with the best scoring average on the PGA Tour, winning his third Vardon Trophy. In late 1994 Norman considered starting what he called the World Golf Tour, a series of eight tournaments. The PGA originally did not like the idea, fearing that players would be drawn away from their events, but finally agreed to try to work out a schedule with Norman.

SECOND AGAIN. Norman suffered two more disappointing losses in 1995. He tied for the lead in the final round of the Masters, only to bogey the seventeenth hole and eventually fall to third. Norman led the U.S. Open going into the final round but finished second for the seventh time in a major tournament, this time losing to Corey Pavin. He played consistently but went 36 holes without making a birdie. "I obviously didn't get the job done making one birdie for 36 holes," Norman admitted. "All in all, I had a good golf tournament."

NUMBER ONE. At the end of 1995, during which he won three PGA tournaments for the first time in his career, Norman led the tour in earnings and held the number one world ranking. The PGA honored him with its Player of the Year award. In his career Norman has won 53 international tournaments and 15 PGA titles. He has also won close to $10 million, the most won by any golfer in history.

OFF THE COURSE. Norman lives in Hobe Sound, Florida, with his wife, Laura, and his two children, Morgan-Leigh and Gregory. He met his wife, a former flight attendant, on a plane. They had dinner after the flight and went from there. "It was chemistry," Norman told *People* magazine. Norman likes to drive his boats and sports cars, hunt, fish, and play snooker, a card game. He also scuba dives.

Norman is still the most popular golfer in the world and makes more money in endorsements than any other athlete

NOT SECOND-BEST

Finishing second so many times in major tournaments has led some experts to call Norman a choker—someone who cracks under pressure. That he has been so close to winning so many major tournaments, however, proves that he plays very well in the most important competitions in golf. Some experts, including Jack Nicklaus, believe that the reason Norman has lost so many times is that he refuses to play safe when the title is on the line. He is a very aggressive player and always goes for his shots. "He's always right there on the edge," ABC golf commentator Jack Whittaker explained in *Esquire*. "Always on the attack. Perhaps that's why he's lost some of the ones he's lost. But it's also why you can't ever take your eyes off him."

except Michael Jordan. He is involved with many charitable causes and hosts the annual Franklin Templeton Shark Shootout.

Norman tries not to let the disappointments of his career get him down. "I've always believed that things happen in life for a reason," he explained in *Golf* magazine. "The shots people made to beat me during that one period, the ups and downs I've had, and definitely my slump. That was a test, and you know what? I passed the test. That, more that anything, makes me feel good about myself."

Sources

Atlanta Journal and Constitution, April 10, 1995.
Esquire, June 1990.
Golf, May 1988; May 1990; June 1990; August 1990; April 1991; August 1993; September 1993; October 1993; July 1994.
Los Angeles Times, June 15, 1986; March 23, 1987.
Maclean's, July 16, 1984; September 13, 1993.
New York Newsday, April 5, 1987.
New York Times, June 20, 1981; July 16, 1984; June 9, 1986; June 14, 1987; June 12, 1989; October 26, 1995.
People, August 20, 1984; April 17, 1987.
Sport, September 1987.
Sporting News, July 26, 1993; August 23, 1993.
Sports Illustrated, August 25, 1986; June 22, 1987; April 24, 1989; July 31, 1989; October 28, 1991; July 26, 1993; August 23, 1993; April 4, 1994; November 28, 1994; July 10, 1995.
Time, November 21, 1988.
Washington Post, April 12, 1988; August 14, 1988.
Additional information provided by the PGA Tour, Knight-Ridder Newspapers, June 18, 1995, and Reuters news service, August 14, 1994.

WHERE TO WRITE:
C/O PGA TOUR,
112 TPC BLVD.,
PONTE VEDRA BEACH, FL 32082.

Dan O'Brien

1966—

D an O'Brien of the United States has earned the title "the World's Greatest Athlete." Three times he has won the gold medal in the decathlon, the most grueling event in track and field, at the World Track and Field Championships. In 1992 O'Brien broke the world record in the decathlon, and several times he has threatened to surpass 9,000 points, a barrier no man has ever reached. Despite his accomplishments, many fans remember him for the competition he did not win—the 1992 U.S. Olympic Trials. A mistake in the pole vault cost O'Brien a chance to win an Olympic gold medal in the decathlon, but he hopes to achieve this goal at the 1996 Summer Olympics in Atlanta, Georgia.

*"His performances are godlike."
—Bruce Jenner, former decathlon world-record holder*

Growing Up

ADOPTED SON. Dan O'Brien was born July 18, 1966, in Portland, Oregon. His parents gave him up for adoption at birth. O'Brien spent his first two years of life in an orphanage. In

1968 Jim and Virginia O'Brien adopted him. The O'Briens, who are Caucasian, adopted six children of different nationalities (including African American, Native American, and Hispanic). Virginia O'Brien also had two children of her own from another marriage. Despite the unusual makeup of his family, O'Brien feels as though he had a normal childhood growing up in Klamath Falls, Oregon. "I never felt like an outcast," O'Brien told in *People* magazine.

O'Brien knows very little about his biological parents. The adoption agency told the O'Briens "that his father was black, 6' 3", and very athletic; that his mother was at least part Finnish; and that one or both of them were college professors," Larry Hunt, O'Brien's high school track coach, explained in *Sports Illustrated*. O'Brien today has no interest in locating his biological parents.

As a child, O'Brien was always very active. "The first thing he did after we got him was jump off a picnic table and start running," Jim O'Brien recalled in *People* magazine. Virginia O'Brien added in the same magazine, "We looked at him and said, 'He's going to be in the Olympics.'" O'Brien had a hard time concentrating and could not pay attention to anything for very long. Because of this, he had difficulty in school. Later doctors learned that O'Brien suffered from attention deficit disorder (ADD). "I couldn't read an article to the end," O'Brien told *Sports Illustrated*. "I couldn't sit in one place for five minutes."

GROWTH SPURT. It took until his sophomore year at Henley High for O'Brien to blossom as an athlete. A growth spurt made him grow almost six inches that year. "He grew so much his bones hurt," recalled Jim O'Brien in *Sports Illustrated*. As a senior (1984), O'Brien won the state championships in the 100-meter dash, the long jump, and two hurdle

events. "He was an exceptional hurdler, long jumper and sprinter in high school," his future coach at the University of Idaho, Mike Keller, recounted in *Boys' Life*. O'Brien also won All-State honors in basketball and football.

NATIONAL CHAMP. Also in 1984 O'Brien finished fourth in the U.S. Junior decathlon, even though he had not paid much attention to pole-vaulting or the track-and-field throwing events. After graduating from high school he wanted to go to the University of Oregon to play football and run track, but the school did not offer him a scholarship. O'Brien could not afford to pay for school, so he accepted a scholarship at the University of Idaho.

BAD HABITS. O'Brien's life took a damaging turn when he went away to college. Never a good student, he had trouble taking his schoolwork at Idaho seriously. "My attitude was, 'A seven-page paper? You're kidding,'" he admitted in *People* magazine. O'Brien began to get into trouble. He stopped

O'Brien clears a vault during a decathlon in Germany.

training, skipped classes, smoked marijuana, and drank heavily. "Drinking was just something I did all the time," O'Brien confessed in *Runner's World.* "I wouldn't have said I was an alcoholic at the time, but I probably was. I also used to smoke pot heavily. Sometimes I'm out of control. I admit that."

Soon O'Brien got into so much trouble that he ran up a $5,000 debt. He wrote checks to pay for things without actually having the money. In late 1987 O'Brien lost his scholarship and campus police came and threw him out of the dorm. He was out of money but was too embarrassed to go home and see his parents. "I was so disgusted with my life that I couldn't face my family," O'Brien recalled in *Runner's World.* "Everyone at school had gone home, but I stayed here all alone, rolling joints and drinking beer. I was so depressed that the only way out I could see was to start training again."

CLIMBING BACK. "It was the lowest point of his life," Keller told *People* magazine. "Danny had to hit rock bottom before he started climbing back up." O'Brien tried to get his life together and asked Idaho for another chance. Keller agreed to give him one last shot. "Dan caused problems, and there was a lot of pressure on Mike to get rid of him," Rick Sloan, another of O'Brien's coaches, told *Runner's World.* "But Mike stuck with him. If he hadn't, Dan would be at the rescue mission up in Spokane. He'd be gone. He would have nothing." Keller paid O'Brien's tuition in junior college and did all he could to help his pupil. "Basically I kept him alive," Keller told *Runner's World.* "I had to. There was no way I could let him die. Any coach would have done the same."

WORKS TO IMPROVE. O'Brien attended junior college and raised his grades. He also worked hard to get in shape and change his attitude. "Rick Sloan and I say to each other, 'We're watching this guy grow up right before our eyes,'" Keller stated in *People* magazine. O'Brien's hard work paid off when he qualified for the 1988 U.S. Olympic Trials. "That was my goal: to qualify for the Trials," O'Brien recalled in *Runner's World.* "But I wasn't prepared. I just got by on my speed." O'Brien hurt his leg in the second event and had to pull out of the competition.

The experience at the Olympic Trials helped O'Brien. "As I was leaving the track in Indianapolis [where the Trials were held] I could see what the other guys were like, and I realized they weren't better athletes than I was," O'Brien recounted in *Runner's World*. "They had more experience and knew the event better. That's all. Right then, I committed to doing better in school and applying myself on the track."

GETS NOTICED. O'Brien burst onto the scene in 1990 by finishing second in a meet sponsored by The Athletics Congress (TAC). At the 1990 Goodwill Games, he began a good-natured rivalry with his teammate Dave Johnson. Johnson defeated his fellow American in the decathlon by 45 points, winning the event in the last race, the 1,500-meters. This was the first time an American had won the decathlon in an international competition since Bruce Jenner won the gold medal at the 1976 Summer Olympics. It was also the first time since 1975 that two athletes from the United States finished first and second in the decathlon.

BEST IN U.S. At the TAC meet in June 1991 O'Brien broke the American decathlon record, set at the 1976 Summer Olympics by Bruce Jenner. He scored 8,844 points at the meet, missing the world record by only three points. "His performances are godlike," Jenner told *Boys' Life*. If O'Brien had run one second faster in the 1,500-meter run or leapt one-quarter inch farther in the long jump, he would have broken the world record set by Daley Thompson of Great Britain at the 1984 Summer Olympics. "People used to say, 'I wonder if Dan is ever going to blossom,'" O'Brien told *People*. "I used to wonder myself. I don't anymore."

THE DECATHLON

The decathlon is the most grueling event in track and field. It includes competition in ten events over two days. The first day of competition includes the 100-meter dash, long jump, shot put, high jump, and 400-meter run. On the second day the decathlete is required to successfully compete in the 110-meter hurdles, discus throw, pole vault, javelin throw, and 1,500-meter run. To win, a decathlete must have speed, strength, and, most important, endurance. Decathletes earn points for their time, height jumped, or distance thrown in each event. It is possible to win a decathlon without winning any of the individual events.

Because the decathlon has so many events that require different skills, experts usually refer to the winner of the Olympic decathlon as the world's greatest all-around athlete. King Gustav V of Sweden first used the title, using it to refer to the great Jim Thorpe, the decathlon champion at the 1912 Olympic Games.

WORLD CHAMP. O'Brien participated in the 1991 World Track and Field Championships in Tokyo, Japan. He won the gold medal in the decathlon—and the title of the world's greatest athlete—by 263 points over his nearest competitor. O'Brien scored 8,812 points, becoming the first decathlete to score more than 8,000 points twice in the same year. He had reached the top of his sport.

Superstar

BIGGEST MISS. Early in 1992 O'Brien suffered a stress fracture in his right foot. The injury forced him to do all his running in a pool so that he would not put too much pressure on his foot. Then, just before the Olympics, O'Brien sprained his ankle throwing the javelin. "The whole year, we haven't been able to train six days in a row," Coach Keller told *Sports Illustrated*.

O'Brien traveled to the 1992 U.S. Olympic Trials in New Orleans, Louisiana, hoping to set a world record. He started fast in the competition, finishing the first five events with a record total of 4,698 points. On the second day of competition, O'Brien did well in the discus and the 110-meter hurdles and seemed on his way to a world record. He led his commercials partner, Johnson, by an overwhelming margin.

NO POINTS. The pole vault worried O'Brien the most of all the decathlon events. He had not vaulted in a meet all spring because of his injuries. Still, O'Brien's personal best vault was 17 feet ³/₄ inches and he had vaulted 16 feet ³/₄ inches in practice. Keller and O'Brien decided to skip the first four heights of the pole vault in an effort to earn more points. The bar stood at 15 feet 9 inches before O'Brien attempted his first vault.

O'Brien missed his first vault but did not worry because he had two more tries. When he also missed his second vault, though, coming down on top of the bar, Keller and Sloan became nervous. O'Brien had to clear at least one height to get any points in the event, and he had only one vault left.

The tension made O'Brien nervous. Twice he ran up to attempt his final vault, and twice he stopped because he knew his footwork was not right. Finally, O'Brien tried his final jump. He knew halfway up to the bar that he would not make it, and he and his Olympic dream fell into the landing pit. O'Brien's failure to clear even one height in the pole vault dropped him to twelfth place in the standings with his two weakest events—the javelin and the 1,500 meters—left in the competition. Soon he and his coaches realized he could not make the Olympic team. "I realized it was over," O'Brien recalled in *Sports Illustrated*. Johnson went on to win the competition.

"I felt numb at first," O'Brien revealed in *Sports Illustrated*. "I wanted to turn to somebody and say, 'Hey, this shouldn't be happening to me. Do something. Somebody do something.'" O'Brien broke down and cried, admitting that the pressure had gotten to him. "I jump that as an opening height in practice," O'Brien explained in *Sports Illustrated*. "I can't remember a day when I didn't clear that height." What made his disappointment worse was that he and his coaches decided to start at a higher height when he might have made a lower jump. "You'd think they'd get something down, some mark, something in the bank," a shocked Jim O'Brien said to *Sports Illustrated* after the meet.

WATCHES OLYMPICS. Robert Zmelik of Czechoslovakia won the 1992 Olympic gold medal in the decathlon, and Johnson finished third. Zmelik's coach, Libor Varhanik, admitted in *Sports Illustrated* that the true champion did not compete in the Olympics. "We both know," Varhanik told Keller, "that if Dan had been at the Olympics, it would have been a different story." O'Brien acted as a commentator for NBC during the Olympics, but his loss cost him a fortune in endorsements and commercials. "I had the opportunity to set myself up, I guess," O'Brien stated in the same magazine. "But I can't be bummed about money I never had."

WORLD RECORD. O'Brien did not let his disappointment stop him from competing. In September 1992 he reestablished himself as the world's greatest athlete. At a meet in Talence, France, O'Brien broke the world record in the decathlon. In four of the ten events he achieved personal best scores, and he finished with 8,891 points. O'Brien became the first American world-record holder in the decathlon since Jenner set his mark in 1976. "The world's greatest athlete has come back to America," an excited O'Brien exclaimed in *Sports Illustrated.*

O'Brien's performance impressed the experts, including Daley Thompson. "He's bigger than me, faster than me, and stronger than me," the former world-record holder stated in *Sports Illustrated.* "He can be anything he wants to be. I see him as a 9,500-point man."

KEEPS WINNING. In March 1993 O'Brien set another world record, this time the indoor record in the heptathlon. (The heptathlon consists of five events.) He further solidified his position as the world's greatest athlete by winning the decathlon gold medal at both the 1993 and 1995 World Track and Field Championships.

THE FUTURE. O'Brien sets high standards for himself. He wants to win a gold medal in the decathlon at the 1996 Summer Olympics in Atlanta, Georgia. "My goal is to win the gold medal," O'Brien stated in *Runner's World.* "If I don't, my career won't be complete." O'Brien also has his sights set on becoming the first decathlete to surpass the 9,000-point mark. He knows he has to improve his performance in his worst event, the 1,500-meters, if he is going to reach this level. "I'm afraid of it," O'Brien told *Runner's World* about his least-favorite event. "The pain scares me. I think I'm gonna die. My legs are shaking, and I have that achy, queasy feeling. My stomach's churning, and I've got the cold sweats because I'm so nervous. But the 1,500 is important because it's the last event, and everybody remembers it."

O'Brien knows that as the Olympics approach more and more people will ask him about his failure in the pole vault at the 1992 Olympic Trials. "As I get closer to Atlanta, everybody's going to start focusing on the pole vault," O'Brien stated in *Runner's World*. "It's something you never forget. Every decathlon, in my first attempt in the pole vault, I always think about what happened in '92. It's my motivation not to make a mistake like that again."

O'Brien's best asset is his speed. He also has great strength, important in the discus, shot put, and javelin throw. O'Brien needs to train hard to compete in so many events. He practices six hours a day, four days a week and usually competes on one of the days he does not train. O'Brien also eats right. "It's important to eat a big breakfast and drink lots of water," O'Brien explained in *Boys' Life*.

OFF THE TRACK. O'Brien enjoys playing golf and video games. After his track career has ended, he would like to try acting. O'Brien has important things to tell children. "I like to show kids that it's cool to get your work done instead of goofing off and being a jerk," O'Brien told *Runner's World*. "So I visit classrooms or walk over to the local school and have lunch with the kids. Nobody really talked to me when I was young. If they had, I would have been a better student. I like to show them there's hope. Look at me. I wasn't a great athlete until I started to work hard." O'Brien helped start the National High School Decathlon Championships in 1994.

O'Brien likes to compete, but not train. "Doing a decathlon is definitely fun, but the training isn't," O'Brien explained in *Runner's World*. "The thing I love about the decathlon is you always get another chance. Plus, you get to do 10 different things." O'Brien is so good that the only competition he has is the world record. "I'm my biggest opponent," O'Brien stated in *Runner's World*. "The decathlon is a competition against yourself."

Sources

Boys' Life, April 1992.
New York, February 10, 1992.
People, August 19, 1991.
Runner's World, May 1992; November 1995.

Sports Illustrated, August 6, 1990; July 6, 1992; July 13, 1992; September 14, 1992; March 22, 1993; July 27, 1994.
Additional information provided by USA Track and Field.

WHERE TO WRITE:
USA TRACK AND FIELD,
P.O. BOX 120,
INDIANAPOLIS, IN 46206.

Mike Piazza

1968—

No one can ever call Mike Piazza a quitter. Despite being the 1,389th player taken in the 1988 major league draft, Piazza, who plays for the Los Angeles Dodgers, has become the best catcher in major league baseball through hard work and determination. Although scouts said he would never make it after his high school career ended, Piazza kept working and proved all the experts wrong. The 1993 National League (NL) Rookie of the Year and an All-Star in each of his three major league seasons, Piazza continues to work hard to improve. Now he has just one goal: to be one of the best catchers in major league history.

"I'll never take this game for granted. Never."
—Mike Piazza

Growing Up

LEARNS VALUE OF HARD WORK. Michael Joseph Piazza was born September 4, 1968, in Norristown, Pennsylvania. Piazza grew up in Schuylkill Township, Pennsylvania, a suburb of Philadelphia. His father, Vince, dropped out of high school at age 16 to help support his family. Vince Piazza started with one used car lot and through hard work built his business into a nationwide empire of 50 automobile dealerships. He expanded his business into real estate and now owns a computer service company. Today, Vince Piazza is worth an estimated $100 million, and in 1992 he tried to buy the San Francisco Giants.

Being the son of a wealthy man was not always easy for Piazza. "People, knowing my father was successful at business, looked on me as a—well, I guess 'dilettante' [unprofessional] is the word," Piazza explained in *GQ*. "I mean, I grew up in a regular house in a regular neighborhood. It wasn't like I was getting oboe [musical instrument] lessons." Having a wealthy father was no replacement for hard work. "It was me that gave Michael the tools, but it was Michael who used them," Vince Piazza told the *Los Angeles Times*.

PLAY BALL. Piazza always loved baseball. "You've got to understand, the only thing Michael ever wanted to do was play baseball," Vince Piazza recounted in the *Los Angeles Times*. "When he was in high school and the other kids were at the dances, Michael was in the batting cage. When he would finish playing a game, he would come home and practice more."

Piazza hit baseballs at a mattress up against the wall in his basement. Sometimes he hit off a batting tee, and his father also pitched to him. When Piazza was 11, he and his father built a pitching machine and batting cage in the backyard. Piazza hit close to 300 balls a day in his backyard, even during the coldest winter days. In the winter he warmed the baseballs on the stove and wrapped tape around the bat handle so it would not sting his hands. As Piazza grew older, his

Piazza (left) tags out Chicago Cubs baserunner Brian McRae. ▶

father built a roof and walls on the batting cage and put in a heater.

He continued to use the batting cage until he graduated from high school. "I was out there every day," Piazza recalled in *Sports Illustrated*. "I would come home from school, get a snack, watch cartoons and then hit. Every spring I would see that I was hitting the ball farther and farther." Piazza knew at a young age that he had to work hard to succeed. "I wasn't blessed with a lot of natural talent," Piazza admitted in *Sports Illustrated for Kids*. "Nothing came easy for me. I had to work to perfect my skills."

FAMILY FRIEND. Piazza's hard work helped him attract the attention of Los Angeles Dodgers manager Tommy Lasorda. Lasorda was a distant relative and childhood friend of Piazza's father's. "I used to let Mike be our batboy when we played in Philadelphia," Lasorda told *Sports Illustrated for Kids*. "I pitched to him and saw the power he had." Lasorda and Vince Piazza joked around about the young slugger someday playing for the Dodgers. "It's something we had hoped would happen," Lasorda admitted in *Sports Illustrated*.

TOO SLOW. Piazza played first base on his Phoenixville High School baseball team. He hit .442 as a senior with 11 home runs and broke the school's career home run record. The team named him Most Valuable Player. Unfortunately, no major league teams were interested in Piazza. "One reason Mike was overlooked [was that] he only played first base here and was slow, and a lot of scouts said, 'I can find someone who can match the offensive performance with better speed,'" Phoenixville High coach Doc Kennedy recounted in *Sport* magazine. It looked like Piazza's dream of playing in the major leagues would not come true. "I have talked to a lot of scouts since then who said they didn't like anything about me," Piazza stated in *Sports Illustrated*. "They said that I couldn't run or hit."

1,389TH As a favor to Lasorda, the University of Miami gave Piazza a place on the Hurricanes baseball team. He did not play much at Miami, going one for nine his freshman season. Piazza transferred to Miami-Dade North Community College and hit .364 his first year there. The Dodgers picked Piazza as a favor to Lasorda in the sixty-second round of the 1988 major league free-agent draft. He was the 1,389th player chosen that year. "I asked the Dodgers to draft him as a favor," Lasorda recalled in *Sports Illustrated*. "And, thank God, they did."

Lasorda and the Dodgers expected Piazza to stay in school, but he asked for a tryout instead. He was impressive, good enough for Los Angeles to sign him. "I just hammered balls into the blue seats," Piazza recounted in *Sports Illustrated*. The Dodgers gave Piazza $15,000, but he said he would have paid them to play.

CATCHING ON. Because there were so many good first basemen in the Dodgers system, Piazza switched to catcher. He spent four years in the minors trying to learn baseball's most physically difficult position. He traveled to the Dominican Republic and Mexico, struggling because he did not know Spanish and could not talk with his teammates. "It was very difficult for me to adapt to that position," Piazza confessed in *Sports Illustrated for Kids*. "But once I did and I started making some progress, I became that much more intense on trying to improve and working to make the big leagues as a catcher."

As Piazza struggled to learn his new position, coaches, players, and fans teased him about his relationship with Lasorda. They said that he only made the team because of his father's friendship with the Dodgers manager. People mistakenly thought Piazza was Lasorda's godson, but that honor actually fell to Piazza's younger brother, Timmy. "I can remember ninety-nine interviews that began, 'Tell me about this godfather thing,'" Piazza stated in *GQ*. One night when playing at Vero Beach he quit the team and went home. Fortunately, he soon returned. "He went through some tough times, boy," Lasorda recounted in the *Los Angeles Times*. "I was just hoping and praying they would leave him alone. I knew he could do it if given the opportunity because he was on such a mission."

DODGERS DANDY. In 1992 Piazza had his best season in the minors. He hit .341 with 16 home runs in 94 games for the Dodgers' top farm club, in Albuquerque, New Mexico. These numbers were good enough for the Dodgers to call him up to the majors in September. Piazza went 3-3 in his first game and batted .232 with one home run the rest of the season. He had earned a chance to make the big league team in 1993.

Superstar

STARTING CATCHER. The Dodgers took a chance before the 1993 season when they did not re-sign 13-year veteran catcher Mike Scioscia. Piazza, with 21 big-league games under his belt, was the most experienced catcher on the Los Angeles roster. He won the starting job with a hot spring training, batting .478 with four home runs. Former Dodgers catcher Roy Campanella helped the young Dodgers backstop, and Piazza said he was "very inspirational to me and helped me out a lot."

Piazza also worked to learn about the Los Angeles pitchers. "I had to earn their respect, no doubt about it," Piazza explained in *GQ*. "The pitchers kind of took me under their wing. I would always talk to them when I wasn't playing. I learned their personalities and the way they think on the mound."

ROOKIE OF THE YEAR. Piazza had a sensational rookie season. He batted .318 (seventh in the NL), set a major league rookie record for catchers with 35 home runs (sixth in the NL), and drove in 112 runs (fourth in the NL). More impressive, Piazza played 146 games behind the plate, a tough workload for a catcher, and threw out a franchise-record 58 runners attempting to steal. The National League named him to the All-Star team.

Piazza topped off his season by hitting two home runs and driving in five runs in the season finale, knocking the rival San Francisco Giants out of the play-offs. The fans at sold-out Dodger Stadium gave him a standing ovation. "I think they were just expressing that they, you know, recognized what I'd done," Piazza explained in *Sport* magazine. "I've fed off them all year. I wish I could individually thank each of them."

Piazza earned unanimous Rookie of the Year honors in 1993, only the ninth player ever to do so. He also won the Silver Slugger Award, given annually to the league's best hitter at each position. After the season he signed a three-year, $4.2 million contract, the largest guaranteed deal ever for a second-year player. Piazza promised to earn his pay and not suffer from the so-called sophomore jinx that often affects second-year players. "I've got to constantly push myself, work twice as hard, constantly prove that I can do it again," Piazza stated in the *Sporting News*. "I had one good year. But I can't put myself in the category of an 'all-time player' or anything like that. Not until I do it year after year."

SECOND-YEAR SENSATION. No sophomore jinx could slow Piazza down in 1994. He batted .319 (tenth in the NL), hit 24 home runs (tenth in the NL), and drove in 92 runs (fifth in the NL) in only 107 games. Piazza earned the starting catcher job for the 1994 All-Star Game and went one-for-four in the mid-summer classic. The only thing that could stop Piazza was a players' strike. The strike, caused by a disagreement between players and owners over such issues as free agency, ended the season in August. Before the 1995 season, Piazza announced that he would donate $100 for every home run he hit to help the ushers, ticket takers, concession workers, and parking cashiers at Dodger Stadium. These people did not get paid during the strike.

BEST SEASON. Piazza continued to improve in 1995. In the first ten games of the season he batted .537 with four home runs and 13 runs batted in (RBI). Piazza fell rounding first

ROOKIE ROSTER

Eight Dodger rookies in the last 17 years have won the National League Rookie of the Year award. Following is a list of these award winners and the year they won the award:

Player	Year
Rick Sutcliffe	1979
Steve Howe	1980
Fernando Valenzuela	1981
Steve Sax	1982
Eric Karros	1992
Mike Piazza	1993
Raul Mondesi	1994
Hideo Nomo	1995

base after a hit, however, and tore ligaments in his left thumb. After missing almost a month with the injury, he returned to take the lead in the National League batting race at .367. Only two catchers in history had ever won an NL batting title, Bubbles Hargrave (1926) and Ernie Lombardi (1938 and 1942).

Piazza again started for the NL in the All-Star Game and hit his first All-Star home run. He finished the season second in the NL batting race behind **Tony Gwynn** (see entry) of the San Diego Padres. Piazza hit a career-high .347, blasted 32 home runs, and drove in 93 runs in only 112 games. He also helped pitcher **Hideo Nomo** (see entry) feel at home in the major leagues and backstopped the pitching staff to the second-lowest earned run average in the NL. The Dodgers won the NL West Division, edging out the Colorado Rockies, but were swept out of the play-offs by the Central Division champion Cincinnati Reds.

WHY SO GOOD? Piazza is a very patient hitter and waits for a pitcher to make a mistake. "He's a very good mistake hitter," four-time Cy Young Award-winning pitcher Greg Maddux of the Atlanta Braves explained in *Sports Illustrated*. "I hung a changeup to him, and he hit it out of the park. He's one of the better hitters in the game right now; he has tremendous bat speed." Piazza has great power and is able to hit home runs to all fields.

Piazza knows he still has to work hard on his defense. "Listen, I know there are times when I'm not great behind the plate," Piazza admitted in the *Sporting News*. "It's fatiguing being behind the plate every game, but because of my bat, they [the Dodgers] can't afford to take me out of the lineup too often."

The most important strength Piazza brings to the field is his intensity. "He takes everything so seriously," teammate Eric Karros told *Sports Illustrated*. Pitcher Tom Candiotti added: "Catching is not a casual thing for him. If I lose a game, he feels like he let me down." Piazza promises to continue to work hard. "I'll never take this game for granted," Piazza said in the *Los Angeles Times*. "Never. I've worked too hard to get here. It's something I've always been taught, and lived by. I know this can be gone as easily as it came."

OFF THE FIELD. Piazza lives in Manhattan Beach, California. His parents now own a house that overlooks Valley Forge National Historical Park, the site where George Washington and the Continental Army stayed during the brutal winter of 1777-78. Washington slept in a farmhouse that is on the property. Piazza has made guest appearances on the television shows *Baywatch, The Bold and the Beautiful,* and *Married With Children.* He also was a guest host on MTV and did a commercial for ESPN. Piazza likes to play golf and is a big hockey fan.

Piazza loves heavy-metal music and stays in shape by playing the drums. He started to play when he was 18 after his father bought him a drum set for Christmas. "I am crazy about it," Piazza confessed in *Sports Illustrated for Kids.* "It's fun and it takes my mind off baseball. I'm an aggressive person and I needed an outlet to vent my frustrations. You know, to hit something." Piazza learned how to play by watching his favorite bands on television. "It's not an easy instrument to play," Piazza explained in the same magazine. "People I know in the music world are surprised that I learned so much just by watching." Some day Piazza wants to record his own album, and the band Anthrax invited him to play with them in concert.

Experts rate Piazza as the best catcher in the major leagues, and some scouts think he may be the most valuable player in baseball. "I was involved in a recent survey, and they asked me if I could pick any player in the National League to start a team, who would I pick," major league scout Mel Didier told the *Los Angeles Times.* "You know I thought about it, went over every player on every team, and came up with only one guy: Mike Piazza. He is that good."

Sources

Baseball Digest, July 1994.
Boys' Life, May 1994.
GQ, May 1994.
Los Angeles Times, April 16, 1995.

Sport, May 1994.

Sporting News, July 27, 1992; February 28, 1994; April 17, 1995; April 24, 1995; September 4, 1995; September 25, 1995.

Sports Illustrated, July 5, 1993; March 21, 1994; September 4, 1995.

Sports Illustrated for Kids, September 1994; June 1995.

Additional information provided by Los Angeles Dodgers.

WHERE TO WRITE:
C/O LOS ANGELES DODGERS,
1000 ELYSIAN PARK AVE.,
LOS ANGELES, CA 90012.

Mary Pierce

1975—

Mary Pierce hits the ball as hard as or harder than any other female tennis player in the world. At the 1995 Australian Open she blew away Arantxa Sanchez Vicario to win her first ever Grand Slam tennis tournament. The victory may finally make people forget the story of Pierce and her father, who abused her while trying to make her a tennis champion. In 1993 Pierce broke away from her father and found happiness—both on the court and off—for the first time by just being herself.

"I think fun is the main word. My life off the court has changed. I'm feeling good inside, so I guess it shows on the outside, too."—Mary Pierce

Growing Up

DUAL CITIZENSHIP. Mary Caroline Pierce was born on January 15, 1975, in Montreal, Quebec, Canada. Her parents, Jim and Yannick, met in Montreal. Yannick was a French exchange student when she met Jim, a U.S. citizen. Because of her parent's nationalities, Pierce is both a U.S. and a French citizen. The family, including Pierce's younger brother,

David, eventually moved to Hollywood, Florida, where Jim Pierce worked as a custom jeweler and jewelry salesman.

TAKES UP TENNIS. As a child, Pierce showed talent as a gymnast and ballet dancer. "And she always liked to play ball—any kind," Yannick Pierce told *Sports Illustrated.* A friend of hers asked her to play tennis one time, but Pierce said no. "I was a bit shy, so I said, 'Maybe next time,'" Pierce recalled in *Redbook.* Soon, however, she started playing. She learned the game of tennis quickly. When Pierce was ten she defeated the twentieth-ranked local player in the 12-and-under division only two weeks after her father had taught her to play. Within two years she was ranked the number-two player in the United States among 12-year-olds.

FATHER BECOMES COACH. Jim Pierce decided after watching his daughter at tennis lessons that he wanted to be her coach, even though he had no experience teaching tennis. Expecting much of his daughter, Jim Pierce pushed her very hard. He began to yell at her and slap her if she lost a match or if she did not practice hard enough. The better Pierce played, however, the meaner her father treated her. "He was always very tough," Pierce recalled in *People* magazine. "But the more and more I was winning, the better I was doing, the tougher he got."

Pierce trained with her father eight hours a day, sometimes until midnight. "For seven years, eight hours a day, I hit 700 serves at Mary," Jim Pierce recounted in the *Sporting News.* "We used to work until midnight. My young son slept by the net. I wouldn't let Mary leave until she got it right. Sure, she cried. I cried, too. So what?" Jim Pierce insisted he knew what was best for his daughter and argued with anyone who disagreed with him. The Hopman Academy asked Pierce to leave because of her father.

Jim Pierce would not let Mary eat cake or candy, drink

soda, or have friends. He even fired coaches and hitting part-
ners if they got too close to her. "As soon as they got friendly
with Mary, he'd get rid of them," David Pierce recalled in
Sports Illustrated. "It was all about control." Jim Pierce even
made Pierce and her first date sit and watch a tennis match.
Pierce tried to tell her mother about what was happening, but
that only caused more fighting. "When I told my mom, that
would cause fights too," Pierce revealed in *Sports Illustrated.*
"So sometimes you're afraid to say anything because of that."

LEAVES SCHOOL. In 1987 Jim Pierce took his children out of school so that the family could travel to tournaments with Mary. "I would like to have stayed in school, gone to a prom," Pierce admitted in *Sports Illustrated*. The family traveled by car and stayed in motels wherever Pierce played. Both Mary and David Pierce took correspondence courses to finish school.

TURNS PRO. Pierce turned professional just three months after her fourteenth birthday in 1989, the youngest player up until that time to do so. (The following year Jennifer Capriati turned professional when she was 13 years old.) She made her professional debut at a tournament in Hilton Head, South Carolina. Pierce won her first professional tournament in 1991 in Palermo, Italy, defeating the two top-seeds on the way to her victory. By the end of 1991 Pierce had moved up to number 26 among women's singles players in the world.

As Pierce moved up the rankings she continued to have problems with her father. During tournaments, Jim Pierce yelled and cursed from the stands, putting down either his daughter or her opponent. Other times he yelled at and even hit the parents of other players. At one point the Florida Tennis Association banned him from their tournaments for six months because of his behavior. Pierce defended her father. "He does it all for the best, you know," Pierce explained to *Sports Illustrated*. "I know that. Other people look at him and say, 'My God.' But I understand."

Because of Jim Pierce's behavior, the United States Tennis Association (USTA) stopped helping his daughter with coaches and financial support. The lack of professional training held Pierce back from becoming a better player. "He [Mr. Pierce] loves his daughter and he knows his daughter best, no argument about that," Stan Smith, former player and USTA director of coaching, stated in *Sports Illustrated*. "But I don't know if he knows how to win the big tournaments. We have coaches who can help Mary get the match experience she needs."

MOVES TO FRANCE. When the USTA withdrew its support from Pierce, the family moved to France in 1990. The French

Tennis Federation offered assistance if Pierce represented France in international competition. The move bothered the young player at the time. "I really didn't understand why we had to leave," Pierce admitted to *People* magazine. Ever since the move Pierce has considered herself a French citizen, despite living in the United States most of the year.

The change of scenery did not affect the way Jim Pierce acted. At the 1992 French Open he punched two fans and then bragged about it to the media. Pierce played for France at the 1992 Summer Olympics in Barcelona, Spain, and lost in the second round. Her father yelled at her so much after the match that she ran to the locker room in tears. Jim Pierce got so angry that he went out and wrecked his rental car. "When I lose, he kind of feels like he lost himself," Pierce tried to explain in *People* magazine. "That's why he gets so mad."

Even though Pierce defended her father, his behavior clearly bothered her. She always seemed nervous and sometimes had anxiety attacks on the court. "I think she is under tremendous pressure to do well," former player Kim Warwick explained in *Sports Illustrated* at the time. "Tremendous pressure to perform for her father." Many times Pierce lost on purpose or simply quit because her father put so much pressure on her. She often yelled back at him and once threw her racket at him. "He would be yelling at me, and I would feel like, 'I'm trying so hard and I'm not doing good enough,'" Pierce revealed in *People* magazine.

Superstar

OUT OF CONTROL. At the 1993 French Open, Pierce had her worst experience yet with her father. Jim Pierce attacked her cousin, Olivier, choking him so badly that doctors rushed him to the hospital. The reason he gave for the attack was that Olivier distracted Pierce from scouting an opponent. Later, Jim Pierce screamed at his daughter during her third-round match after she lost a set to a lower-ranked opponent. Tournament officials ejected him from the stadium.

In June 1993 the Women's Tennis Council (WTC) passed a new rule—now known as the Jim Pierce Rule—that allows the organization to ban disruptive members of a player's family or coaching staff. The WTC banned Pierce's father from the tour. "It was an accumulation of things over the past four or five years," Pierce stated in *People* magazine. "You know, things keep boiling up and get to a point where you just can't take it anymore." At every tournament officials gave security guards pictures of Jim Pierce and ordered them to keep him out of the stadium.

Also in June 1993, Pierce finally broke away from her father. She wrote him a letter asking for her freedom. "I considered doing it before, but I was always wondering if it was the right time," Pierce explained in *People* magazine. Later in the year Yannick Pierce divorced her husband. "Things accumulate," Yannick Pierce explained in *Redbook*. "It's like a drop of water falls into a glass every day, and one day the glass spills over." At the time Pierce was ranked fourteenth in the world.

NEW COACH. Pierce signed Nick Bollettieri, who had previously worked with Pierce only to be forced out by her father, as her coach. Bollettieri had coached many great players, including Andre Agassi, Boris Becker, and Monica Seles. "Nick opened my eyes and made me rethink my priorities," Pierce revealed in *Tennis* magazine. Bollettieri told *Redbook*: "It's always been my philosophy not to dwell on the past. If I can't change something, I'm not going to spend energy and time on it. The best you can do is use it as a barometer to not repeat mistakes. We talked about what we could do as a team to help her live up to her potential."

Pierce slowly began to improve. She broke a 19-match losing streak against players ranked in the top ten when she defeated Martina Navratilova and Gabriella Sabitini at the Virginia Slims Championships in November 1993. "She no longer lets herself be subjected to pressure from her entourage, and she's no longer afraid of the consequences of losing," Yannick Pierce told *People* magazine. Mary Pierce added in *Sports Illustrated:* "It's like a weight is off me. When I miss a shot, it's not the end of the world anymore."

MORE PROBLEMS. Jim Pierce did not give up on trying to get back together with his daughter. "My daughter owes everything to me, and I want her back," Jim Pierce said in an interview. He stalked Pierce and her family through France and Italy, forcing them to hire bodyguards. Jim Pierce came to tournament sites and once, according to Yannick Pierce, stole his family's passports at an airport. Another time he attacked a bodyguard with a knife while Pierce hid in the bathroom. When Jim Pierce threatened to kill Pierce and her family, Pierce took legal action against her father. She asked for restraining orders, forcing her father to stay away from her, in cities where tournaments were held.

"You never know what he's capable of," a frightened Pierce told *Sports Illustrated.* "One reason I hesitated to break away was that you just don't know what he might do." Reporters discovered at this time that Jim Pierce had a dangerous past. His real name was Bobby Glenn Pearce, and he had been convicted of a felony. At one time Jim Pierce had entered a psychiatric hospital and doctors had diagnosed him as having a mental illness.

NEW ATTITUDE. Despite still fearing her father, Pierce began enjoying her life, both on and off the court. "Just the general things that everybody gets to do, the things I was never allowed to do before: going to the movies, shopping with my girlfriends, talking to friends on the phone." Pierce told *People* magazine. Just after breaking away from her father, Pierce attended her first rock concert, seeing Aerosmith.

BREAKTHROUGH. Pierce's new attitude and confidence showed at the 1994 French Open. The French fans loved her, cheering her on because of her French citizenship. Pierce crushed opponent after opponent, losing only six games in her first five matches, and appeared to be having fun playing. She smiled at her family, friends, and fans and skipped to the back of the court after winning a point. "I'm so happy," Pierce

PLAYS FOR HERSELF

Her performance at the French Open was a turning point for Pierce. It taught her that tennis was more fun when she played for herself, not for others. "All of this was new to me, much newer than most people would think, given the fact that I've played a lot of tennis so far in my life," Pierce explained in *Tennis* magazine after the French Open. "But one very important part of what happened here is that I really found meaning in what I do, and the meaning really kept opening more and more doors inside myself. In the past, I was always pushed. Obviously, my dad was the major factor there, but it had to do with a lot of other people who also wanted me to succeed. When I started to push myself, I began to see how much more satisfying that was for me. It really opened my eyes."

admitted to *Sports Illustrated.* "Of course, I'm glad I'm winning, but it's not like it means everything. I'm healthy. Everything in my life is good."

In the semifinals Pierce faced the almost unbeatable Steffi Graf, who had beaten her both times they had played. "Oh, god, I'd just die if I won this," Pierce confessed in *Sports Illustrated* concerning her match with Graf. In an amazing demonstration of power, Pierce blew Graf off the court, winning 6-2, 6-2. "I don't know what I could have done about it," a defeated Graf told the same magazine after the match. "What tactic can you have when she puts away every point." Pierce set a record for women by losing only ten games on her way to the final.

Pierce played Arantxa Sanchez Vicario of Spain in her first ever Grand Slam final. (The Grand Slam tournaments are the Australian, French, and U.S. Opens, and Wimbledon.) She got off to a fast start, winning two out of the first three games. Rain, which had delayed the start of the match for four hours, soon started to fall again, forcing postponement of the rest of the match to the next day. The layoff seemed to hurt Pierce, who lost the match in straight sets, 6-4, 6-4.

"I was so nervous," Pierce admitted in *Sports Illustrated* after the match. "I kept telling myself, 'When are you going to have another chance?' I didn't want to let it slip away. I wasn't as calm as on the other days. I was too serious. I thought about it too much." Pierce moved up to number seven in the world.

Pierce planned to play in the 1994 Wimbledon tournament but pulled out two days before her first match. She does not like playing on the grass surface at the Wimbledon tourna-

DEALING WITH DAD

Pierce is still trying to figure out how to deal with her father. "He's my father," she explained in *People* magazine. "I just want to establish a relationship with him as father and daughter, not as a tennis coach. That's something that will take time." Pierce does give her father some credit for her success. "He pushed me hard every day," she stated in the same magazine. "He gave me a tough mental attitude to keep fighting and a hard work ethic." Pierce visited her father in December 1993. She still pays his bills, but insists that he will never again be involved in her tennis. "We don't see each other very often or talk about much," Pierce told *Redbook*. "And when we do, it has nothing to do with tennis anymore. That's what ruined our relationship in the first place. Sometimes it can start to be a little weird, but I just try to not let it upset me."

ment and also worried that her father might show up to cause problems. "It's a variety of reasons, including her father's behavior, the media, the fact that she's been under a lot of pressure generally," a representative of the All England Club, where the tournament is held, told reporters.

BIG WIN. Pierce's big breakthrough came at the 1995 Australian Open. In the six weeks leading up to the tournament, she worked out hard, preparing herself for the hot temperatures in Australia. Bollettieri also told his young pupil to do what she does best—hit the ball hard—and not worry about strategy.

Pierce took Bollettieri's advice and rolled to the finals. In the championship match, Pierce again faced Sanchez Vicario. Nerves bothered Pierce at the beginning of the match, causing her to double-fault twice in her first serving game. She got herself together quickly, however, and began knocking shots past Sanchez Vicario on the way to a 6-3, 6-2 victory. "I just haven't realized what has happened yet," Pierce explained to *Time* magazine after the match. "I'm still reeling from it."

The victory moved Pierce up to third in the world and established her as one of the game's great players. "Everybody said, 'Mary can play, but can she play well all the time?'" Pierce stated in *Sports Illustrated*. "This was important for me."

The rest of 1995 was disappointing for Pierce on the court—she failed to reach any more Grand Slam finals—but her personal life kept improving. "It's simple," Pierce explained in *People* magazine. "I think fun is the main word. My life off the court has changed. I'm feeling good inside, so I guess it shows on the outside, too. I feel that I'm just beginning now. Every day I get stronger."

OFF THE COURT. Pierce lives most of the year in Bradenton, Florida. Someday she would like to be a model and has posed in *Tennis Match* magazine. Pierce likes to go out dancing, play backgammon, cards, and miniature golf, cook, read, and watch MTV. Other sports she enjoys are biking, jet skiing, and swimming. Her favorite actors are Tom Cruise and Nick Nolte, and her favorite actress is Demi Moore. Because Pierce must work so hard at tennis, she does not have much time for dating.

For now, Pierce is happy with her life. "I'm finally becoming Mary Pierce the player," Pierce explained to *Sports Illustrated*. "It was always Mary Pierce and her father did this or Mary Pierce and her father did that. Now it's just Mary Pierce. The true me is finally coming out."

Sources

New York Times, June 28, 1995; July 24, 1995; August 18, 1995; August 19, 1995.

People, September 7, 1992; June 27, 1994.

Philadelpia Inquirer, November 7, 1994.

Redbook, September 1995.

Sporting News, November 15, 1993.

Sports Illustrated, May 7, 1990; August 23, 1993; June 13, 1994; June 27, 1994.

Sports Illustrated for Kids, September 1993.

Tennis, August 1994.

Time, February 6, 1995.

Additional information provided by Women's Tennis Association.

WHERE TO WRITE:
C/O WOMEN'S TENNIS ASSOCIATION,
215 PARK AVE., SUITE 1715,
NEW YORK, NY 10003.

Mike Powell

1963—

In 1991 Mike Powell of the United States broke the longest-standing track-and-field world record—in the long jump. In the same event he also defeated one of the great athletes of all time—Carl Lewis of the United States—for the first time. The victory established Powell as the best long jumper in the world, a title he held until 1995. An incredible athlete and fierce competitor, he hopes to win the one award he has never received—an Olympic gold medal in the long jump—at the 1996 Summer Olympic Games in Atlanta, Georgia.

"If somebody tells me I can't do something it just makes me work harder."
—Mike Powell

Growing Up

JUNIOR JUMPER. Michael Anthony Powell was born November 10, 1963, in Philadelphia, Pennsylvania. His father, John, worked as a roofer, and his mother, Carolyn, is an accountant. Powell was the youngest of three children. He was always a good jumper. "I'd go out the front door and leap right over the steps onto the sidewalk," Powell recalled in the *Philadelphia Daily News*. "I could hear my mother shouting, 'Michael!' The neighbors would call and say, 'Your son jumped over our car again.' I'd hear my mother say, 'I'll talk to him about it.'"

Other kids teased Powell about his skinny legs, but this just made him try harder to prove he was a good athlete. "I think my motivation today still comes from the other kids calling me Skinny," Powell confided in *People* magazine. "I had these real thin legs, and the other kids would say 'Hey, there's Skinny. Look at Skinny.'"

When Powell was in elementary school, his family moved from their West Philadelphia neighborhood to another area in the city. Mike remained in his old neighborhood, however, and lived with his maternal grandmother, Mary Lee Eaddy. Eaddy made sure Powell went to Baptist church every Sunday. She also taught him to be a good person and to always be honest. Powell has remained close to his grandmother throughout his life.

CALIFORNIA BOUND. Powell's parents divorced and Mike moved with his mother to West Covina, California, a suburb of Los Angeles in 1974. He starred in several sports at Edgewood High School. Powell played point guard on the varsity basketball team and showed his excellent jumping ability by leaping over the centers of the other team. In track he excelled at the high jump, leaping higher than seven feet, an outstanding achievement for a teenager. Powell was also one of the state's top performers in the triple jump and long jump. An excellent student, he earned All-American honors in the classroom.

Despite being a top high school athlete, Powell did not receive much attention from college recruiters. "Even people I had beaten were getting better scholarship offers than I was," Powell recalled in *Sports Illustrated*. "I couldn't understand it. I had a 3.2 grade point average, scored over 1,000 on my SATs, and made academic all-American. Maybe they thought the skinny kid just got lucky." Finally, Powell accepted a track scholarship from the University of California at Irvine.

STICKS TO TRACK. Because the basketball and track seasons overlapped, Powell had to choose one sport. He picked track. Powell competed in the high jump during his freshman year, but his coach, Blair Clausen, soon realized that his best event was the long jump. The young athlete trained hard to earn a shot at making the 1984 U.S. Olympic team. The U.S. Olympic Committee invited Powell to attend the Olympic Trials, but he finished sixth in the long jump, not good enough to make the team. He did work at the 1984 Olympics in Los Angeles, California, however, acting as a chauffeur for Swedish sports reporters.

ONE-MAN TEAM. Powell transferred to the University of California at Los Angeles (UCLA) before his senior year (1986). He was a one-man track team at UCLA. Powell competed in the long jump, high jump, and triple jump. He also ran the 100- and 200-meter dashes and the 400- and 1,600-meter relays. Powell's performance earned him the Ducky Drake Award as the team's most valuable athlete.

MIKE FOUL. Soon Powell established himself in international competition. In 1985 he jumped 26 feet 9½ inches, a jump that put him in the top ten in the world. He began working with coach Randy Huntington with the 1988 Summer Olympics as his goal. Huntington helped Powell cut down on his fouls and carry more speed into his jumps. Powell fouled so often in competitions that other long jumpers gave him the nickname Mike Foul. (A foul occurs in the long jump when a competitor begins his jump past a certain point on the runway.)

In 1987 Powell moved up to number six in the world. He finished first in that year's World University Games and jumped farther than 27 feet for the first time. Just six weeks before the 1988 U.S. Olympic Trials, however, Powell had an emergency appendectomy, a major surgery. He recovered in time to compete in the trials and made the team with his last jump. Powell finished third in the competition, behind 1984 Olympic champion Carl Lewis and Larry Myricks.

GETS MEDAL. Seoul, South Korea, hosted the 1988 Summer Olympics. Powell had the best jumps of his career at the competition but could not defeat Lewis, who had the three longest jumps of the meet. Powell did win a silver medal, however, with a jump of 27 feet 10¼ inches. "I was like, Wow, I'm just happy to be here and now I've got a medal," Powell recalled in *Seventeen*. The United States swept the medals in the event when Myricks took the bronze.

To improve his jumping ability, Powell changed his long jump technique after the Olympics. He began using the hitch kick technique, in which a long jumper pedals his feet when in the air. The new technique had almost immediate results for Powell. In the spring of 1989 he leapt more than 28 feet, only the seventh athlete to do so. In 1990 Powell posted the longest jump of the year—28 feet 5 inches.

WHO'S NUMBER ONE? Powell won 15 events in 1990, more than any other competitor. Still, experts did not consider him the best long jumper in the world, because he lost to Lewis the only two times they met that year. At the 1991 U.S. Track and Field Championships, Lewis again defeated Powell when his last jump was one-half inch longer than Powell's best. Despite winning more meets than any other competitor during 1990 and 1991, Powell still could not defeat Lewis. In his career he had lost to Lewis all 15 times the two faced each other. "Carl always being out there gave him something he could reach for—a line in the sand," Huntington explained in *Sports Illustrated*.

Superstar

HISTORIC JUMP. The competition between Powell and Lewis came to a head at the 1991 World Track and Field Championships in Tokyo, Japan. Both men had one goal beyond winning the gold medal: to break the world record in the long jump. Bob Beamon of the United States had set the record—29 feet 2½ inches—at the 1968 Summer Olympics in Mexico City, Mexico. He had broken the previous record by more than two feet but never again jumped close to the same distance. Beamon had set the record in high altitude, where the thin air helped him travel farther. Because of this advantage, most experts believed the record would never be broken. In 1991 Beamon's jump was the longest-standing world record in track and field.

Some experts thought that if anyone broke the world record, it would be Lewis. He had won 65 straight long jump competitions and had not lost in the event since 1981. In both 1984 and 1988 Lewis won Olympic gold medals in the long jump. Powell was angry that no one gave him a chance to break the record. "All my life I've had people tell me I couldn't do certain things," Powell told *Sports Illustrated*. "They said Carl would probably break the record, and I took it as a personal insult. People would tell me right to my face I couldn't do it, without knowing anything about me."

The wind swirled through the stadium on the day of the world championship competition. (A long jump does not count as a world record if the wind is blowing too strongly from behind the jumper. Too strong a wind blowing from the front of the jumper can knock valuable inches off a jump.) If either Powell or Lewis was going to break the record, he would have to be lucky enough to have the wind on his side.

Powell struggled on his first four jumps of the six-jump competition and could not come close to the record. "Something went wrong on every jump," Powell explained in *Time* magazine. In fact, Powell wanted to defeat Lewis so badly he hyperventilated before his first jump. "I was so hyped up to beat Carl, I couldn't even breathe," Powell recounted in *Sports Illustrated*. On his fourth jump Lewis leapt 29 feet 3¾

LIVING ROOM LEAP

Powell often acted out a world-record long jump in his living room. "Sometimes I would just be sitting there on the couch, and all of a sudden here came Mike," Powell's girlfriend at the time, Karen Koellner, recalled in *Sports Illustrated*. "He would come running through the living room, take off, then the minute he landed he'd throw his hands in the air and start jumping up and down. He always broke the record. Every time." Powell added in the same magazine: "I could actually feel it, feel the rush in my head. I've imagined that moment in my living room a hundred times."

inches, surpassing the world record. However, the wind from behind Lewis was too strong. The jump counted for the competition, but not for the world record.

BREAKS RECORD. With Lewis jumping so well, Powell knew he would need the jump of his life on his fifth attempt to win the gold medal. "At the top of the runway, I went over the jump in my mind," Powell recalled in *People* magazine. "I tried to [ignore] the crowd. I told myself I wasn't as fast as Carl, so I had to feel not just fast but springy. When I ran, I let out a yell. I'm not sure why."

Powell knew right away he had a chance to break the record. "I knew it was far, and I knew it was close to Carl's," Powell recounted in *Time* magazine. "When I looked at it, I thought it might be a world record." Powell had leapt 29 feet 4½ inches, and the wind had not affected his jump. "I imagined that moment so many times," Powell explained in the *Village Voice*. The jump was almost a foot longer than his lifetime best and two inches longer than the world record.

Powell then had to wait because Lewis had two jumps remaining. "I thought he was going to beat me, to tell you the truth," Powell admitted in the *Washington Post*. "I've been conditioned so long for him to come from behind and win, I figured, 'Why not tonight?'" On his last jump, Lewis jumped 29 feet, still short of Powell's new world record. Lewis lost the competition despite having four of the seven best jumps in history. "I am living a fantasy," Powell told *Jet* after the meet. "I always said I could break the world record with the perfect situation—a perfect track, a big meet, and me being behind." Powell felt like he could have gone farther, but he was not used to being so high in the air.

Lewis cried after the competition and said some mean things about Powell at a press conference. "Mike had one great jump," Lewis said, according to *Sports Illustrated*. "He may never do it again. I could have gone farther on my last jump. But I didn't. That's something I have to accept." The fact that Lewis did not acknowledge his achievement bothered Powell. "For him not to really acknowledge what I did kind of made me upset, but I understand. After a while, he'll be at peace with it."

Beamon congratulated Powell on breaking his record. "Mike is the kind of person I'd like for my son and daughter to emulate [be like]," Beamon explained in the *Philadelphia Daily News*. "He has great character and integrity." Powell won the 1991 Sullivan Award, given annually to the best amateur (unpaid) athlete in the United States, and the Jesse Owens International Trophy. His grandmother was proud of his accomplishment. "I told you you'd do it, Mike, if you were a good person," his grandmother told Powell, according to *Sports Illustrated*.

GETS RESPECT. The win over Lewis finally established Powell as the best long jumper in the world. "Probably the biggest reason I jumped as far as I did was we are both competitors and we didn't want to lose," Powell explained to the *Washington Post*. "I wasn't thinking so much about breaking the record as about beating him." The record, however, also put pressure on Powell. "Carl has been unbeaten all these years," Powell told *People* magazine. "It's tough to get to the top, but harder to maintain it. So now we'll find out what kind of jumper I really am."

Powell tried not to become too overconfident, however. "I always remind myself I'm jumping in dirt," Powell explained in the *Village Voice*. "That's all it is." Media from around the world wanted to talk to Powell, and he got very little sleep in the days following his record-breaking jump. The record also meant that he would make a lot of money from appearance fees and endorsements.

Breaking the record placed enormous pressure on Powell to live up to his new fame. Leading up to the 1992 U.S. Olympic Trials, he injured his back when he did not land correctly on a jump. The injury prevented Powell from jumping until five days before the Olympic Trials began. He still defeated Lewis for the second straight time.

SILVER STREAK. In July 1992 Powell leapt 29 feet 6 inches in a meet at Sestriere, Italy. Because of a strong wind at his back,

COMPETITORS

Many great athletes are fierce competitors who train hard to win. This desire to win often helps them achieve more than they ever imagined they could. Powell is such a person. His competition with Lewis made him a better long jumper because he wanted to defeat the great champion. At times, though, Powell also hated Lewis. Once he set the world record, however, he changed his mind about his archrival. "In the past, I had even looked at him as Carl Lewis, bad guy," Powell admitted in the *Philadelphia Inquirer.* "I was using that to get myself ready to compete, to get myself fired up. After Tokyo [where Powell set the world record] I started thinking, 'Man, he's never really done anything bad to me, never really said anything bad about me, so I'm not going to do that anymore.' I'm not going to talk bad about him; he's an O.K. guy. He's not my best friend, but that's not what his job is."

the jump did not count as a new world record. Powell entered the 1992 Summer Olympics in Barcelona, Spain, as the favorite. Lewis, however, did not give up, and he leapt 28 feet 5 $^3/_4$ inches on his first attempt. Powell started slowly but steadily jumped farther and farther while Lewis failed to improve on his first jump.

Coming down to his last jump, Powell still trailed Lewis. Powell had his best jump of the Olympics on his final try, but he still came up short. Lewis won his third Olympic long jump gold medal, and Powell settled for the silver for the second time. Fellow American Joe Greene won the bronze, finishing another American sweep. "I began to jump well at the end, but it was too late," Powell admitted after the competition.

STILL FLYING. Powell continued to dominate the long jump after the Olympics. In 1993 he won the gold medal in the long jump at the World Track and Field Championships for the second straight time. (Lewis did not compete.) He ranked number one in 1994 but lost a meet for the first time in 34 competitions. In 1995 a back injury and sore toe slowed Powell down and he finished third in the world championships, won by Ivan Pedroso of Cuba. "It's been a tough year for me," Powell said. "I've always been on the rise. Now I'm taking a few steps back. I have to go home and reinvent myself."

OFF THE TRACK. Powell lives in Alta Loma, California, just east of Los Angeles. He has been a spokesperson for Nike, Foot Locker, and RayBan sunglasses. Powell enjoys bowling and playing basketball and chess. He has donated money to the United Negro College Fund. Some day Powell would like to be a teacher. He graduated from UCLA with a degree in sociology.

In 1990 Powell won the Foot Locker Slam Fest basketball dunking contest, and in 1992 he won television's Superstar competition. He once appeared in a fashion article for *GQ*. Powell continues to compete in the hopes of winning a gold medal in the long jump at the 1996 Summer Olympic Games in Atlanta, Georgia. He is no longer the favorite and in 1995 he also lost his world record to Pedroso, who leapt 29 feet $4^3/_4$ inches at a meet in Sestriere, Italy. Do not count Powell out, however. As he told *Seventeen,* "If somebody tells me I can't do something it just makes me work harder."

Sources

Chicago Tribune, June 19, 1992.
Jet, September 23, 1991.
New York Times, September 1, 1991; July 30, 1995.
People, September 16, 1991.
Seventeen, July 1992.
Sporting News, September 9, 1991.
Sports Illustrated, September 9, 1991; September 16, 1991.
Time, September 9, 1991.
Track and Field News, November 1991; March 1992.
Village Voice, February 11, 1992.
Washington Post, August 31, 1991; September 1, 1991.
Additional information provided by USA Track and Field.

WHERE TO WRITE:
C/O USA TRACK AND FIELD,
PO BOX 120,
INDIANAPOLIS, IN 46206.

Manon Rheaume

1972—

Goalie Manon Rheaume has always been a trendsetter. She was the first woman to play junior hockey in Canada, the first woman to play in the National Hockey League (NHL), and the first woman to play professional roller hockey. Throughout her career, experts have told Rheaume to quit because she was not good enough. She has ignored the critics and continues to play the game she loves. Rheaume hopes that some day fans accept her as a fine goalie, not just as the best woman hockey player in the world.

Growing Up

ALL IN THE FAMILY. Manon Rheaume (ma-No ray-OME) was born in 1972 and grew up in Lac Beauport, a suburb of Quebec City, Quebec, Canada. Her father, Pierre, coached hockey and ran the city's outdoor ice rink. Rheaume learned to skate at age three on a rink in the back of her house. Her mother, Nicole, took her down to the rink each day to watch her brothers, Martin and Pascal, play. Soon Rheaume played with her brothers on the family's ice rink. "I was the youngest and the smallest, so they made me play goal," Rheaume recalled in the *Sporting News*. "I always played with the boys."

WHY NOT? One day Pierre Rheaume's team needed a goalie. Manon, age five at the time, grabbed her opportunity to play. "I said to my father, 'I would like to be your goaltender,'" Rheaume recalled in *People* magazine. "He laughed. But then he said, 'Why not? You take shots from your brothers at home.'"

Rheaume loved to play sports and participated in baseball and skiing. She also enjoyed ballet. By age 12, however, hockey was Rheaume's full-time sport. "I didn't just play hockey," Rheaume recounted in *People* magazine. "It was my passion."

Rheaume always played on teams with boys because there were no teams for girls. "Every year, the boys found it special to have a girl on the team, but after the first day, they didn't look at me as a girl," she told *Sports Illustrated*. "They saw me as a player." Despite loving hockey and growing up in Canada, where the game is very popular, she never dreamed of playing in the NHL. "[When] I was growing up watching NHL games on TV, I never saw a girl playing, so I didn't think I could," Rheaume told the *Sporting News*.

WANTS TO PLAY. At 11 years old, Rheaume became the first girl to play in the International Pee Wee Ice Hockey Tournament in Quebec, Canada. Soon, however, it appeared her hockey career was over. "There had never been a woman in junior hockey before," Rheaume explained.

The junior leagues in Canada were the training grounds for future NHL players, and Rheaume wanted a chance to play. She got her chance when an injury sidelined the starting goalie for the Trois-Rivieres Draveurs, a team in a Junior A league. She played in three games and earned a third-star selection in one of those games. "She didn't get to this level because she's a girl," Draveurs captain Paolo Racicot told *Sports Illustrated.* "She got here because she's good."

Being a pioneer proved to be difficult for Rheaume. The boys she played with often played harder against her. "Some players tried to make me afraid with some very high shots," Rheaume recalled in *People* magazine. One shot hit her in the face, broke her mask, and cut her eyebrow. "The blood started running," Rheaume recounted in the same magazine. "But I continued to play. I didn't want anyone to say I stopped because I'm a girl."

WORLD BEATER. In 1992 Rheaume helped the Canadian national team win the second Women's World Hockey Championship in Tampere, Finland. Canada defeated the United States 8-0 in the final. Tournament officials named Rheaume to the All-Tournament team. She gave up only two goals in three games.

Superstar

LIGHTNING LADY. The Tampa Bay Lightning, an expansion team preparing to play its first season in the NHL, invited Rheaume to its first training camp in 1992. She became the first woman ever invited to an NHL training camp. "I wasn't really sure at first [about going to the tryout]," Rheaume admitted in the *Sporting News.* "But then I thought that I did not want to look back 20 years from now and wonder if I could have done this. I just didn't want any regrets." She added in *Sports Illustrated:* "I'd like to test myself against the best."

Some people claimed inviting Rheaume was a publicity stunt designed to gain attention for the new team. "I'd be a liar to say I wasn't using this for publicity," Phil Esposito, former player and then-president and general manager of the

Rheaume makes a save during her professional debut with the Tampa Bay Lightning.

Lightning, admitted in *People* magazine. "But I don't care if she is a woman. If there were a horse with skates and it could stop a puck, I'd put it in there."

Rheaume impressed her coaches in practice but tried not to get too excited. "I'm very realistic," Rheaume explained in *Sports Illustrated.* "I take this tryout for what it is and do my best." She understood that part of her role was to get fans interested in the new team. "I understood why I was invited to camp," she admitted in the *Sporting News.* "But I felt like I could not pass up the opportunity. How many girls, or even how many boys, would get the chance that I did? I did this to get better and to make myself a better goalie."

The level of play with the Lightning was much better than what Rheaume was used to. "Here the players are much faster and bigger and the shots are much harder," she explained in the *Sporting News*. "I have never faced this kind of shot before, so I was very nervous at first. But you concentrate on the puck, not the shot and that makes it easier to stop."

NHL FIRST. On September 23, 1992, Rheaume became the first woman to play in the NHL. She started in an exhibition game for the Lightning against the Saint Louis Blues. Rheaume played one period, made seven saves, and gave up two goals. Saint Louis won the game 6-4. "One goal I should have stopped," Rheaume confessed in the *Sporting News* after the game. "But I was pleased because I learned from it. The players played very well in front of me. I have to give them a lot of the credit for me doing so well. But the most important thing is that I learned from it. It was a great experience and now I can work to get better."

"If you didn't know she was a woman, then you wouldn't have known by watching her play," hockey writer Tom Jones told *Women's Sports and Fitness* magazine. "She did a respectable job. She played as well as any goaltender would have. She doesn't have a problem reacting to shots or making saves. She has a good glove hand."

Her position as role model was not the most important thing to Rheaume. "I really don't think about being the first woman [to play in an NHL game]," she told the *Sporting News*. "It doesn't matter to me if I'm the first woman, or the second, or whatever. I came here because I love hockey and it is a great opportunity. If this helps women's hockey or brings it more attention, then great. I hope it does. But the history doesn't really mean much to me."

SIGNS CONTRACT. Before the regular season began, the Lightning signed Rheaume to a three-year contract to play with their Atlanta Knights minor league team. "She earned the chance to go to Atlanta," Esposito told *Women's Sports and Fitness*. "She did well during the preseason, and she earned a spot on the roster." The news thrilled Rheaume. "This I could not believe," she confessed in the *Sporting*

News. "They're actually going to pay me to play hockey, the game I love. It is more than I ever imagined."

Rheaume was the third-string goalie for the Knights and rarely got into a game. She did not mind, however. "Yes, I'm happy to be with Atlanta because I have a good chance to get experience, to learn more," Rheaume explained in *Women's Sports and Fitness* magazine. "I didn't try to be the first woman to do this, I just want to play. I never before had the chance to practice every day. It's normal to be the number three goalie, because I'm just 20 years old. The two other goaltenders are 24 and 25, and they have a lot more experience than me."

KEEPS TRYING. Rheaume has struggled to get playing time with minor league teams. From 1992 through 1995 she played only nine games and had a 5-3-1 record. In 1994 Rheaume played in the East Coast Hockey League, where she posted a 5-0-1 record. The Las Vegas Thunder of the International Hockey League gave her a tryout in 1995. "[She is] a phenomenal athlete, the hardest-working player we have on staff, bar none," Chris McSorley, the Thunder's assistant coach, stated in *Saturday Night*. "She's where she is today because of her work ethic. She's competent enough to hold the pipes in this league, and I believe in three or four years she'll have a chance to play a regular-season game in the National Hockey League." Rheaume played two periods for the Thunder and gave up three goals.

ROLLER RECORD. In 1994 Rheaume achieved another first when she became the only woman to play professional roller hockey. She played goalie in 1994 and 1995 for the New Jersey Rockin' Rollers of Roller Hockey International. Roller hockey helps Rheaume train for ice hockey. "The roller-hockey puck is light and the shots are fast," she explained in *Sports Illustrated for Kids*. "It's good for improving my reflexes."

THE FUTURE. Rheaume has considered moving to Europe to play in a professional league. She looks forward to playing for

FOLLOWING IN HER FOOTSTEPS

Little girls ask Rheaume for her autograph and say she has inspired them to play hockey. "You're going to see a lot more girls and women turning to ice hockey now," Katie Michel, the captain of the Yale University women's team, told *Women's Sports and Fitness.* "A girl's going to see Manon and say, 'Mom, Dad, I want to play ice hockey, not figure skate.'" Rheaume says that girls should follow their dreams. "Do what you want to do," Rheaume stated in *Sports Illustrated for Kids.* "If someone tries to stop you, just try harder."

Canada at the 1998 Winter Olympics in Nagano, Japan. Women's ice hockey will be a medal sport for the first time in 1998. As for playing in the NHL, Rheaume knows that may never happen. "I'm realistic," she told *Saturday Night.* "I just said I'll go as far as I can go."

No matter how well she plays, reporters and other players still call her a publicity stunt. "You know, since I started people have always said it's just for publicity," Rheaume complained in *Saturday Night.* "I don't face hundred-mile-an-hour shots every day and I don't have bruises everywhere on my body to have publicity. I make so many sacrifices because I love the game and I want to get better. And when people still ask and ask this question, it's hard."

Rheaume, at five feet six inches and 120 pounds, is small for a goalie and cannot block as much of the net as bigger goaltenders. "I think her skill level and her talent are quite exceptional," Las Vegas teammate and former NHL goalie Clint Malarchuk told *Saturday Night.* "But she's small in stature and she's not as strong as a man." Her lack of size also makes it difficult when another player hits her, accidentally or intentionally. Rheaume also has trouble clearing the puck and making passes to teammates. She works out with weights to improve her upper-body strength and has excellent speed and reflexes, important qualities for a goalie.

OFF THE ICE. Rheaume likes softball, badminton, and tennis. She also likes to shop and read. Much of Rheaume's time is spent doing charity work. She once made an appearance on the *David Letterman Show.* Playing goalie does not scare Rheaume. "I don't think about getting hurt when I'm on the ice," Rheaume told *Women's Sports and Fitness* magazine. "It wouldn't be good for a figure skater to think about getting hurt if she misses a move. I just think about doing my job."

Playing goalie is a tough job, but Rheaume loves it. "If the defense makes a mistake, there is the goaltender," Rheaume stated in *Sports Illustrated for Kids*. "But if the goaltender makes a mistake, there is no one. The feeling you have when you stop a puck, when you win a game. It's great."

Sources

New York Times, October 19, 1992.
People, September 28, 1992.
Saturday Night, February 1995.
Sporting News, October 5, 1992; September 26, 1994.
Sports Illustrated, December 30, 1991; May 4, 1992; September 28, 1992.
Sports Illustrated for Kids, September 1993; August 1995; September 1995.
Time, October 5, 1992.
Village Voice, October 13, 1992.
Women's Sports and Fitness, January/February, 1993.

 WHERE TO WRITE:
C/O NEW JERSEY ROCKIN' ROLLERS,
ONE PALMER TERRACE,
CARLSTADT, NJ 07072.

Glenn Robinson

1973—

> *"I would like to be the type of player to take over down the stretch."*
> —Glenn Robinson

Glenn "Big Dog" Robinson is not one of the biggest players in the National Basketball Association (NBA). At six feet seven inches tall and 220 pounds, Robinson is one of the smaller men working in NBA arenas. What *is* big about him, however, is his game. Equally dangerous inside and beyond the three-point line, Robinson has always been the best at what he does. He won both the high school and college Player of the Year awards during his career. Now the best professional basketball players in the world feel the Big Dog's bark and bite.

Growing Up

LISTENS TO MOM. Glenn Allen Robinson Jr. was born January 10, 1973, in Gary, Indiana. His mother, Christine Bridgeman, was unmarried and only a teenager when her son was born. Despite being so young, Bridgeman worked to see that her son grew up right. Once, when his grades were not up to her standards, Robinson's mother pulled him off the high school basketball team until they improved.

Robinson's father, Glenn Robinson Sr. was not involved with his son and had several run-ins with the police. "I didn't get to know him like a son should know a father, because he wasn't really around," the younger Robinson confessed to *Sports Illustrated.* "But I'm not ashamed of my father. A lot of people have said that when I see him, I turn away. That's not true. I would never turn away from my own father."

Growing up was not easy on the tough streets of Gary, where crime and drugs were everywhere. "There are two sides of the street," Robinson told *Sports Illustrated,* describing his hometown. "You can choose to be on one side of the street—or you can go [to] the other side. I get along with people on both sides of the street." This ability to play both sides of the street enabled Robinson to survive. He earned money by carrying tools and doing cleanup work at an air-conditioning and refrigeration shop.

STARTED AS A PUPPY. Basketball did not always come easy to Robinson. He was so bad that he refused to go out for his seventh grade team. "He wasn't very good," his future Roosevelt High School coach Ron Heflin told *Sports Illustrated.* "People don't understand how hard that kid worked. He hasn't always been a good ballplayer."

MR. BASKETBALL. Robinson's game improved enough that he made the junior varsity team as a high school freshman and the varsity team as a sophomore. He continued to improve, and as a senior led Roosevelt to a 30-1 record and the state championships in the tough Indiana high school basketball tournament as a senior. Robinson averaged 25.6 points and 14.6 rebounds per game as a senior. After his senior season Robinson was named Indiana's Mr. Basketball for 1991. He shared National High School Player of the Year honors that

BIG DOG

Robinson got his nickname, "the Big Dog," when he first arrived at Purdue. Charles McDonald, the building manager at Lambert Fieldhouse, the Boilermakers' home arena, recalled in *Sport* magazine how the nickname came into being. "I was asked to take a look at the new recruits playing a pickup game, and one player reminded me of a dog amongst a bunch of puppies, you know the way the rest of 'em just sit back and watch the big dog eat. So I called him 'the Big Dog,' and it sure fit. I told the coach that they'd never have any trouble with the big one, no sir." Robinson liked the name so much he had a bulldog tattooed on his chest.

same year with **Chris Webber** (see entry) from Detroit Country Day High School in Michigan.

MAKING THE GRADES. Many colleges tried to recruit Robinson. Unfortunately, Robinson did not achieve a high enough score on the Scholastic Aptitude Test (SAT) to qualify for an athletic scholarship. He finally entered Purdue University under Proposition 48 of the National Collegiate Athletic Association (NCAA). Proposition 48 allows student athletes to enter college with a scholarship despite not receiving high enough scores on the SAT. These student athletes, however, may not play sports their freshman year and must prove that they can meet the university's academic standards during their first year.

Not playing on the team his first year was hard on Robinson. He ate a lot to make himself feel better. "I almost gave up and went home," Robinson admitted in *Sports Illustrated.* "I looked in the mirror and I had this big old stomach." Robinson also believed that people cared about him only as a basketball player. "People would tell me, 'You've got to get eligible so you can play,'" Robinson told *Sports Illustrated.* "They never asked me how I was, or how my family was. They weren't concerned about anything like that."

Robinson kept his basketball game sharp by playing in the Malcolm X Summer League in Chicago, Illinois. "I've played with guys like [NBA players] Tim Hardaway and Kevin Duckworth," Robinson explained to *Sports Illustrated.* "There's no fooling anybody out there. You find out quickly if you can play."

PURDUE POWERHOUSE. Robinson finally got his chance in his sophomore year (1992-93) to show what he could do. He did not disappoint Purdue fans. Robinson averaged 24.1

points and 9.2 rebounds per game. He was the only player in the Big Ten to finish in the top ten in the conference in scoring, rebounding, steals, blocked shots, field goal percentage, and free throw percentage. "Superman," Illinois coach Lou Henson called Robinson in the *Sporting News*. "I can't recall anybody coming in to make such an impact on our league."

Robinson could only do so much for the Boilermakers. They finished 18-10 his first year and lost in the first round of the NCAA Basketball Tournament to Rhode Island, 74-68, despite 36 points from Robinson. This loss had a lot to do with Robinson's decision not to go pro after his first season. "I felt we didn't really accomplish anything," Robinson explained in *Sports Illustrated*. "I felt I would have left my teammates hanging if I had gone out on that note." Robinson also realized he might not have been ready for the high-pressure NBA. "I wasn't mature yet," Robinson confessed in *Sports Illustrated*. "I wasn't ready to go off into that big world yet. Out there you have to be able to deal with girls, agents, people trying to give you drugs—all that stuff."

Superstar

THE BEST. Robinson was the best player in college basketball his junior year at Purdue (1993-94). He led the nation in scoring with 30.3 points per game and led the Big Ten in rebounding with 10.1 per contest. Robinson was the first player since 1978 to lead the Big Ten in both categories. "There's really no way to guard him," Ohio State center Gerald Eaker told *Sports Illustrated* after the Big Dog burned him for 40 points. "All you do is try to contain him. I've never played against anybody like that." Robinson won virtually every award as the National College Basketball Player of the Year, including the prestigious Naismith and Wooden Awards.

Robinson was also well on his way toward earning a degree in physical education. "I've always been kind of tickled at people who assume he's not a very good student," Purdue coach Gene Keady told the *Sporting News*. "They couldn't be further from the truth. If he wanted to, he could go past his B.S. [Bachelor of Science] degree."

SHUT DOWN. The Boilermakers were national championship contenders. They won the Big Ten basketball championship and finished the 1993-94 season at 29-5 overall. Purdue entered the NCAA tournament as a favorite, and Robinson was ready. He scored 44 points in a game against the University of Kansas, the highest single-game total in the tournament that year. Purdue's title quest ended, however, in the Southeast Regional Finals. Duke shut down the Boilermakers, and **Grant Hill** (see entry) shut down Robinson. He scored only 13 points, 17 under his average, in the loss.

GOES PRO. Robinson had a big decision to make. If he stayed at Purdue, his team had a chance to go all the way to the NCAA championship. If he left school, however, he would be the number one pick overall in the NBA Draft. Robinson finally decided that he was ready to go to the next level. The Milwaukee Bucks held the first pick in the draft, and they rejected numerous trade offers and picked Robinson. The choice thrilled the Bucks. "It's tough to guard him one-on-one during long periods of time during a ball game," Bucks coach Mike Dunleavy said in *Sport* magazine about his young superstar. "And when he gets the basketball, you're gonna get burned."

The next problem for Milwaukee, however, was signing their new star. Robinson missed training camp, and his contract became part of a political campaign. Bucks owner Herb Kohl is also one of Wisconsin's U.S. senators. Along the campaign trail, reporters asked Kohl about Robinson as well as the major issues of the day. Kohl tried to keep his sense of humor. "He can have the franchise and I'll take his contract," Kohl joked in *Sport* magazine. Robinson finally signed a ten-year contract for $68.15 million only one hour before the Bucks' opening game.

"I'm still the same normal, quiet guy from Gary [Indiana]," Robinson said after signing the contract. "Am I worth it? If I wasn't, I don't think I'd have this contract," Robinson explained to *Sport* magazine. "If a player is going to be paid $500 million or whatever, I think if you're performing to that level, they'll pay you for it. I don't think it's gotten out of hand at all."

Missing training camp hurt Robinson early in the season. His shooting touch was missing as he struggled to get used to the physical NBA game. "Teams are going to want to keep me from playing the game well, having the great game, keeping me under control," Robinson explained to *Sport* magazine. "They don't want me goin' crazy or scoring 35 points, and that's just a sign of respect. I kind of knew it was going to be like this, hearing people talk about me and the kind of player I am."

When Robinson got going, however, there was no stopping him. Robinson led all rookie scorers with 21.9 points per game, and he pulled down 6.4 rebounds per contest. He finished second in the voting for NBA Rookie of the Year behind cowinners Grant Hill of the Detroit Pistons and **Jason Kidd** (see entry) of the Dallas Mavericks. The NBA recognized Robinson as among the best players in the league by naming him to represent the United States on the "Dream Team III" squad, which will play in the 1996 Olympics in Atlanta, Georgia.

OFF THE COURT. Robinson is single and lives in Gary during the off-season. His community activities include the Holiday Food Baskets project, Boys' and Girls' Club Basketball Clinics, and the NBA Stay in School program. Robinson also sponsors an annual all-star game in Gary to benefit local charities and an annual summer basketball camp.

On the court, Robinson knows what he wants. "I know what I can do on the court," Robinson told *Sport* magazine. "I'm not a fancy player and I don't try to showboat. I would like to be the type of player to take over down the stretch. I

HOMETOWN HERO

Gary, Indiana, has the reputation of being a dangerous city, but Robinson says that is not a complete picture of his hometown. "People come to Gary expecting to be shot," Robinson complained in *Sports Illustrated.* "You hear a lot of bad things about Gary, but a lot of people who say those things have never been there." The people of Gary are Robinson's biggest fans. "When Glenn plays, all the TVS in Gary are on," family friend Rayfield Fisher told *Sports Illustrated.* "Everybody here owns Glenn: he's our Glenn Robinson." The City of Gary honored Robinson by proclaiming August 4, 1994, "Glenn Robinson Day."

always want the ball in the clutch, that's how I've always played."

Sources

Sport, April 1995.
Sporting News, November 29, 1993; March 28, 1994; April 25, 1994; November 14, 1994.
Sports Illustrated, December 14, 1992; March 14, 1994.
Additional information provided by Milwaukee Bucks.

 WHERE TO WRITE:
MILWAUKEE BUCKS,
1001 N. FOURTH ST.,
MILWAUKEE, WI 53203.

Patrick Roy

1965—

Chants of "Rooooo-ah, Rooooo-ah" greeted Montreal Canadiens goaltender Patrick Roy whenever the goalie takes his place between the pipes at the Montreal Forum. Ever since Roy led the Canadiens to a Stanley Cup in his rookie season of 1986, he had been an institution in the French-speaking city. Roy won the Conn Smythe Trophy as the most valuable player (MVP) in the 1986 National Hockey League (NHL) play-off's and repeated the feat in 1993 when he once again led the Canadiens to the Cup. In addition to his play-off heroics, Roy has won the Vezina Trophy, awarded to the NHL's best goaltender, three times. Roy continues to be a strong contender to add more trophies to his case in the years to come, now for his new team, the Colorado Avalanche.

"He's the best goaltender in hockey."—Montreal Canadiens team president Ronald Corey

Growing Up

RUNS IN THE FAMILY. Patrick Roy (Wah) was born October 5, 1965, in Quebec City, Quebec, Canada. His father, Michael, is a vice president of the Quebec Automobile Insurance Board. His mother, Barbara, is a real estate agent and swimming coach. Athletic ability ran in his family. His father was a good enough baseball player that the then-Brooklyn Dodgers scouted him. His mother was a competitive synchronized swimmer. The Minnesota North Stars drafted Roy's brother, Stephane, fifty-first overall in the 1985 NHL Draft.

CAREER CHOICE. Roy decided early in his life he wanted to be a goalie. "I liked the pads," Roy recalled in *Sports Illustrated.* "I saw all that equipment and I wanted to wear it." His grandmother, Anna Peacock, was a huge Montreal Canadiens fan. She was also a fan of legendary Canadiens goalie Ken Dryden. His grandmother would watch games on television while giving Roy his dinner. "The last time I saw Anna in the hospital, she was watching the Islanders play Vancouver in the [1982] Cup finals," Roy told *Sports Illustrated.* "She was a real big hockey fan."

CANADIEN'S CHOICE. Roy, like many French Canadian boys, always dreamed of playing for the Canadiens. His dream came true in 1984. Roy dropped out of school in eleventh grade and played for three years with Granby in the Quebec Major Junior Hockey League. He compiled a 45-54 record with a whopping 5.32 goals-against average. The Canadiens picked Roy with the fifty-first overall choice in the 1984 NHL Draft. The chances of his making the Canadiens did not seem bright.

Montreal sent Roy to its American Hockey League farm team in Sherbrooke, Quebec, Canada. It was there he met Francois Allaire, the team's goaltending coach. Allaire worked to refine Roy's raw talent and taught him the right and wrong ways to block shots. Roy continues to work with Allaire today.

Roy helps the Canadiens beat the Boston Bruins with this save.

ROOKIE SENSATION. The Montreal Canadiens are one of the most dominant teams in the history of professional sports. They have won 22 Stanley Cups, far and away the most of any team. In 1986, however, the Canadiens were in a slump. They had not reached the Stanley Cup Finals in six seasons and had changed coaches five times during that period. It was obvious that the team needed a spark to get them going.

That spark was Roy. The Canadiens called him up midway through the 1985-86 season as a 20-year-old rookie. He posted a 23-18-3 record and a 3.35 goals-against average during the regular season. Montreal finished second in the Adams Division, but no one considered them a threat to win the Cup. Their chances seemed especially slim with a rookie goalie. Most experts considered an experienced goaltender to be a must to win a championship.

Roy proved the experts wrong. In one of the most remarkable performances ever, he posted a 15-5 record and 1.92 goals-against average in 20 play-off games. The Canadiens stormed past the Boston Bruins, the Hartford Whalers, and the New York Rangers to reach the Stanley Cup Finals. Once there, they defeated the Calgary Flames to regain their position at the top. The media recognized Roy's performance by awarding him the Conn Smythe Trophy as the most valuable player of the NHL play-offs.

The NHL named Roy to the All-Rookie team following his fantastic first season. He worried that people would expect too much of him because of his rookie success. "I have my two feet on the ground," Roy told *Sports Illustrated* following the season. "I know this is all a dream. I understand that. So I lived with my family this summer, and I have the same friends. We still do the same things we've always done: play deck hockey, softball. It's important not to change. I don't want to be a one-year player. I want to have a long, successful career. And the way to do that is to not forget how you got successful in the first place."

BEST IN THE LEAGUE. Roy continued to post impressive statistics the next few seasons, although the Canadiens were unable to duplicate their Cup victory. He lowered his goals-against average to 2.93 in the 1986-87 season and to 2.90 in 1987-88. During the 1988-89 season the NHL recognized Roy as the best goalie in the league when he won the Vezina Trophy, awarded annually to the league's best goaltender. He compiled an amazing 33-5-6 record that season with a league-leading 2.47 goals-against average. Roy was a first-team All-NHL pick.

In 1990 Roy repeated as the Vezina Trophy winner. He led the NHL with 31 victories and a 2.53 goals-against average. Roy won his third Vezina in 1992 when he posted his lowest ever goals-against average, 2.36. Despite having the best goalie in the NHL, the Canadiens floundered in the playoffs. Montreal had lost in the first or second round of the playoffs each year since their Stanley Cup victory in 1986. The team's problem was that they could not score enough goals to support Roy.

Montreal previously had not gone more than seven years without winning the Stanley Cup. Many fans blamed Roy for the team's slump. His critics said Roy, despite his great statistics, gave up easy goals in big games. Some fans even wanted the Canadiens to trade Roy. He did not let the pressure bother him. "I know it sounds odd when I say that I've never felt any pressure playing for the Canadiens," Roy told *Saturday Night*. "But hockey has always been fun for me."

Superstar

RETURN TO THE TOP. Coach Jacques Demers took over the Canadiens just before the 1992-93 season. Demers, a native of Quebec, had been successful with both the Saint Louis Blues and the Detroit Red Wings and was a popular choice with the Canadiens' French Canadian fans. Demers preached a more wide open offense, with less emphasis on the tight defensive game Montreal had been used to playing. Demers depended on his All-Star goalie to stop the other team. Roy, used to a strong defense in front of him, struggled. "Pat's struggles this year were new to him," teammate Kirk Muller said in *Sports Illustrated*. "Obviously people in Montreal expect a lot from him, and he can't really have a bad game—ever. But I think the struggle made him better."

Roy's goals-against average under Demers went from 2.36 the previous season to 3.20, his highest since 1988. Roy failed to be one of the three finalists for the Vezina Trophy. Demers knew, however, that his team would succeed or fail with Roy between the pipes. He resisted pressure in the local media to replace Roy as his starting goalie, and, as it turned out, Demers made the right choice. "The one thing as a coach I'll take credit for, is I stood with Patrick," Demers explained in *Sports Illustrated*.

GOALPOSTS LISTEN. Roy decided to change his luck before the play-offs started. A very superstitious player, he had a routine he went through before each game. Roy would face the net after the national anthem was played and tell the goalposts that "they're all going to play wonderful hockey, allowing no little black objects to enter" the net. Then he would stare at the goal until he could see it getting smaller.

SUDDEN DEATH. Roy continued to talk to the goalposts, but he changed the way he skated around the face-off circles before warming up. "Prest-o, change-o, Roy's goalposts began to listen to him again," E. M. Swift wrote in *Sports Illustrated*. The Canadiens, with Roy playing like his old self, reeled off a record-tying 11 straight play-off victories. Seven of the victories came in sudden death overtime, the most pressure-packed situation imaginable. One mistake by Roy and the Canadiens could have lost these games.

"We didn't mind going into overtime," Roy explained to *Sports Illustrated*. "I knew my teammates were going to score goals if I gave them some time. My concentration was at such a high level. My mind was right there. I felt fresh, like I could stop everything."

STANLEY CUP II. The Canadiens once again reached the Stanley Cup Finals. There they faced the Los Angeles Kings, led by the great one, Wayne Gretzky. The Candiens won three of the first four games. Roy was the difference in the series, constantly frustrating the high-powered Kings' offense. He stopped 40 shots in Game Four, including 10 in overtime. This performance ran his playoff overtime shutout streak to an amazing 96 minutes and 39 seconds, during which he stopped 65 shots without allowing a goal. "I'm just seeing the puck really well," Roy said in the *Detroit Free Press*. "My concentration is easy. It's tiring playing all these overtimes, but I don't think about the overtime record. It's fun."

Before Game Five, Roy predicted the series would end that night. He was right. Roy stopped 18 shots and allowed only one goal in a 4-1 victory. "When Patrick Roy makes a promise, he keeps it," teammate Mike Keane said after the game. "He isn't an outspoken guy, but he said he was going to shut the door tonight, and he did."

SECOND SMYTHE. As the Canadiens celebrated by carrying the Stanley Cup around the ice of the Montreal Forum, the top of the scoreboard read "Superpatrick." Roy was the undisputed most valuable player of the play-offs. He posted a 16-4 record in the play-offs with a 2.13 goals-against average. These numbers were more than good enough for Roy to win his second Conn Smythe Trophy. "On a Stanley Cup winner, you have to have great goaltending," Demers told the *New York Times*. "Patrick Roy has been outstanding. When he got that trophy, it was deserved. I don't think there was any one player who did not want him to win it." Roy became only the fifth player to win the Conn Smythe Trophy two times. "It's awesome," Roy explained in the *Detroit Free Press*. "Nobody would believe [the feeling]."

STAYS IN MONTREAL. Roy signed a big contract after the Canadiens' Stanley Cup victory. He could have left Montreal, but Roy decided that was where he wanted to stay. "It's always been important to me to play in Montreal and to finish my career in this city," Roy told the *Montreal Gazette*. "Everything about playing in the city fits in with what I want to do with my life." The Canadiens were glad to keep him. "He's the best goaltender in hockey," team president Ronald Corey told the same newspaper. "Fans have made him the most popular player on the team. He's got the respect of everybody on the team."

The Canadiens once again entered a rebuilding period following Roy's second Stanley Cup victory. The probable future Hall of Famer continues to shine however. During the

SPECIAL DELIVERY

Montreal lost Game One of the 1993 Stanley Cup play-offs, but Roy had something more important on his mind. He drove his wife, Michele, to the hospital after the game. She gave birth to their daughter, Jana, at 7:50 A.M. the next day. Roy was unbeatable the rest of the series.

strike-shortened 1994-95 season, Roy posted an impressive 2.97 goals-against average but finished with a losing record, 17-20-6, for the first time in his career. Roy's overall record at the end of the 1994-95 season was an extraordinary 277-166-65 with a career 2.76 goals-against average.

BIG TRADE. The Canadiens got off to slow starts at the beginning of the 1995-96 season under new coach Mario Tremblay. Roy was unhappy with the way the team was playing and argued with Tremblay. Montreal suspended Roy after he gave up 11 goals in a loss to the Detroit Red Wings. The suspension made Roy angry and embarrassed.

Finally, on December 6, 1995, Montreal traded Roy and forward Mike Keane to the Colorado Avalanche (formerly the Quebec Nordiques) for goalie Jocelyn Thibault and forwards Martin Rucinsky and Andrei Kovalenko. "Three days ago [when Roy was suspended] it was a sad day for me," Roy told the *Chicago Tribune*. ["This] is a happy moment. Colorado was my first choice for many reasons."

OFF THE ICE. Roy lives in the Montreal suburb of Rosemere with his wife, Michele, and their three children, Jonathan, Frederick, and Jana. He has an ice rink in the basement of his house. Roy collects hockey cards and enjoys playing golf. He is also well-known for working with children' charities.

In addition to talking to his goalposts, Roy has other routines he follows before games. He eats spaghetti and drinks water at one P.M. and bounces the same puck in the dressing room. And even though he plays great under pressure, Roy always seems nervous. He constantly twitches his face and shoulders and cannot stay still during breaks in the action. "He makes everybody nervous," Montreal sports journalist Red Fisher told *Saturday Night*.

When Roy signed a new contract after the 1992-93 season, he said the four-year deal would be his last. "I will have been in the league for 12 seasons at the end of this contract," Roy explained in the *Montreal Gazette*. "I'll be 32. I've got to be prepared for a life after hockey."

Sources

Chicago Tribune, December 7, 1995.
Detroit Free Press, June 1, 1993; June 2, 1993; June 8, 1993; June 9, 1993; June 10, 1993; September 15, 1993.
Montreal Gazette, September 14, 1993.
New York Times, May 18, 1986; May 19, 1989; June 10, 1993.
Saturday Night, March 1995.
Sporting News, May 2, 1994.
Sports Illustrated, October 13, 1986; June 21, 1993.
Additional information provided by Montreal Canadiens.

WHERE TO WRITE:
C/O COLORADO AVALANCHE, MCNICHOLS SPORTS ARENA, 1635 CLAY ST., DENVER, CO 80204.

Junior Seau

1969—

Linebacker Junior Seau of the San Diego Chargers is one of the most intense competitors in the National Football League (NFL). Seau has an incredible combination of speed and strength, a package that has made him one of the best linebackers in football. Seau is also a success off the field, acting as a role model for persons from American Samoa and for kids living in tough inner-city neighborhoods. Seau says he wants to be remembered as the best linebacker who ever played the game. No linebacker in history has ever worked harder than Seau to reach that goal.

Growing Up

SAMOAN SUCCESS. Tiaina (Tee-eye-EE-nuh) Seau (SAY-ow) Jr. was born January 19, 1969, in San Diego, California. Seau was the fifth of six children. His parents were born on the island of Aunuu, a part of American Samoa, a group of seven islands in the South Pacific Ocean. The Seaus moved to California five years before Junior was born because their oldest child, David, needed special medical treatment for a lung disease. Seau's father took the name of his paternal grandmother, Seau, as a gesture of respect to the family they were leaving behind in Samoa.

Seau lived in Samoa for a brief time when he was young but returned to the United States just before entering grade school. His father, Tiaina, worked at a rubber factory and then as a school custodian. His mom, Luisa, worked in a laundry and at a store on a military base. People called Seau "Junior" because they could not pronounce his real first name.

BIG DOOR. The Seaus lived in a small house. Seau and his three brothers slept in the garage with only a portable heater to keep them warm on chilly nights. "My sisters, who lived inside the house, always bragged that they had a carpet in their bedroom," Seau recalled in *Sports Illustrated.* "But we'd say, 'So what? We have the biggest door in the whole place.'" Seau grew up in a tough neighborhood filled with crime and violence.

SAMOAN CUSTOMS. The family spoke only the Samoan language at home and followed the customs and traditions of Samoa. "Samoans are very family oriented," Seau explained in *Sports Illustrated for Kids.* "People respect their elders. That's very important. You respect your elders, no matter if they are right or wrong. Samoans are also very religious." Before breakfast and after dinner the Seau family prayed on straw mats in their living room. Mr. Seau acted as a deacon at the First Samoan Congregational Church and led his family in Samoan hymns.

Samoan customs go beyond language and religion. The Seau boys wore wraparound skirts called *lavalavas,* which were made by their father. The girls wore floor-length dresses called *muumuus,* made by their mother. The boys learned the Samoan slap dance, and the girls the hula. The family ate a traditional Samoan food: green bananas.

Trying to keep their culture alive had some bad side effects on the Seau children. Seau did not learn English until after elementary school. "I can't blame them [his parents] for pushing their language over English," Seau confessed in *Sports Illustrated.* "They didn't understand that you can't bring the Samoan culture here and live it. If you want to be something in America, you have to convert to American ways."

Seau has been to Samoa four times. "It's a small island," Seau said in *Sports Illustrated for Kids.* "They don't have the luxuries that we have in the States. You get the true feeling of the tropical natives hanging out. It's green and blue, and there are reefs all around the island."

STRICT DAD. Mr. Seau tried to bring his children up right. "Dad taught us about morals, values and goals," Seau revealed in *Sports Illustrated.* "Having a tight-knit family was impor- tant to him. The one question he always asked us was, 'How do we protect the Seau name?'" Seau's father was very strict. "There were a lot of spankings—with sticks, shoes, whatever was laying around," Seau's older brother, Savaii, remembered in *Sports Illustrated.* "If we even thought about going to the right after he told us to go to the left, we got our whippings."

His father sometimes frightened Seau. "He had killer eyes—one goes one way, the other the other way," Seau recalled in *Sports Illustrated.* "You don't know if he's looking at you when he's speaking to you, and when he's sitting to your side, one eye follows you. It's intimidating. My friends used to be so afraid of him that they'd stand in the middle of Zeiss Street and call for me to come out and play."

SEAU SIBLINGS. Seau bodysurfed and played sports with his three brothers. He worked out hard, trying to keep up with his

Seau (number 55) and his teammate tackle O. J. McDuffie of the ▶
Miami Dolphins during the 1995 play-offs.

more muscular siblings. He lifted weights and did push-ups and chin-ups from a big tree in the backyard. His brothers called him "Jarhead" as a child because of the haircuts his father gave him. Seau made money by selling balloons at the Circus Vargus at the Sports Arena in San Diego. "I sold those big, long balloons, and I got a nickel for every one I sold," Seau remembered in *Sports Illustrated for Kids*.

QUARTERBACK SEAU? When Seau began playing football, he wanted to be the quarterback. His fantasy is still to throw a 50-yard pass, run down and catch it, and score a touchdown. Seau started playing football for a Pop Warner (little league) team. His brother Savaii bought him a cheeseburger every time he scored a touchdown. Seau's father gave him money when his team won, but the son got the silent treatment when his team lost. "If we lost, Dad acted like we were failures," Savaii Seau recounted in *Sports Illustrated*. "He'd say, 'You're lazy.'"

HIGH SCHOOL STAR. At Oceanside High School Seau was a star football and basketball player and ran track. In football Seau played linebacker on defense and quarterback and tight end on offense. "I played quarterback in high school, and I wanted to be a quarterback," Seau stated in *Sports Illustrated for Kids*. "The quarterback was always the main man." Football, however, was not Seau's favorite sport. "Basketball was my true love," he admitted in *Sports Illustrated for Kids*. "I was a shooting forward. I played basketball all the way through my senior year of high school." San Diego sportswriters named Seau the San Diego Section Basketball Player of the Year in his senior season.

Seau led Oceanside to the city 2A championship in football his senior season, an amazing feat because the team had only 18 players. Sportswriters named Seau the Most Valuable Defensive Player of San Diego County and the Most Valuable Offensive Player of the Avocado League. *Parade* magazine named him to their All-American team.

TROJAN TERROR. Recruiters from every college football power showed interest in Seau. In 1987 he received a football scholarship to the University of Southern California (USC). Unfortunately, he could not play with the Trojans his freshman season because he did not achieve high enough scores on the Scholastic Aptitude Test (SAT). "Everything I'd worked for, everything my family had stood for was gone," Seau recalled in *Sports Illustrated*. "I was labeled a dumb jock. I went from being a four-sport star to an ordinary student at USC. I found out who my true friends were. Nobody stuck up for me—not our relatives, best friends or neighbors. There's a lot of jealousy among Samoans, not wanting others to get ahead in life, and my parents got an earful at church: 'We told you he was never going to make it.'" Seau made a special trip back to his high school to apologize to his coaches, teachers, and principal.

Seau earned the respect of his USC teammates by winning the annual Superman contest. The competition included eight events and tested an athlete's speed and strength. Seau also earned above-average grades in the classroom his freshman year, clearing the way for him to play football.

ALL-AMERICAN. An injury to Seau's right ankle before his sophomore season further delayed his football career. Finally, in his third season (1988), Seau became a starter and an instant star. He recorded 19 sacks and 27 tackles for the Trojans. He played so well that he earned Pacific-10 Defensive Player of the Year and All-American honors.

TURNS PRO. Seau decided to turn professional after his junior season at USC. The San Diego Chargers chose him with the fifth pick in the first round of the 1989 NFL Draft. Joining the Chargers turned out to be a learning experience for Seau. San Diego moved him to inside linebacker, a big change from the outside pass-rushing position he played at Southern California. The new position forced Seau to learn how to cover running backs on pass plays and plug the holes in the Chargers' run defense.

THE NUMBER GAME

How did Seau pick his number 55? Was it a lucky number? Did one of his favorite players wear the same number? The answer is none-of-the-above. "My father turned 55 when I went to college," Seau recalled in *Sports Illustrated for Kids*. "I chose his age to be my number."

Seau learned quickly. He started 15 games as a rookie and made 85 tackles, second on the team. Seau's fellow NFL players named him an alternate to the All-Pro game. He followed up his great rookie season with an even better second year. Seau led the Chargers in tackles in 1991 with 129 and earned a starting position in the Pro Bowl.

CHARGING BACK. The Chargers hired a new coach for the 1992 season. Bobby Ross, a coach who had won a college national championship with the Clemson Tigers, took over. San Diego started slowly, losing their first four games, and seemed out of play-off contention. In a remarkable turn-around, the Chargers went 11-1 the rest of the regular season and finished with an 11-5 record and the American Football Conference (AFC) West division title. The comeback was the biggest season turnaround in NFL history. San Diego qualified for the play-offs for the first time since 1982.

Seau was the heart and soul of the Chargers defensive unit which finished fourth in the NFL. He led the team with 102 tackles during the season and encouraged his fellow defensive players to hold hands in the huddle, promoting team unity. Seau also congratulated the offense, running off the bench when the Chargers scored. The AFC named him its Defensive Player of the Year. San Diego defeated the Kansas City Chiefs in the first round of the NFL play-offs but lost 31-0 to the Miami Dolphins the next week. Seau contributed a career-high 19 tackles in the loss to Miami and took out a full-page ad in a local paper thanking the San Diego fans for their support during the season.

LETDOWN. San Diego fans expected a Super Bowl appearance from their team in 1993, but the Chargers finished 8-8 and failed to make the play-offs. "Disappointing is too mild a word," Seau exclaimed in *Sport* magazine, describing the 1993 season. "I can sit here and make a number of excuses—injuries, in particular—but the fact is we just weren't good enough to reach the level we did in '92." Seau led the Chargers in tackles for the third straight year, with 129.

SUPER CHARGERS. The Chargers turned their fortunes around in 1994. San Diego won the AFC West Division after experts predicted a last-place finish before the season. Seau finished with a career-high 155 tackles and had eight games in which he had ten or more stops. He was named the NFL's Linebacker of the Year. Seau accomplished all this despite a painful pinched nerve in his neck that made his left arm all but useless for tackling.

SEAU SHINES. The 1994 play-offs brought out the best in Seau. San Diego faced the Miami Dolphins and the great Dan Marino in their first play-off game. Marino led the Dolphins to a 21-6 lead in the third quarter, but the Chargers came back to take a 22-21 lead with little time left on the clock. Marino moved the Dolphins down field, but a 48-yard field goal by kicker Pete Stoyanovich fell short. San Diego had survived without playing its best game. Seau had four tackles in the victory.

The Chargers now faced the Pittsburgh Steelers in the AFC championship game. The Steelers were confident of winning the game and advancing to the Super Bowl. Pittsburgh players predicted a shutout and discussed a Super Bowl rap video. The Chargers listened and became more determined. Ross talked to his players the night before the game. "No one gives us any respect," *Sports Illustrated* reported Ross as telling his team. "No one has given us any respect all year long. You can't just talk a game, though. You have to go out and play."

Seau set the tone for the game when he threw down Steelers running back Barry Foster on the second play of the game. He jumped to his feet after the tackle and shouted encouragement at the San Diego bench. "He was quiet before the game, just sitting in here and waiting, and then, when the game started, he exploded," teammate Stanley Richard related in *Sports Illustrated.* "Seeing him, you told yourself, I need to get out and start playing, because he's stepping up."

Seau finished the game with 16 tackles and led the Chargers with his intense determination. San Diego took the lead late in the game, 17-13, and then held on. Seau's last tackle came with only 1:22 left in the game. He stopped Pittsburgh fullback John L. Williams on the Chargers' three-yard line on third down. Linebacker Dennis Gibson batted away a fourth-down pass, giving San Diego the victory.

The Chargers held the NFL-leading Steelers' rushing game to only 66 yards. "You can never measure character," Seau explained in *Sports Illustrated*. "You can never measure heart. You saw it out there today. You don't know whether to cry, to laugh, to smile." The Chargers were in the Super Bowl for the first time in their history.

BLOWN OUT. The San Francisco 49ers had a mission in the 1995 Super Bowl. They were out to win a record-setting fifth Super Bowl, and the 49ers were unstoppable. San Francisco scored early and often on the way to a 49-26 victory. Seau had 11 tackles and one sack in the rout. "A Super Bowl victory would have been great, but it was an honor just being there," Seau said after the game. "I hope I get the chance to compete again soon."

ANOTHER COMEBACK. Expectations were high for the Chargers in 1995 coming off their Super Bowl season. The team struggled, however, beginning the season 4-7. San Diego, led by Seau, would not quit. The Chargers won their last five games and not only qualified for the play-offs but earned a first-round home game against the Indianapolis Colts. The Colts ended the Chargers' winning streak and season with a 35-20 victory. Although San Diego lost, Seau made 11 tackles and intercepted a pass against Indianapolis.

TOUGH JOB. Playing linebacker in the NFL is a tough job. Linebackers have to possess the strength to fight off 300-pound linemen trying to knock them down. They also have to be fast enough to cover speedy running backs and keep them from catching passes. Seau does all these things, and does them well. He possesses a rare combination of size, speed, and desire. Seau can bench-press 500 pounds, run the 40-yard dash in 4.61 seconds, and leap three feet in the air from a standing start. "He chases down plays, he plays the run, he plays the pass," Cleveland Browns coach Bill Belicheck explained in *Boys' Life*. "He's a guy nobody's really been able to stop."

Seau wants to be the best. "I'm afraid of being average," he admitted in *Boys' Life*. "I have a real fear of being just another linebacker." Seau takes losses hard, especially when he feels like they are his fault. After one game, he broke down crying when he tried to apologize to the team. "People don't hold themselves accountable for what they do," Seau stated in *Sports Illustrated*. "I wanted to stand up and say, 'It's my fault.'" Teammate Bill Plummer told the same magazine that Seau had nothing to apologize for. "He's the last person anybody would blame for a loss. Junior expects perfection out of everybody, but especially himself."

OFF THE FIELD. Seau lives in La Jolla, California, with his wife, Gina, and their daughter, Sydney Beau. He likes the trumpet and has played the instrument since fifth grade. Seau likes all kinds of water sports, including skiing and body surfing. He has two dogs, a golden retriever named Trojan and a rottweiler named Heisman. In school Seau's favorite subject was math.

Seau sponsors the Junior Seau Foundation, which helps kids in San Diego by supporting programs that fight drugs, alcohol, and child abuse. Seau also sponsors the Junior Seau Celebrity Golf Classic and Junior Seau's Drug-Busters Basketball Team. "Too many athletes are living in a tiny window," Seau stated in *Sports Illustrated*. "They have no vision for themselves—what they can

FAMILY AFFAIR

Seau has personal experience with what gangs can do to a family. His brother Tony did not escape the old neighborhood like Seau did. Tony joined a gang, and the police arrested him for assault. "He got caught up in the wrong crowd," Seau confessed in *Sport* magazine. "I feel bad for Tony. He has to live with the expectations of doing as well as the older brother, and that's hard on a young kid. He's only 15. He rebelled. It says a lot about where I come from, the neighborhood I lived in. The influences of the 'hood are powerful—even for a soft-hearted kid like Tony. I preach to Tony what I've preached to all groups I've spoken to. We can go out and try to guide them, try to set an example, but we can't make their choices. They must. And they must live with those choices. Luckily for Tony, he's alive. He gets a second chance. He didn't get shot. He didn't die. Now the choice is his: a life his family has for him or a lifestyle the gangsters have for him. To me, the choice is easy." Seau believes he is a good role model for inner-city kids, as he explained in *Sports Illustrated for Kids*: "I'm living proof that you can make it out of the ghetto."

be outside of football and what they can mean to a community. They just don't know any better. My hopes and dreams are unlimited." The NFL recognized Seau's charitable work in 1994 by giving him the Edge NFL Man of the Year award.

Seau is happiest when he takes the field. "Coming out on the field is always an exciting time," Seau revealed. "That's the moment you know it's time to perform. I'll always just love playing the game."

Sources

Boys' Life, December 1994.
Sport, October 1994.
Sporting News, January 16, 1995; January 23, 1995; January 30, 1995; February 6, 1995; January 8, 1996.
Sports Illustrated, September 6, 1993; February 6, 1995.
Sports Illustrated for Kids, November 1993; November 1994; September 1995.
Additional information provided by San Diego Chargers.

WHERE TO WRITE:
C/O SAN DIEGO CHARGERS,
P.O. BOX 609609,
SAN DIEGO, CA 92160.

Bruce Smith

1963—

The quarterback sack is the most devastating weapon for a defensive football team. The best at getting to the quarterback in the history of the American Football Conference (AFC) is defensive lineman Bruce Smith of the Buffalo Bills. Smith was one of the main reasons the Bills won four straight AFC championships (1990-93), and he continues to shine as an All-Pro after 11 grueling National Football League (NFL) seasons. A marked man by opposing offenses, Smith has one goal: to be the best defensive lineman in NFL history.

"There's no way a human being should do what he does."—Buffalo Bills center Kent Hull

Growing Up

ROLE MODELS. Bruce Bernard Smith was born June 18, 1963, in Norfolk, Virginia. He was the youngest of three children. His father, George, was a shipping clerk and a truck driver. His mother, Annie, worked at a variety of jobs, including driving a city bus. "I've been trying to make her quit driving the bus, but she won't," Smith related in *Sports Illustrated*. Both of Smith's parents played sports. His father boxed, and his mother played center on her high school basketball team.

Smith credits his parents with bringing him up right and teaching him values. "My role model was the man I saw at home every day," Smith declared in *Sports Illustrated*. He and his father fished and hunted together, and his dad taught him some valuable lessons, including the value of hard work. "I admired my father because he was a hard worker at the minimum wage," Smith recalled in *Inside Sports*. "He worked ten to twelve hours a day, and yet he'd always find the time to watch me play sports. He was always there for me."

BIG EATER. Smith always had a big appetite. "As a kid I'd eat at my mother's house, then go down the road to my girlfriend's and eat, and then sometimes go to my friend's house and eat again," Smith confessed in *Sports Illustrated*. "I could gain five pounds in a day. In a week, there wouldn't be a scale to weigh me." By the time he was a high school sophomore, Smith weighed 270 pounds.

Other children teased Smith because of his weight, and local bullies beat him up. "Those were hard times growing up, dealing with my size and my situation," Smith recalled in the *New York Times*. "We didn't have a great deal of money though we were able to get necessities. You see your mother and father working two jobs apiece, and making the best out of everything, somehow, someway. I was too big, too slow and too fat for sports. Little success came easy for me in anything. I lacked in confidence. It was a struggle."

HIGH SCHOOL STAR. Smith's size helped him become a two-sport star at Booker T. Washington High School. He earned All-American honors as a lineman in football and played cen-

ter on the 1980 Virginia state championship basketball team. When it came time to pick a college, Smith wanted to attend the University of Virginia. Unfortunately, recruiters for the Cavaliers told Smith he did not have enough speed to play for their team.

TECH TERROR. Virginia Tech University had no problem with Smith's speed. They signed the young lineman, and he went on to be a star. In four seasons Smith recorded 180 tackles, including 46 quarterback sacks and 25 other tackles for losses. Smith's teammates twice named him the team's Most Valuable Player. Smith earned All-American honors as a senior and won the prestigious Outland Trophy, awarded annually to the nation's best collegiate lineman. Tech earned a berth in the Independence Bowl in Smith's senior year (1984) but lost to the Air Force Academy, 23-7.

TOP PICK. After finishing with a 2-14 record in 1984, the Buffalo Bills held the first pick in the 1985 NFL Draft. Look-

Smith (number 78) tries to sack Phil Simms of the New York Giants.

ing to beef up their defense, the Bills selected Smith. The rookie lineman made an immediate impact with the Bills. He recorded a team-leading 6.5 quarterback sacks and recovered four fumbles. Several times Smith also played fullback on offense in short-yardage situations. Experts named Smith the AFC Defensive Rookie of the Year.

Despite Smith's rookie success, the Bills still lost 14 games in 1985. Their fortune soon changed, however. The team signed quarterback Jim Kelly, who had been playing in the United States Football League, a professional league that competed for a short time with the NFL. Buffalo also made a coaching change, bringing in Marv Levy to run the team.

MVP. The Bills steadily improved. Smith had 15 sacks (tied for second in AFC) in 1986, but Buffalo won only four games. A players' strike shortened the 1987 season by one game, but Smith made the most of the games he played. Smith led all AFC linemen with 12 sacks and earned Defensive Player of the Year honors from United Press International (UPI). He also earned election to his first Pro Bowl game. Smith showed he belonged with the best players in the world when he earned Most Valuable Player honors in the game.

The Bills broke through in 1988. They finished 12-4 and won the AFC East Division title. Smith again led Buffalo with 11 sacks and earned All-Pro honors. The Bills advanced to the AFC Championship Game but lost to the Cincinnati Bengals, 21-10. Buffalo won the AFC East title for the second time in 1989 with a 9-7 record, and Smith recorded 13 sacks. The Bills lost 34-30 in the first round of the play-offs to the Cleveland Browns.

GROWING UP. The Bills were now one of the NFL's most talented teams. To reach their potential, however, the Buffalo players, including Smith, needed to grow up and learn to work together. The team had earned the nickname "the Bickering Bills," and Smith admitted he had not been in shape and had gotten by on talent alone. He also served a suspension in 1988 for using drugs. Smith now admits he made a mistake but hopes people can forgive him. "It's not how you fall down, it's how you get back up," Smith related in *Sports Illustrated.*

"I was losing my relationship with God and I kind of pushed it aside," Smith admitted in the *New York Times.* "My values had diminished. I had to regroup. I guess I was still maturing and I didn't handle success as well as I should have. In this business, I learned that you have to grow up in a hurry. You have to mature much quicker than you would in a normal life."

To improve, Smith began a tough workout routine to get in shape. He gave up the fast foods he had loved since he was a child and ate only a high-energy, low-fat diet of pasta and fish. "I haven't had a Big Mac in three or four years. Whopper about the same," Smith told *Sports Illustrated* in 1991. It's all about discipline." The diet helped Smith reduce his weight to 265 pounds, and his workouts helped him increase his strength. "Now he's got the body fat of a wide receiver," Levy related in the *New York Times.* "Really, you look at him now and he looks like he's been carved out of wood. It has improved his endurance and his liking for the game."

Superstar

SO CLOSE AND THEN SO FAR. The next four years the Bills dominated the AFC. In 1990 Buffalo finished 13-3, led by Smith on defense and the powerful no-huddle offense run by Kelly and running back Thurman Thomas. Smith finished with 19 sacks, despite being double- and triple-teamed all season. He earned NFL Defensive Player of the Year honors.

Buffalo continued to dominate in the play-offs, defeating the Los Angeles Raiders 51-3 in the AFC Championship Game. The victory put the Bills in the Super Bowl for the first time. There they faced the National Football Conference (NFC) champions, the New York Giants. The game featured two of the best defensive players in the NFL, Smith and linebacker Lawrence Taylor of the Giants.

WIDE RIGHT. Buffalo kept the game close throughout and had a chance to win with only seconds left on the clock. Kicker

Scott Norwood, however, missed a game-ending 47-yard field goal, giving the Giants a 20-19 victory. Smith scored two points in the game when he sacked Giants quarterback Jeff Hostetler in the end zone for a safety. Despite his disappointment, Smith told Norwood the loss was not his fault. "Afterward he [Smith] gave me a big hug at the hotel, telling me it wasn't me who lost the game," Norwood recalled in *Sports Illustrated*. "It meant a lot to me."

RECORD BREAKERS. The Bills returned to the Super Bowl the next three seasons, setting a record for consecutive appearances in the NFL's biggest game. Unfortunately, Buffalo also set a record by losing four straight Super Bowls. Smith missed 11 games in 1991 following knee surgery and a recovery period that limited him throughout the play-offs and the Super Bowl. He had additional surgery before the 1992 season but came back strong during the 1992 season with 14 sacks. In 1993 Smith had his best all-around season. He finished second in the NFL with 14 sacks and collected a career-high 108 tackles. *Pro Football Weekly* named him the Defensive Player of the Year.

DRIVE FOR FIVE. The Bills' reign as AFC champions ended in 1994, because their 7-9 record was not good enough to qualify for the play-offs. Smith again suffered a painful injury, this time to his shoulder. He still recorded ten sacks, however, and earned All-Pro honors.

OUT WITH THE OLD. There were several changes to the Bills' roster before the 1995 season. Only 11 players remained from the first Super Bowl team, and Smith's best friend on the team, linebacker Darryl Talley, signed as a free agent with the Atlanta Falcons. "It's a lonely feeling, so to speak," Smith admitted in *Football Digest*. "Darryl and I had been together for the last ten years, and we had a lot of great moments and great experiences. The fact that he's not here is just another indication in life that everything can't always stay the same."

The Bills also added some players, including linebacker Bryce Paup from the Green Bay Packers and pass-rushing specialist Jim Jeffcoat from the Dallas Cowboys. "I finally have some defensive line help to take away from a lot of double- and triple-teams," Smith told *Football Digest*. In addition to new players, the defense got a new coach—Wade Phillips— who was formerly head coach of the Denver Broncos. Phillips brought a new aggressive style to the Bills' defense, a style perfectly suited to Smith's skills.

The team's new defense helped the Bills return to the play-offs. Buffalo finished the regular season with a 10-6 record, and Smith once again took a leadership role. He finished with 10.5 sacks, and his presence allowed Paup to lead the NFL with 17.5 sacks. Buffalo won the AFC East Division title and earned a first-round home play-off game against the Miami Dolphins. Buffalo easily handled the Dolphins, 37-22, but lost on the road in the second round to the Pittsburgh Steelers. Smith missed the Pittsburgh game because of the flu. The virus weakened Smith and made him too dizzy to play.

WHY SO GOOD? Smith has worked hard to be the best, and his coaches and teammates appreciate his determination. "Bruce is the classic example of a guy that's matured over five, six, seven years," Levy explained in the *Washington Post*. "He was somewhat self-indulgent when he came in, overweight. He had been able to totally dominate, I'm sure, all the way back to grade school. But somewhere when he got hurt, he began to realize the value of conditioning. Now, no one works out harder."

Smith also has improved his attitude. He no longer celebrates after every sack, realizing that team goals are more important than individual achievements. "Smith used to stomp to the sidelines and scream at his teammates and coaches, begging them to change the system so that he could get more sacks and more attention and more personal accolades," Jennifer Frey reported in the *New York Times*. "Now he won't even whisper a

SACK MEN

The NFL has been keeping quarterback sacks as an official statistic since 1982. In 1995 Smith ranked third all-time in this important statistic. The top three sack men as of the end of the 1995 season are shown below.

Player	Sacks
Reggie White	157
Lawrence Taylor	132.5
Bruce Smith	126.5

TOUGH SPORT

Playing football takes a toll on the body, and many players suffer from injuries long after they retire from the game. Smith feels the risk is worth it. "Let's face it, the human body is not made for football," Smith explained in *Sports Illustrated*. "When you play, you have to accept that. I'm not complaining. I get an awful lot of good things out of football. I chose to be a football player, and I accept everything that goes with that decision— the pain, the injuries, the pressure. Basically I'm giving my body up to support a better lifestyle for me and everyone close to me."

complaint." His teammates noticed the change. "He really has changed," Bills center Kent Hull told the same reporter. "At times you see him do things to help another defensive lineman that puts himself at risk. And I don't think you would have seen him doing things like that before."

Smith has a unique combination of speed and strength that has made him one of the best defensive linemen of all time. "You're talking about a guy who is stronger than a three-hundred-pounder and faster than a linebacker," teammate Hull stated in *Sports Illustrated*. "His speed around the corner is unreal. And if you move out, he'll take one step upfield, spin inside and he's gone. I think he's double-jointed. He'll line up over me, and I'll try to hit him, and there's nothing there—he's going back and coming forward at the same time. I can't even explain it. There's no way a human being should do what he does."

OFF THE FIELD. Smith lives with his wife, Carmen, and their son, Alston, in Norfolk, Virginia. He built a home for his parents in nearby Virginia Beach. Smith hopes his son will be his biggest fan someday. "I'm not just playing for myself or my wife anymore," Smith explained in *Football Digest*. "I'm playing for my entire family. That's the addition of Alston, and just to look into his eyes—right now he can't envision [understand] this, but when he gets a little older, he'll be able to look at my accomplishments and be proud of his father."

Smith majored in sociology at Virginia Tech. In 1987 he donated $50,000 to set up a scholarship fund at his alma mater. Someday, Smith hopes, experts will recognize him as the best defensive lineman of all time. "I'll let people judge me off my play," Smith explained in *Football Digest*. "I'm trying to let my actions speak for themselves and let others put it in perspective."

Sources

Chicago Tribune, January 13, 1994.

Football Digest, November 1995.

Inside Sports, August 1991.

New York Times, December 9, 1990; January 27, 1991; July 6, 1992; January 27, 1993.

Sporting News, January 24, 1994; January 31, 1994; February 7, 1994; January 8, 1996; January 15, 1996.

Sports, August 1991.

Sports Illustrated, September 2, 1991; December 14, 1992; August 9, 1993; February 7, 1994.

Washington Post, December 22, 1990; January 14, 1993.

Additional information provided by Buffalo Bills.

WHERE TO WRITE:
C/O BUFFALO BILLS,
ONE BILLS DR.,
ORCHARD PARK, NY 14127.

John Stockton

1962—

Point guard John Stockton is a conductor on the court. Teaming with power forward Karl Malone, Stockton directs the beautiful music made by the fast-break offense of the Utah Jazz. In 1995 Stockton established his name firmly in the record books when he broke Earvin "Magic" Johnson's record as the leading career assist man in National Basketball Association (NBA) history. In 1992 Stockton played on the greatest basketball team ever assembled, the "Dream Team," which won the gold medal at the Summer Olympics in Barcelona, Spain. Today, Stockton continues to add to his record and solidify his position as one of the best point guards of all time.

Growing Up

HOMETOWN BOY. John Houston Stockton was born March 26, 1962, in Spokane, Washington. He is the second and youngest son of Jack and Clementine Stockton, who also have two daughters. Jack Stockton owned Jack and Dan's Tavern, located near Gonzaga College, a small college located in Spokane. Stockton's family was always close. "John was just a member of the family," Mr. Stockton recalled in the *Sporting News*. "He always appreciated that. He's never been babied. His NBA career and his youth all sort of blended in."

BASKETBALL BOYHOOD. Stockton played basketball early and often as a child. "In rain and snow," Mr. Stockton remembered in *Sports Illustrated*. "Day and night." Mark Rypien, who also grew up in Spokane and went on to be an NFL quarterback, recalled knowing Stockton. "I remember driving by Stockton's house in high school," Rypien related in *Sports Illustrated*. "Ten, eleven o'clock at night, and he was out on the driveway, dribbling a basketball." The Seattle Supersonics gave Stockton a thrill by having him as their ball boy.

Stockton learned toughness early. His brother, Steve, and other boys in the neighborhood roughed him up. "Those were rough games and I'd get knocked around when I played in other games in the neighborhood," Stockton admitted in the *New York Times*. One day Stockton came home crying and talked to his father. "My father said, 'Maybe you shouldn't play with those boys, maybe they're too tough,'" Stockton recalled in *Sports Illustrated*. "He said it in a kindly way, but it made me take it as a challenge. Maybe I was stupid, but I went back out to show them I could play."

HOOP DREAMS. Being one of the smaller boys forced Stockton to learn how to handle the ball and pass over and around his bigger opponents. He took these skills to Gonzaga Prep, where he started at guard on the basketball team. Still, Stockton did not impress college recruiters. He could only dream about the NBA. "The only person in the world who thought

John would play in the NBA was John," Mr. Stockton confessed in *Sports Illustrated*.

GONZAGA GUNNER. Stockton enrolled at his father's alma mater, Gonzaga University. His basketball career started slowly at Gonzaga, but he became a regular by his sophomore season, averaging 11.2 points and 5 assists per game. He raised both totals as a junior (13.9 points and 6.8 assists) and NBA scouts took notice for the first time. Stockton became a full-fledged star during his senior season. He scored 20.9 points—first in the West Coast Athletic Conference—and dished out 7.2 assists per game. Stockton beefed up during his years at Gonzaga, going from a skinny 145-pound kid to a solid 175-pound player.

The U.S. Olympic Committee invited Stockton to try out for the 1984 U.S. Olympic team. Despite his lack of experience, Stockton more than held his own among the best college players in the country. Bob Knight of Indiana University, the coach of the national team, made Stockton one of the last cuts from the squad. "Deep inside he knew he was as good as most of the players there," Steve Stockton related in the *Sporting News*. Stockton used the experience as a confidence booster, convinced in his heart that he could play with the best players in the world. NBA scouts began to take Stockton seriously as a future star.

ONE OF THE BEST. The 1984 NBA Draft was one of the strongest of all time. It included such superstars as Michael Jordan, Hakeem Olajuwon, and Charles Barkley. "There are a lot of great players in the NBA today," Barkley explained in *Sport* magazine. "But not one of [the players from a previous draft] can say that [his rookie] class matches the talent we had in '84." The Utah Jazz drafted Stockton with the sixteenth pick in the first round. Many people thought that Utah took a risk, using a high draft choice on a small (by NBA standards) guard from a small school.

Stockton played backup point guard for Utah in his rookie season of 1984-85. He averaged 5.6 points and 5.1 assists his first season. The Jazz struggled, finishing second to

Stockton (left) tries to pass to his teammate.

last in the Midwest Division. Their poor finish allowed Utah to pick Stockton's longtime running mate, Karl "The Mailman" Malone, in the NBA Draft. The next two seasons, with Malone's help, Stockton became one of the best assist men in the league. He wheeled and dealed for 7.4 assists per game in 1985-86 and 8.2 in 1986-87.

Superstar

LEADS LEAGUE. Stockton became a full-time starter in 1987-88 and his career took off. He finished the season with 1,128 assists, shattering the single-season record set by Isiah Thomas of the Detroit Pistons and becoming only the third player in NBA history to surpass the 1,000 assist mark in a single season. Stockton averaged 13.8 assists per game to lead the NBA for the first time, beating out the great Earvin "Magic" Johnson. He also finished third in the league in steals and averaged 14.7 points per contest. The Jazz, now one of the best teams in the NBA, reached the Western Conference Finals, losing to the eventual NBA champion Los Angeles Lakers in seven games.

The Jazz won the Midwest Division title in 1988-89, winning 51 games during the regular season. Stockton once again led the NBA in assists, averaging 13.6 per game, and was tops in steals, with 3.2 a contest. He also increased his scoring average to 17.1 a game. Unfortunately, the Jazz were swept in the first round of the play-offs by California's Golden State Warriors. Stockton dished out a career-best 14.5 assists in 1989-90, but the Jazz once again suffered a first-round defeat in the play-offs. In the 1990-91 season, Stockton broke his own NBA single-season assist record, setting the standard that still stands—1164.

DREAM TEAMER. In late 1991 the U.S. Olympic Committee named Stockton to represent the United States on the first "Dream Team," set to play in the 1992 Summer Olympics in Barcelona, Spain. Stockton, who had been remarkably durable during his career with the Jazz, suffered a broken leg during the early stages of Olympic qualifying. The injury restricted his play during the Olympics, but it did not matter. The "Dream Team" overwhelmed the best opposition the rest of the world had to offer and won the gold medal.

HOME COURT ADVANTAGE. Stockton received another thrill when the NBA held the All-Star Game in 1993 on the Jazz's home court in Salt Lake City, Utah. He teamed up with Malone to lead the Western Conference to a thrilling 135-132 overtime victory. Stockton dished out a game-high 15 assists, and Malone led all scorers with 28 points. Reporters covering the game named the two teammates jointly the game's Most Valuable Players.

RECORD BREAKER. Stockton set two incredible records during the 1994-95 season. On February 1, 1995, he passed Magic Johnson to become the NBA's all-time assist leader. The record-breaking assist came on a basket by Malone. "I think it will mean something later on," Stockton explained in *Sports Illustrated.* "Right now, I just want to play." Johnson gave Stockton his due and told the *Sporting News:* "Nobody can distribute the ball plus lead his team like John Stockton. Because his whole thing is to get everybody involved."

Stockton also tied the immortal Bob Cousy of the Boston Celtics when he led the NBA in assists for the eighth consecutive season. He is expected to break the all time record for steals in a career held by Maurice Cheeks. His credentials put Stockton up with the greatest point guards of all-time. But Stockton does not believe the hype. "I don't think of myself near those other point guards; the record is just a stat," Stockton admitted in *Sport* magazine. "Once you start thinking you're good, that's when you get hammered."

WHY SO GOOD? Unlike some other point guards, Stockton is not a specialist at the flashy play. He leads the Jazz offense

TEAMMATES

Malone and Stockton will forever be linked in the record books. Few partnerships in the NBA have been as successful. Experts disagree about which player is better, but together they are unstoppable. "If Stock and I happen to go to the Hall of Fame, I'm sure they'll try to work it in both our schedules that we're there at the same time because we're bonded together for life," Malone told *Sport* magazine. "I couldn't think of a better guy to be bonded with. He always tries to go out and make his teammates All-Stars. People ask me what I would be without him, and I don't even want to think about it."

with quiet precision. "When I first came into the league, I thought I could take him pretty easily," NBA point guard Johnny Dawkins told the *New York Times*. "But I learned that you can't relax for a second with him. He sees everything on the court, and he's aware of everything. You stand up for a moment and he's got that quick first step and he's got you on his hip, and he's either laying the ball in the hoop or dishing off to somebody for a basket. And then when you least expect it, when the game is on the line, he'll pull up for a three-pointer and hit one at the buzzer." Stockton has large hands, allowing him to palm and control the ball better than most point guards.

Stockton's quiet style often causes fans to overlook his play. "He's so good, you begin to take him for granted," Malone related in the *New York Times*. "I've just come to always expect the perfect pass from him, and I get it. And I was thinking not long ago, even I don't appreciate him as much as I should." Even though he does not get angry or trash-talk, Stockton is a fierce competitor. "Stockton's as mean as they come," Dennis Rodman, one of the toughest players in the NBA, told *Sports Illustrated*. "Everybody might think he's a choirboy, but he'll slip an elbow when the refs aren't looking, or he'll talk some junk."

The biggest disappointment of Stockton's career is that he has never led the Jazz to the NBA Finals. Always a threat, Utah has never made that final step. Stockton does not think a championship is the most important thing. "I'd like to win one, but if that's the only way you can put a positive value on yourself, then you're in big trouble," Stockton explained in *Sport* magazine.

OFF THE COURT. Stockton lives with his wife, Nada, in the house next door to where he grew up in Spokane. The couple has three sons—Houston, Michael, and David—and one daughter, Lindsay. Stockton met his wife, a former volleyball player, in college. He loves to spend time with his children.

Stockton is a spokesperson for Nike and sponsors an annual youth basketball camp during the summer. Going against the current fashion, Stockton refuses to wear the baggy shorts that are now so popular in the NBA. "I go with what feels comfortable," Stockton told the *Sporting News*. In the summer he plays recreation league basketball in Spokane, sometimes on a team with his older brother, Steve.

Stockton hopes to finish his career in Utah, even though he might get more recognition in a bigger city. "I was drafted by this team, and I've spent my entire career with the Jazz, so I'll give everything I can for 'em until they ask me to quit," Stockton explained in *Sport* magazine. "You never know what any other team or NBA city would have been like—and I don't want to find out."

Sources

Chicago Tribune, January 26, 1994.
New York Times, January 23, 1995.
Sport, December 1991; February 1993; July 1994; February 1995.
Sporting News, May 2, 1988; November 4, 1991; February 20, 1995; April 10, 1995.
Sports Illustrated, July 27, 1992; May 30, 1994; February 6, 1995.
Additional information provided by Utah Jazz.

WHERE TO WRITE:
C/O UTAH JAZZ, DELTA CENTER,
301 W. SOUTH TEMPLE,
SALT LAKE CITY, UT 84101.

Elvis Stojko

1972—

Figure skater Elvis Stojko can do amazing things on skates. On his way to gold medals in two straight World Figure Skating Championships (1994 and 1995), he has introduced a new, more lively style to the often old-fashioned sport. Stojko, whose parents named him after the king of rock and roll, Elvis Presley, has jumped his way to the king's throne in men's figure skating. He hopes to add one more trophy to his collection—the gold medal at the 1998 Winter Olympics in Nagano, Japan.

Growing Up

NAMED AFTER ROYALTY. Elvis Stojko was born January 22, 1972. His father's name is Steve, and his mother's name is Irene. Stojko (Stoykoe) grew up on a 50-acre farm in Richmond Hill, Ontario, Canada, in an area just north of Toronto. Steve Stojko moved to Canada from Slovenia at the height of Presley's popularity in the 1950s. "My dad was in a Slovenian singing group, and he really liked Elvis' music," Stojko recalled in the *Chicago Tribune*.

DAREDEVIL. Stojko always liked to take risks. At age seven he began participating in motocross on a minibike. Because he was so young, he had to step on a block of wood to reach the seat of the bike. Fearing that an injury might end his skating career, Stojko gave up motocross racing. When he was ten, he took up karate. By the age of 16 Stojko had earned his blackbelt.

HITS THE ICE. Stojko first became interested in skating when he was three. His parents made him wait, but at age five they let their son take to the ice. "They thought it was a phase," Stojko recounted in the *Chicago Tribune*. "It is a very long phase."

Stojko took his daredevil attitude onto the ice. One time he landed flat on his face when he tried to do a backflip, a jump that is banned in competition because it is too dangerous. Doctors needed nine stitches to close a cut on his eyebrow, a spot where he still has a scar. "I'm lucky it wasn't a lot worse," Stojko admitted in the *Chicago Tribune*.

Soon Stojko began training with Doug Leigh. Leigh had helped make Brian Orser, also from Canada, into a world champion (1987) and Olympic silver medal winner (1988). From the beginning, Stojko's strength was his jumping ability. "Growing up, I was always consistent with the jumps," Stojko recalled in *Maclean's*. "They didn't just come to me—I worked hard at them—but I enjoyed doing them, so that made it easier."

GETS NOTICED. Stojko first burst onto the national scene in Canada when he finished second to world champion Kurt Browning in the 1990 Canadian Figure Skating Championships. His performance earned him the right to compete at the 1990 World Figure Skating Championships in Halifax, Manitoba, Canada. In his first performance on the world stage, Stojko finished a respectable ninth.

Stojko skates towards the silver medal during the 1994 Olympics in Lillehammer, Norway.

BIG JUMP. At the 1991 World Figure Skating Championships in Munich, Germany, Stojko became the first skater to successfully land a quadruple-revolution jump, a quad salchow, in combination with another jump, a double toe loop. The move required him to complete four revolutions in the air followed by another jump immediately after landing. Stojko moved up to sixth in the world during the competition. "He's known as a great jumper, and he does them all," Leigh explained in *Maclean's*. "He doesn't really have a weak jump."

FIRST OLYMPICS. In 1992 Kurt Browning missed the Canadian Figure Skating Championships with a back injury. Experts expected Stojko to win the championship, but Michael Slipchuk surprised him. Stojko made several mistakes in his long program, many caused by a broken bone in his left foot. His second-place finish, however, qualified him to compete in the 1992 Winter Olympics in Albertville, France.

In his first Olympic competition, Stojko finished sixth in the short, or technical program. (In the short program the rules require a skater to complete certain jumps and maneuvers.) He then skated flawlessly in his long, or free-skating, program. (In the long program, a skater can choose which jumps and maneuvers to include.) Even though Stojko was the only one of the top five skaters not to make a mistake in the long program, he fell to seventh in the final standings. The reason for his poor showing was that judges gave him low marks for artistic impression. "He was on the doorstep at the Olympics, but he got left on the doorstep," a disappointed Leigh complained in *Maclean's*.

SECOND BEST. Stojko won the bronze medal at the 1992 World Figure Skating Championships in Oakland, California. Victor Petrenko, the 1992 Olympic gold medalist, won the competition, ending Kurt Browning's three-year reign as world champion. Stojko and Browning—who won the silver medal—became the first Canadian skaters to win medals at the same world championship competition. "I'm absolutely thrilled," Leigh exclaimed in *Maclean's*. "I can't think of a better way to top off a season than to win a medal at the world championships."

WORKS TO IMPROVE. To improve his artistic marks, Stojko began working with choreographer Uschi Keszler after the 1992 World Figure Skating Championships. (A choreographer is a person who develops dance routines and sets them to music.) With Keszler's help, his artistry improved. Stojko trained hard, five days a week at the Mariposa School of Skating in Barrie, Ontario, Canada. "I want to improve my whole package," Stojko explained in *Maclean's*. "The summer is when we do all our work."

Stojko and Browning again represented Canada at the 1993 World Figure Skating Championships in Prague, Czechoslovakia. "We'll compete against the rest of the world," Stojko told *Maclean's*. "We'll cheer each other on." By now Stojko had included karate kicks and chops into his skating routine. He won the silver medal, with Browning taking the gold.

In 1994 Stojko finally defeated Browning at the Canadian Figure Skating Championships after finishing second four times, three times behind his teammate. For the first time he took advantage of his name and skated to the music of Elvis Presley. Stojko wore a black leather jacket with Elvis written on the back in red letters and skated to "Jailhouse Rock." "Last winter, it just seemed the right time had arrived," Stojko explained in the *Vancouver Sun,* explaining why he finally decided to dedicate a performance to Presley.

SO CLOSE. Experts expected experienced skaters such as Brian Boitano (1988 Olympic champion), Victor Petrenko (1992 Olympic champion), and Browning to dominate the 1994 Winter Olympics in Lillehammer, Norway. Stojko looked forward to the challenge, especially competing against Boitano. "I always thought it would be awesome to compete against him, but I thought I never would," Stojko stated in the *Chicago Tribune.*

Despite his second-place finish at the 1993 world championships, not many experts listed Stojko as a medal favorite. "I'm in a no-lose situation," he explained in the *Chicago Tribune.* "There is no pressure on me. If I don't win a medal, it's no big deal. I have to enjoy what I'm doing. I just want to push myself to the limits."

The past champions stumbled in their short, or technical, programs. Boitano finished eighth, Petrenko ninth, and Browning a disappointing twelfth. Alexsei Urmanov of the Ukraine, a skater who had never won an international competition, finished first in the short program. Stojko was right on his heels in second place. "There were a couple of generations out there, and when somebody said, 'Step up to the plate,' the new generation did," Leigh stated in *Sports Illustrated*. "The Olympics [are] about rising to the occasion and not waiting for your turn."

"I just enjoyed every second out there, but it was a shock to see where the big guns placed," Stojko admitted in *Maclean's* after his short program. The young Canadian promised fireworks in his long program, saying he would try to be the first skater to successfully complete a quadruple jump, triple jump combination. "That is the daredevil side of me," he explained in the *Chicago Tribune*. "I like being on the edge. I'm not doing it to win. I'm doing it because I can and because I'm challenging myself."

SILVER STREAK. Stojko's long program included a tribute to the late martial arts star Bruce Lee. He wore a leather outfit with metal studs hand-sewn by his mother. In the heat of competition, Stojko left out his quadruple toe loop, triple toe loop combination. He made up for his omission by adding a triple axel, triple toe loop near the end of his program. Stojko received seven near-perfect scores of 5.9 for technical merit, but the judges again marked him down on his artistic impression scores. Urmanov skated flawlessly and narrowly edged his Canadian rival for the gold medal. Phillipe Candeloro of France, who skated to music from the movie *The Godfather,* finished third.

"I didn't feel very good about it at first," Stojko confessed in *Maclean's* about finishing second. "But all I can do now is smile and say, 'Hey, I won a silver medal for Canada and it's proof that all those hours sweating through workouts really paid off.'"

ARTISTIC ARGUMENTS

Figure skating is one of the few sports that require an athlete to make an "artistic impression" on judges. Skaters receive two scores in every competition, one for technical merit and one for artistic impression. While most everyone agrees on what it takes to complete a jump successfully, there are no rules for what makes a performance artistic. Skaters like Stojko, Phillipe Candeloro, and **Surya Bonaly** (see entry) of France have suffered in international competitions because judges do not like their style of skating. Stojko believes judges should be more open-minded. "You can't stop evolution," he told the *New York Times*. "Things have changed with kung fu and *The Godfather*. All skaters don't look alike. They have to realize that there is more than one style of skating, and not always will the classical win over. There are many different styles out there."

Superstar

WORLD CHAMP. Stojko took his place among the best male figure skaters in the world when he won the 1994 World Figure Skating Championships in Chiba, Japan. "Before I won, I used to wonder what it would be like to be world champion, but now that I'm there, I'm more interested in what's next," Stojko said in the *Vancouver Sun*.

Stojko edged out Phillipe Candeloro; he thought the two skaters had finally broken through with the judges. "We are a force to be reckoned with," Stojko stated in *Maclean's*. "One style is not the ultimate. I've opened the door for younger skaters to come up and do their own things." In honor of his achievements, Stojko won Canada's Male Athlete of the Year award in 1994. "It's quite an honor to be chosen for the award," Stojko confessed in the *Vancouver Sun*. "It hasn't really sunk in yet, but it's pretty amazing."

REPEAT. Just eight weeks before the 1995 World Figure Skating Championships in Birmingham, England, Stojko tore a ligament in his right ankle. "I still couldn't pull on my boot," Stojko told the *Los Angeles Times* five days after the injury. "The foot was swollen like a balloon."

Stojko lands his jumps on his right leg, and the injury made it difficult for him to compete. "They told me I wouldn't be ready [for the 1995 world championships]," Stojko told the *Los Angeles Times*. "They said it couldn't be done. They said I was making a dumb move to even try." Stojko had to skip the Canadian Figure Skating Championships because of his injury.

Stojko proved all the experts wrong. "He's just tough," Leigh told the *Los Angeles Times*. "Very tough." Stojko successfully defended his title, beating out second-place finisher Todd Eldredge of the United States and bronze medal winner Candeloro. Eldredge led after the short program but fell late in his long program trying to land a triple axel.

WORLD CHAMPIONSHIP II. When he took the ice for his long program, Stojko trailed. "It was a test, almost of survival," Leigh told the Reuters news agency. "When he went on the ice, he said to me: 'Right, I'm going to do it for us.' He was so quiet within himself, it was unbelievable." Halfway through his long program, Stojko fell during a quadruple toe loop. "Trying the quad was such a risk," Stojko's choreographer, Uschi Keszler told *Maclean's*. "If he'd landed that the wrong way he would have been out of there. But the only way Elvis knows how to compete is to go for broke."

After the fall, Stojko had to do something special to win. He decided to do a triple lutz, triple axel combination during his final minute on the ice, a point during his program when he was already exhausted. "I knew that after missing the quad, I needed something more," Stojko admitted in *Maclean's*. "So I took a breath, gathered my energy and went for it."

When the public-address announcer read the scores of the judges, Stojko knew he had won. Despite his fall, the judge from France gave him a perfect mark of 6.0. "I'm glad I went through those eight weeks [of rehabilitation] to have what I have now," a happy Stojko explained in *Maclean's*. "It is hard to put into words what this means. It is a sweet victory. I trusted myself. I knew I could do it, and I proved that to myself."

THE FUTURE. Stojko plans to continue to compete until the 1998 Winter Olympics in Nagano, Japan. He currently skates in exhibitions and ice shows. "Elvis is wearing his own shoes, doing it his way," Leigh told *Maclean's*. "He has gone way beyond the criticism of a few years ago—that he lacked the

OH, CANADA!

Over the past nine years, Canadian men have won the gold medal in the World Figure Skating Championships seven times. Brian Orser began the streak in 1987. Kurt Browning won the championship four times (1989, 1990, 1991, and 1993), and now Stojko has won back-to-back titles.

style, the artistic side. He will only be 25 at the next Olympics."

OFF THE ICE. Stojko is single and lives in the Toronto, Ontario, Canada, area. He still practices karate and rides dirt bikes. Despite his success Stojko continues to work hard. "I guess I just want to be the best," Stojko explained in *Maclean's*. "It's the same with the other things I do, like the martial arts or motorbiking. Some days I get bored with training, but that's when I'm not looking for new things to do. I have to set new goals all the time, higher and higher, better and better."

Sources

Calgary Herald, March 10, 1995.
Chicago Tribune, February 17, 1994.
Los Angeles Times, March 10, 1995.
Maclean's, February 3, 1992; April 6, 1992; March 15, 1993; February 14, 1994; February 28, 1994; April 4, 1994; March 20, 1995
New York Times, February 18, 1994; February 20, 1994.
Sporting News, February 28, 1994.
Sports Illustrated, February 28, 1994.
Vancouver Sun, December 27, 1994.
Additional information provided by Reuters news service, March 9, 1995.

WHERE TO WRITE:
C/O CANADIAN FIGURE SKATING ASSOCIATION,
1600 JANE NAISMITH DR., #804,
GLOUSTER, ONTARIO, CANADA K1B 5N4.

Picabo Street

1971—

P icabo Street is never at a loss for words. An extremely outgoing person, her personality and her silver medal in the downhill at the 1994 Winter Olympics in Lillehammer, Norway, made Street a star. During the 1994-95 season, she accomplished a feat no American woman had ever achieved—winning the World Cup international championship in the downhill. Street has overcome a bad temper and poor training habits to become one of the best skiers in American history.

"I always just try to go out there and have fun."
—Picabo Street

Growing Up

"SHINY WATERS." Picabo Street was born April 3, 1971, in Triumph, Idaho. Her father, Roland "Stubby" Street, is a stonemason, and her mother, Dee, is a music teacher. Street's parents moved from Reno, Nevada, to Idaho in 1969 to escape from big-city life. They call themselves "hippies," and have always been very free-spirited. "[We] were kind of anti-establishment," Stubby Street admitted in the *Los Angeles Times*. "We rebelled against the eight to five, working for someone else."

BABY GIRL STREET. The Street's first child was a boy, Roland (nicknamed Baba), and Street was born two years later. Street was a "blue baby" at birth and had not started breathing on her own. The nearest hospital was 12 miles away, so her father gave her mouth-to-mouth resuscitation. The maneuver worked, and soon Street began to breathe just fine.

When their daughter was born, the Streets decided they would let her pick her own name. Her birth certificate lists her name as "Baby Girl Street." However, the U.S. government required a name before giving her a passport. The Streets picked the name Picabo, taken from a local town named after a Native American word meaning "shining waters." "She loved playing peek-a-boo," Dee Street recalled in *People* magazine. "We decided it fit her personality."

Her name sometimes caused Street pain. Children at school teased her, calling her "Peekabugger" and "Sneak-a-peak." The teasing caused her to come home several times in tears. "It taught me patience," Street recounted in *People* magazine. She added in the *Los Angeles Times:* "I started coming up with stuff like, 'Well, at least my name's not Jim, like everyone else in the world.' It started to sink in that it was pretty cool my name isn't like that. I kind of enjoyed it. It made me stand away and out from the rest."

ONLY GIRL IN TOWN. Triumph, Idaho, was a very small town when Street was a child, with a population of only 13. She was the only young girl in the entire town and quickly learned to become one of the boys. "Once, I got hit in the forehead and knocked out with a baseball, and they [the boys] just said, 'Ah, c'mon,' and kicked me around and got me back up," Street recalled in the *Los Angeles Times*. "So I just had to hack it and be tough. I think that's what made me as tough as I was, growing up in that atmosphere and having the name that I did."

Street always had a lot of energy and had a hard time staying still for very long. "She's been a risk-taker from the start," Dee Street told *Newsweek*. "My quest has been to keep her alive." Her parents did let Street have the freedom to make her own mistakes and learn from them. "They'd let us splatter into a brick wall so we could see how it felt," Street recalled in *Newsweek*. "They'd smile and say, 'Do you believe me now?'" Dee Street added in *Sports Illustrated:* "Happy is all we hoped they'd be, and we pulled it off. They're happy."

MOUNTAIN LIVING. The Street family did not have many modern conveniences. Street learned to cook on a wood stove and only watched television five times during her childhood. The family took camping and fishing trips and ate healthy foods. "I spent all my time with my family," Street told the *Los Angeles Times*. "I never had a baby-sitter. My parents never left us."

The family was very close. "We started out as a close-knit community of four, and that closeness paid off," Dee Street explained in *Skiing* magazine. "We went through a lot of adversity, and we learned we were a team." Street credits her father with giving her her determination. "I don't ever start anything without finishing it and giving it my all, and he taught me that from the get-go," Street stated in *Skiing* magazine.

HITS THE SLOPES. The first time Street skied, at age five, she cried all the way up the chairlift because she was afraid of falling. To keep up with her father and brother on the slopes, Street always skied flat out. "I just started chasing my brother and my dad around the mountain," Street recalled in the *Los Angeles Times*. "I had to keep up or get left behind." Street told her father at an early age that she would win an Olympic medal some day.

Street won her first race at age six at the nearby Sun Valley ski resort. Soon she was beating older competition in her

Street glides downhill during the 1994 Olympics in Lillehammer, Norway.

local area. By the time she was 15 years old, Street had earned a spot on the U.S. junior team. In 1988 she won the U.S. junior downhill and super giant slalom championships. Her parents made economic sacrifices for Street, including moving the family to Utah so she could attend the prestigious Rowmark Ski Academy. Street stayed only one year, because she did not like the schoolwork at the academy.

GOING DOWNHILL. In 1989 Street suffered a serious injury in a ski accident that kept her off her skis for six months. She fell out of shape and thought about giving up the sport. In 1990 U.S. Alpine ski coach Paul Major kicked Street off the national team. He complained that she did not work hard enough and reported to training camp out of shape. "I had gotten to the point where I was sick of being told what to do with my life," Street admitted in *People* magazine. Street returned home to her parents, but her father put her on a strict workout schedule. She had to do 100 sit-ups and 50 push-ups in the morning and at night.

Soon Street was ready to "start doing what was necessary." As she explained in *Redbook:* "I knew my attitude had to improve if I wanted to make it on the team. I had to rededicate myself and make a lot of sacrifices. I couldn't go partying with friends. I had to go to sleep early and stay on a program. It was really hard. There were a lot of obstacles to overcome and a lot of mixed feelings. But I focused and went back with a new attitude and a new love for skiing."

GETTING NOTICED. Street began to have success when she returned to the U.S. national team, winning the North American Championship Series in 1991 and 1992 and capturing the 1991 U.S. giant slalom title. She graduated to the international World Cup circuit in 1992.

Street first gained attention on the international scene by winning a silver medal in the Alpine combined event (downhill and slalom) at the 1993 World Alpine Ski Championships in Japan. Six weeks later she finished second in a World Cup downhill in Norway. "Being up on the podium was like tasting candy to her," Major explained in *People* magazine. "She's going to do what it takes to get back up there."

OLYMPIAN. Street was confident leading up to the 1994 Winter Olympics in Lillehammer, Norway. "Whoever can learn [the course] the fastest and then put their guts to it is going to pull it off," Street told *People*. Street tried to relax before to her run, listening to music on her Walkman and waiting for her turn. She raced down the hill and took the lead, but her time did not hold up. Katja Seizinger of Germany beat her time and won the gold medal.

Street settled for second place and the silver medal. "Picabo means silver water in Indian," Stubby Street explained in the *Chicago Tribune*. "And now she has a silver medal. Pretty cool." Street congratulated Seizinger, kissing her on the cheek and saying: "Now you're the queen."

Street had the chance to win the combined competition, finishing second in the downhill portion of the event. Unfortunately, she did not do well enough in the slalom portion to win a medal. Street's name, red hair, freckles, and outgoing personality made her a media star and the fans loved her. Her medal earned her a trip to the White House to meet President Bill Clinton and First Lady Hillary Clinton. "It was so cool," Street confessed in *Women's Sports and Fitness* magazine. "I don't think I took a single breath the whole time I was there."

Superstar

WORLD CUP WONDER. Before her Olympic performance, Street had had little success on the World Cup international skiing circuit. She had finished in the top three in a race only once. "I'm absolutely nowhere on the World Cup," Street admitted in *Sports Illustrated*. "Once in a while I'll pop in and then, like you know, wig out. Just because I won an Olympic silver medal, that doesn't mean [anything]."

Before the 1994-95 season, Herwig Demschar took over as the U.S. women's skiing coach. Demschar helped the team loosen up. "He's encouraged us to have more fun," Street told *Sports Illustrated*. "He told us that when we showed up at a race, he wanted us to fall out of the van laughing and having a good time. It would give us an edge, and the Europeans would go nuts." The strategy worked, as Street told the same magazine after a race. "I was loose," she explained. "I was telling my opponents, 'I'm having fun.'"

AMAZING AMERICANS. Street and teammate Hilary Lindh dominated the World Cup downhill season. Lindh won the first race of the season, in Vail, Colorado. Street won the second race, with Lindh second. This was the first time since 1982 that American women finished first and second in a World Cup downhill race.

WORLD CHAMP. Street won five of six downhill races in Europe during the season and six out of nine races overall. (Lindh won two others.) At one point she won five races in a row. Street clinched the World Cup downhill title by capturing her fourth straight race on March 11 in Lenzerheide, Switzerland. She became the first American and the first non-European to win the World Cup downhill season title. "When they handed me the trophy, I started crying," Street admitted in *Sports Illustrated*. "Crying and laughing at the same time." Street also finished fifth in the overall World Cup standings, based on points earned in all skiing events.

"The World Cup means consistency, perseverance, greatness," Street explained in *Sports Illustrated*. "This puts you in a special, elite category. I've been looking at the trophy. Holding it. I think this summer when I'm home and having a mellow moment, I'll look at it and go, 'Wow.'"

Street knows it will be hard to repeat her success. "I'm going to try and do that again," Street told the *New York Times*. "But if it doesn't happen, I'll be all right with that because, really, it was kind of a Cinderella story season. There aren't that many people who've had that kind of season."

PERSONALITY PLUS. Street has an extremely outgoing personality and talks freely about whatever is on her mind. "One thing I can say about Picabo is that you know she's around at all times," a former coach, Ernst Hager, told the *New York Times*. "In the hotel, in the airplane, at the table. Wherever you are, you know."

Street's temper has always been a problem. She has fought with coaches and gets angry sometimes when she does not perform as well as she thinks she should. "I don't have

FEARLESS

In 1994 Ulrike Maier of Austria died during a World Cup downhill race. The event contains very few turns and requires the skier to go as fast as possible to win. Despite Maier's accident, the danger of her sport does not scare Street. "I don't really feel fear," Street explained in the *Los Angeles Times.* "That's not something that I ever encounter. And if I do, it means that something's going on, and I have to open my eyes and be more aware than normal. But usually, it's not something that enters my brain, not when I'm skiing anyway. I can't go fast enough or catch enough air, so I'm definitely not afraid. You can lose control every once in a while, for sure, but there are usually warning signs you'll feel if you're pushing it to the point where something could happen and you wouldn't have enough recovery time to get out of it without crashing."

control over it," Street admitted in the *Los Angeles Times.* "I used to let it fly a lot worse. I used to freak out whenever I didn't ski as well as I wanted to. I didn't care who was around watching. I'd just throw my stuff around, throw a little temper tantrum. I've learned you can't do that."

To become successful, Street also had to become more dedicated to her training. "It took about three years to get her into shape," Hager said in *Skiing* magazine. "But now she's here, and it's easier to keep her going. But when we first got her, every time off the ski hill, we'd have to drag her out of bed. She's not a workhorse. Picabo likes to have a snooze and, you know, it's just Picabo. She likes to have a good time."

OFF THE SLOPES. Street bought a house in Portland, Oregon. She has appeared on the television shows *Sesame Street* and *American Gladiators.* Street has an Australian cattle dog, Dougan, and a Ford pickup truck and likes in-line skating. She is a spokesperson for Nike, which plans to introduce a Street running shoe, the first time a winter-sports athlete has received this honor. Someday Street wants to build a year-round sports park next to her old elementary school.

In 1995 Street did a photo shoot for *Vogue* magazine. "It was great," Street said in the *New York Times.* "They plucked my eyebrows because they wanted to make it a real chic looking picture. They let me have some of the Polaroids. They were unbelievable. I was blown away when I saw them."

Her name helps fans recognize Street. "Yeah, I get recognized quite a bit in ski areas, especially in Europe, and little kids know who I am," Street stated in the *Los Angeles Times.* "But I've tried to maintain myself as a person and just be me, just keep skiing. I feel a responsibility to bring attention to my sport and to be a positive role model for the kids, and I see more in it than just competing and doing well, and having that experience and that's that."

Street hopes to continue skiing through the 1998 Winter Olympics in Nagano, Japan. "I just had the most stellar season, one of the best seasons in the history of U.S. skiing, and I feel like I haven't skied my best yet," Street admitted in *Skiing* magazine. "I want to win the title again. And I want to be in the top three in Super G [super giant slalom] consistently, and I want to podium [win a medal] in every downhill, unless I crash. And I want to win the overall [World Cup title]. I know it's going to take a couple, three years to pull it off, but I figure I have to set my goals high. Why should I set them any lower? I just won six out of nine. Why should I say I only want to win four next year? What's the use in that?"

Street has a good attitude about competing. She told the *Los Angeles Times,* "I always just try to go out there and have fun."

Sources

Chicago Tribune, February 21, 1994; January 26, 1995.
Los Angeles Times, February 8, 1994; February 17, 1995.
Newsweek, February 14, 1994.
New York Times, March 7, 1995.
People, February 7, 1994.
Redbook, November 1995.
Rocky Mountain News, December 2, 1994.
Seattle Times, March 16, 1995.
Skiing, September 1995.
Sports Illustrated, February 28, 1994; December 19, 1994; January 30, 1995; March 27, 1995.
Time, March 27, 1995.
Women's Sports and Fitness, July-August 1994.

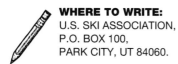

WHERE TO WRITE:
U.S. SKI ASSOCIATION,
P.O. BOX 100,
PARK CITY, UT 84060.

Sheryl Swoopes

1971—

"When I'm shooting well, it's like the basket is as big as this table. I can't seem to miss."—Sheryl Swoopes

Basketball fans have many reasons to remember the name Sheryl Swoopes. One is that her last name rhymes with hoops. However, the best reason to remember the former Texas Tech Lady Raider is that she is one of the best female basketball players in the world. Swoopes led her Texas Tech team to the National Collegiate Athletic Association (NCAA) championship in 1993 and earned recognition as the Female College Player of the Year. Swoopes has also earned the honor of representing the United States as a member of the women's national basketball team which will compete at the 1996 Summer Olympics in Atlanta, Georgia.

Growing Up

RHYMES WITH HOOPS. Sheryl Denise Swoopes was born March 25, 1971, in Brownfield, Texas. Brownfield is a small farming town in western Texas. Swoopes was the third of four children, and the only girl, born to Louise Swoopes. Swoopes learned to play basketball by playing with boys, including her three brothers. Her idol was her brother James. "He was a good athlete and he's a great person," Swoopes said. Seeing her mom raise four kids on her own taught Swoopes that "no matter how tough things get, never give up."

PLAYER OF THE YEAR. Swoopes attended Brownfield High School, where she was a three-sport star. She played volleyball and ran track in addition to playing basketball. As a junior Swoopes led her team to the state championship in 1988 and earned the Texas girls' basketball Player of the Year award. In her senior year three different high school All-American teams picked Swoopes. She averaged 26 points, 14 rebounds, and five assists as a senior. The U.S. Olympic Committee invited Swoopes to participate in the 1989 U.S. Olympic Festival Trials.

When it came time to pick a college, Swoopes decided to stay in Texas. She signed to play basketball at the University of Texas. Unfortunately, Swoopes was only there three days when she got so homesick that she left and went back home. She then enrolled at South Plains Junior College, which was closer to home. Swoopes earned national Junior College Player of the Year honors at South Plains in 1991 and was an All-American her two seasons at the school. She set 28 school records at South Plains and averaged 25.3 points per game.

LADY RAIDER. After graduating from South Plains, Swoopes decided to attend Texas Tech University in nearby Lubbock. She became an instant star at Tech, starting 31 of her first 32 games. Swoopes averaged 21.6 points and 8.9 rebounds per game her first season (1991-92). The Southwest Conference named her Player of the Year. Her play helped Texas Tech University's Lady Raiders win their first ever Southwest Con-

Swoopes goes up for a shot.

ference title. Swoopes became a big hit with Tech fans, many of whom would scream "Swoooopes!" after every spectacular play. Texas Tech won their first ever NCAA tournament game and advanced to the final 16 for the first time.

Swoopes's play at Texas Tech earned her an invitation to try out for the 1992 U.S. Olympic team. A knee injury slowed her down and kept her from making the team. "I was just a baby at it," Swoopes recalls. "I was very young and honestly, I never really played against so many great, talented players."

Superstar

PLAYER OF THE YEAR, AGAIN. Swoopes and the Lady Raiders were unstoppable during the 1992-93 season. Swoopes averaged an amazing 28.1 points per game (second in the nation) and grabbed 9.2 rebounds per contest. She finished her career at Tech as the school's second-leading scorer (1,645 points) in just two seasons. The Lady Raiders had a 58-8 record in Swoopes's two seasons, participated in two NCAA tournaments, and won two Southwest Conference titles. Texas Tech retired her number 22 jersey.

Nearly every organization named Swoopes the national Player of the Year, and she won the prestigious Naismith Award, given annually to the best college basketball player in the country. "I can't tell you what Sheryl has meant to this program," Texas Tech coach Marsha Sharp told *Sports Illustrated*. "She'll be a legend in women's basketball, but not just because of her play. She has a charisma that the crowd loves. You never doubt that she is a team player."

Swoopes was only warming up during the regular season. She torched Texas, the school she originally attended, for 53 points in the Southwest Conference championship game. Her outburst broke the Reunion Arena record for most points in a basketball game, formerly held by professional players Larry Bird and Bernard King. The Lady Raiders then tore through three opponents in the NCAA Basketball Tournament to reach their first Final Four.

NATIONAL CHAMPS. Texas Tech took the Final Four by storm. The Lady Raiders defeated Vanderbilt, 60-46, in the semifinals. Vanderbilt had been rated number one throughout most of the season. Swoopes scored 31 points and pulled down 11 rebounds.

Swoopes saved her best for last. The Lady Raiders faced Ohio State University in the national championship game at the Omni in Atlanta, Georgia. The game was close throughout, and Swoopes kept her team in it. Texas Tech won the game, 84-82, and Swoopes shattered the record for most points in an NCAA championship game. She scored 47 points, more than any player—male or female—had ever scored in a championship game. "You don't appreciate Sheryl Swoopes until you have to stop her," Ohio State coach Nancy Darsch admitted in *Sports Illustrated* after the game.

"When I'm shooting well, it's like the basket is as big as this table," Swoopes explained to *Sports Illustrated*. "I can't seem to miss." Swoopes's play earned her the tournament's Most Valuable Player award after she averaged 35.4 points and 9.6 rebounds during the NCAA play-offs. She set four Final Four records, four NCAA championship game records, and five NCAA tournament records. She was also second in two others. Swoopes gave credit to her teammates. "I'm surrounded by such great players that I just try my best to be better than they are," Swoopes explained to *Sports Illustrated*. The Associated Press named Swoopes Female Athlete of the Year, the Women's Sport Foundation named her Sportswoman of the Year, and she also won the Babe Zaharias Female Athlete of the Year Award.

DRAFTED. In April 1993 Swoopes became only the second woman drafted by the U.S. Basketball League, a professional league for men. Unfortunately, the NBA was not a possibility for Swoopes. She headed to Europe, where there are many professional women's teams. "I don't like the idea of leaving the States, but it'll give me more international experience," Swoopes explained in *Sports Illustrated*.

Swoopes signed to play with the Basket Bari professional team in Italy. Despite averaging 23 points per game in the team's first ten games, she came home again after the team failed to live up to things they had promised in her contract. During the next two years she played only 12 organized games. She helped the United States win the bronze medal in the 1994 World Basketball Championships in Australia and the gold medal in the 1994 Goodwill Games. Swoopes also won a spot on the 1995 U.S. Pan-American team, but organizers canceled the competition when too few countries signed up to play.

MAKES NATIONAL TEAM. Swoopes continued to practice, preparing herself for the 1996 Olympics. In May 1995 U.S.A. Basketball named Swoopes to the U.S. women's national team. "I'm really looking forward to getting back into the flow of playing," Swoopes said. "I would like to think I'm probably in the best [physical] shape I've ever been in."

Swoopes missed a tour of Europe with the national team in the summer of 1995 because she was busy planning her wedding to Eric Jackson. She was married in July 1995. Swoopes says the strain of being away to prepare for the 1996 Olympics would not affect her new marriage. "It's only a year; it's not a lifetime," Swoopes said. "Of course I'll miss him and he'll miss me. But you have to make sacrifices. I'm not going to let anything get in my way of playing in the Olympics, and he [her husband] understands that."

The U.S. national team was scheduled to play a tough series of exhibition games leading up the 1996 Olympics. "In a way, it's kind of like being back in college—without the class work," Swoopes explained. "Training with the same group of players and the same coach every day."

OFF THE COURT. Swoopes lives with her husband in the Lubbock, Texas, area. She works part-time for the Plains National Bank of West Texas. Swoopes once played one-on-one with Michael Jordan. She majored in exercise and fitness. A team of eight- and nine-year-old girls from Shallowater, Texas, gave Swoopes her biggest honor when they named their team the Swoopesters.

Swoopes knew it would take hard work for her to reach her goal. "There's always something every day you can get

HER AIRNESS

Swoopes is a spokesperson for Nike, which released "Air Swoopes" basketball shoes in 1995. She became the first woman to have basketball shoes named after her. "I've got several pairs, and I definitely wear them," Swoopes said.

better at, things you can work on," Swoopes said. "Of course you get tired, and it's really hard to get out there and to keep going all the time. But you have to remember, in the back of my mind, all I'm thinking of is '96, gold medal. I just make myself come out every day and push myself."

Sources

Jet, November 29, 1993; February 7, 1994.
Sporting News, December 6, 1993; May 22, 1995.
Sports Illustrated, March 15, 1993; April 12, 1993.
Sports Illustrated for Kids, June 1993; December 1995.
Time, April 19, 1993.
Additional information provided by Texas Christian University and USA Basketball.

WHERE TO WRITE:
C/O USA BASKETBALL,
5465 MARK DABLING BLVD.,
COLORADO SPRINGS, CO 80918.

Derrick Thomas

1967—

Linebacker Derrick Thomas of the Kansas City Chiefs loves to sack quarterbacks. During his seven seasons in the National Football League (NFL) he has developed into one of professional football's most feared defenders. In 1990 Thomas set an NFL record with seven sacks in one game, and his fellow players, coaches, and fans have voted him to the Pro Bowl all-star game for seven consecutive seasons. Besides being an all-star on the field, Thomas has earned many awards for his community service. He has achieved all this after overcoming the loss of his father and his own difficulty in learning to read.

"I want kids to score a touchdown in life. And learning how to read is the way to do it."
—Derrick Thomas

Growing Up

LOSES DAD. Derrick Vincent Thomas was born January 7, 1967, in Miami, Florida. His father, Robert James Thomas, an air force captain, died in Vietnam when the North Vietnamese shot down his B-52 bomber on December 17, 1972. The air force called his father's mission "Operation: Linebacker Two." Thomas was only five years old at the time. Although his father's body has never been found, the U.S. government declared Mr. Thomas legally dead in 1980.

TROUBLE READING. Thomas says the most important people in his life are his mother, Edith Morgan, and grandmother, Annie Adams. The two women raised him after his father's death, in a tough, South Miami neighborhood. Thomas had difficulty learning to read when he entered school. Because of this problem, he had a hard time in school. Soon Thomas started skipping classes and hanging out with the wrong crowd at night.

Two teachers at Palmetto Middle School tried to help Thomas. "Willie McIntosh, my seventh-grade science teacher, came to my house each morning to get me up to go to school," Thomas told *Sports Illustrated for Kids.* "And Miriam Williams, my eighth-grade English teacher, really worked hard with me."

Williams tutored Thomas in reading and talked with him. She used his dream of playing football to motivate her student. "I told him it was okay to be an athlete, but not a dumb athlete," Williams recalled in *Sports Illustrated for Kids.* In 1991 Williams won the NFL Teacher of the Year Award.

TURNS LIFE AROUND. Thomas reached a crossroads as a high school sophomore. Police arrested him for breaking into a store. The judge sentenced him to the Dade Marine Institute, a school for troubled kids. Thomas did not want to go, but now says the experience helped him. "It was the best thing that ever happened to me," Thomas confessed in *Sports Illustrated for Kids.* "The people there cared. They helped me to set goals, to strive to achieve those goals, and to see that if you believe in yourself, you can achieve anything." He completed the six-month program at the institute in only four months.

'BAMA BOUND. Football helped Thomas grow up. He idolized the immortal Lawrence Taylor of the New York Giants and played running back, tight end, and finally linebacker at South Miami High School. Thomas earned All-League honors in high school and attracted recruiters from major football universities. After graduation from high school, Thomas decided to attend the University of Alabama.

Thomas (left) sacks quarterback Dave Brown of the New York Giants.

During Thomas's junior and senior seasons with the University of Alabama's Crimson Tide, experts considered him the best pass rusher in the country. Thomas set Alabama career records with 52 quarterback sacks and 74 tackles behind the line of scrimmage. He also set the school season record with 18 sacks his junior year. In his senior year Thomas earned All-American honors and the 1988 Butkus Award, given annually to the nation's best collegiate linebacker.

CHIEFS' CHOICE. The Kansas City Chiefs won only four games in 1987 and four games in 1988. Trying to turn the team around, Kansas City hired coach Marty Schottenheimer before the 1989 season. Schottenheimer was a proven winner, guiding the Cleveland Browns to two straight American Football Conference (AFC) championship games.

Schottenheimer specialized in defense, and one of his first moves was to improve the Chiefs in this vital area. Professional scouts rated Thomas the top linebacker in the 1989 NFL Draft, and the Chiefs chose him with the fourth overall pick. Proving that Kansas City made the right choice, he started every game and recorded 10 quarterback sacks in his first ten games during his rookie season. The Chiefs improved their record to 8-7-1, and Thomas earned a spot in the Pro Bowl game. He has been so honored every season since. Thomas also won many Defensive Rookie of the Year honors.

Superstar

SACK MAN. Remarkably, Thomas topped his rookie sack total in 1990 by sacking the quarterback 20 times, earning the nickname "Sack Man" from his teammates. This was the fifth-highest single-season sack total since the NFL began keeping the statistic in 1982. Thomas also set an NFL record with seven sacks in one game, against the Seattle Seahawks. "I saw quite a bit of him that day," Seahawks quarterback Dave Krieg said in *Boys' Life*. "He was really something." Thomas played extra hard that day, because before the game a squad of fighter jets flew over Arrowhead Stadium in Kansas City in honor of Veterans Day. "I felt he [Thomas's father] was with me,"

Thomas confessed in *Boys' Life,* explaining that he played that game for his father.

The Chiefs finished with 11 wins in 1990, but lost in the first round of the play-offs to the Miami Dolphins. Thomas again recorded double-digit sack numbers in 1991 and 1992 (13.5 and 14.5), but he received a scare in 1991 when he experienced an increased heart rate. Doctors corrected the condition, and Thomas played the next week. Despite the outstanding play from their All-Pro linebacker, however, the Chiefs could not reach their potential. Each season the team won ten games but did not advance very far in the play-offs.

CHIEFS' CHANGES. Kansas City decided to make some changes before the 1993 season. The Chiefs made a big trade, acquiring the legendary quarterback Joe Montana from the San Francisco 49ers. Schottenheimer also decided to make defensive changes. To take advantage of Thomas's pass-rushing ability, Schottenheimer moved him to defensive end from his line-backer position. Thomas did not like the move. "I was frustrated every day because I was playing somewhere I didn't want to be," Thomas admitted in *Football Digest.* "I ain't no defensive end. The great defensive ends are big people. I couldn't compete with people in that category."

Thomas had a career-low eight sacks in 1993, but the Chiefs won the AFC West Division title with an 11-5 record. Kansas City had an exciting play-off run. The Chiefs won their first play-off game, 27-24, in overtime against the Pittsburgh Steelers. In the second round Kansas City came back from a 20-7 deficit at the end of the third quarter to defeat the Houston Oilers 28-20. Thomas starred in the defeat of the Oilers, recording two sacks of Houston quarterback Warren Moon and forcing two fumbles.

The Chiefs' magic ran out, however, in the AFC Championship Game against the Buffalo Bills. The Chiefs knew

SINGLE-SEASON SACKERS

Since the NFL began keeping track of quarterback sacks as an official statistic in 1982, only five players have recorded more than 20 sacks in a season. Those players and their sack totals are given below.

Player	Sacks
Mark Gastineau	22
Reggie White	21
Chris Doleman	21
Lawrence Taylor	20.5
Derrick Thomas	20

they had to stop the Bills from running, but they could not stop running back Thurman Thomas. The result was a 30-13 defeat of the Chiefs. Schottenheimer pulled Thomas from the game in the second half because Buffalo repeatedly ran successfully on his side of the field in the first half.

COMEBACK. His performance in 1993 disappointed Thomas. Things got worse when *Inside Sports* magazine rated him one of the most overrated players in the NFL. "I know that upset him," teammate and friend Neil Smith stated in *Football Digest*. "But he's come back this year [1994] as focused as I've ever seen him. And I think he's got his confidence back, too, now that he's in his old position."

Schottenheimer realized his experiment had not worked and moved Thomas back to his familiar linebacker position. For his part, Thomas dedicated himself to working just as hard on stopping the run and pass defense as on rushing the quarterback. "I think I'm growing up," Thomas admitted in *Football Digest*. "I've become more consistent, especially in rush and pass defense as well as rushing the passer. My first couple of years I had a great deal of success that came from playing with athletic ability and emotion. But at some point you have to [increase] your knowledge of the game. I really think I'm a better student of the game now. What I went through [in 1993] inspired me to try harder, made me want it that much more."

The Chiefs struggled in 1994 but slipped into the play-offs with a 9-7 record. Thomas returned to form with 11 sacks and a career-high 86 tackles. His teammates voted him Most Valuable Player. Kansas City ran into a hot Miami Dolphins team, however, in the first round of the play-offs and lost 27-17. The game was the last for Montana, who retired shortly after that. Thomas had six tackles and a sack in the loss.

BEST RECORD. All the pieces came together for the Chiefs in 1995. Lifetime backup quarterback Steve Bono took over for Montana and the offense did not miss a beat. The defense remained tough, led by defensive end Neil Smith and

THIRD AND LONG FOUNDATION

Thomas had his life turned around by a special program. To help others Thomas formed the Third and Long Foundation, a reading and tutoring program, in 1990. Thomas and other NFL stars spend their free Saturdays reading with children ages nine to 13 in inner-city Kansas City libraries. The foundation also offers after-school tutoring, summer reading programs, and other help. The name of the foundation is a football term meaning that the offense is in trouble and needs a big play. Thomas hopes the foundation is that big play for troubled kids.

Thomas got the idea for the foundation when he was a senior at Alabama. "I was about to enter the NFL, and I promised myself that if I was successful, I would give something back to the community," Thomas explained in *Sports Illustrated for Kids.* "I spoke with a lady who said, 'Derrick, if you really want to help kids, teach them to read.'" Thomas says the program really works. "We've had a lot of success," Thomas told the same magazine. "We've had kids go from making Cs and Ds in school to making the honor roll. They want to do well because they know we care."

In 1993 the NFL honored Thomas for his community service by giving him the Edge NFL Man of the Year Award. President George Bush honored Thomas when he named him a Point of Light in 1992. In June 1995 the NFL Player's Association gave Thomas the Byron White Humanitarian Award for service to team, community, and country. The goal of the foundation is simple. "I want kids to score a touchdown in life," Thomas declared in *Sports Illustrated for Kids.* "And learning how to read is the way to do it."

Thomas says he hopes his program will spread to other NFL cities. "Twenty years from now, I'd like someone to say to me, 'Do you remember when I was in your reading program? Well, now I'm a doctor or a lawyer or a state representative.' Those are the things that would mean the most to me," Thomas explained in *Football Digest.*

Thomas, who finished with eight sacks. Kansas City finished the season with the best record in the NFL at 13-3.

UPSET. Experts made the Chiefs a favorite to reach the Super Bowl. Kansas City played the Indianapolis Colts in the first round of the play-offs. The Colts had barely squeaked into the play-offs with a 9-7 record and the week before had defeated the San Diego Chargers. No one gave Indianapolis much of a chance to beat the Chiefs, especially since All-Pro running back **Marshall Faulk** (see entry) missed the game with an injury. The Colts proved the experts wrong, winning 10-7 in subzero temperatures. Kicker Lin Elliot missed three field goals for the Chiefs, including a 43-yarder with seconds left that would have tied the game.

THE FUTURE. Thomas says he wants to someday break the all-time sack record, currently 157, held by Reggie White of the Green Bay Packers. "[It's] a number I don't even know yet because Reggie White keeps jacking it up," Thomas explained in *Football Digest*. "I've got to get him out of the game." At the end of the 1995 season Thomas had 85 sacks in only seven seasons and had forced more than 30 fumbles in his career. "Derrick is without a doubt the fastest linebacker that I've ever seen play this game," Schottenheimer told *Boys' Life*.

OFF THE FIELD. Thomas is single and lives in Independence, Missouri. He honored his father in 1993 when he gave a speech at the Vietnam Veterans Memorial in Washington, D.C. President Bill Clinton was in the audience. Thomas is a spokesperson for a local Ford truck dealership and hosts a weekly radio show. He is friends with Deion Sanders, country singer Hank Williams Jr., and former MTV host "Downtown" Julie Brown. Thomas likes seafood and has his own clothing line. He currently is taking courses at the University of Missouri-Kansas City to finish his college degree.

Some people say that Thomas spends too much time doing community activities and that it leaves him too tired to play football. "There was a time a couple of years ago when I was trying to do so many things that I began to slack off," Thomas confessed in *Football Digest*. "Third and Long, for some reason, didn't seem so important. I found myself wanting to go play golf on Saturday afternoons rather than going to the library. But then I started asking myself, 'What are you really here for? What's your real purpose?' I had a long talk with myself and decided that my real purpose was to make a difference. I could still play golf and enjoy life, but my real source of enjoyment would come from seeing others succeed. I made a promise to myself in college that if I was ever successful, I would give something back and make a difference. And that didn't mean giving back for just one year. That meant giving back for as long as I was in a position to make a difference."

Thomas has set high goals for himself. "My challenge now is to find out how good Derrick Thomas can be, and I don't know the answer to that yet," Thomas told *Football Digest.* "I've yet to run into an obstacle in my playing career that I couldn't overcome. And yet the things that have come before me in sports are minute [small] compared to the things I've faced in life. Sure, I'd like to be remembered for what I did on the field and maybe one day have the opportunity to make it into Canton [the Professional Football Hall of Fame]. But I'd also like to be remembered for the things I did off the field when I was in a position to make a difference."

Sources

Boys' Life, October 1992.
Football Digest, February 1995.
Jet, February 21, 1994.
Sporting News, January 17, 1994; January 24, 1994; January 31, 1994; January 9, 1995; January 15, 1996.
Sports Illustrated for Kids, February 1993.
Additional information provided by Kansas City Chiefs.

WHERE TO WRITE:
C/O KANSAS CITY CHIEFS,
ONE ARROWHEAD DR.,
KANSAS CITY, MO 64129.

Gwen Torrence

1965—

Gwen Torrence is the fastest woman in the world. She won that title at the 1995 World Track and Field Championships by crossing the finish line first in the women's 100-meter dash. A native of Atlanta, Georgia, Torrence is a favorite to return to her hometown in 1996 and earn an even bigger prize—an Olympic gold medal. Ranked the number-one U.S. female sprinter in both the 100- and 200-meter dashes, Torrence says she only hopes she will not be too shy to stand on the podium and collect her prize.

Growing Up

GOING PLACES. Gwendolyn Lenna (Li-NAY) Torrence was born June 12, 1965, in Atlanta, Georgia. She grew up in a housing project. "Before Gwen came along, I had two boys and two girls, and I thought, that's it," her mother, Dorothy, recalled in *Sports Illustrated*. Torrence is seven years younger than her next-youngest sibling (brother or sister). She was born with her umbilical cord wrapped around her neck, a serious problem that forced her to spend her first five days of life in an incubator.

Dorothy Torrence knew right away that her daughter was special. "The first time I laid eyes on Gwen, she had this look in her eyes," Dorothy Torrence recounted in *Sports Illustrated*. "I didn't tell anybody, but I said to myself, This baby's going places. She didn't want to lie down like a baby. So I carried her on my shoulder." Torrence walked at seven months and talked when she was only one year old.

TRAGEDY STRIKES. When Torrence was seven, her brother Charles was paralyzed while playing football in the street. She claims that he is her inspiration, and he is Torrence's biggest fan. Only a year later Torrence's father died of a stroke. After her husband's death, Dorothy Torrence worked as a housekeeper and nanny to support the family.

BROTHER KEEPS HER. While her mother worked, Torrence's brother Willie watched her. "If there was something Gwen didn't want to do in school, she would run home, and Willie would take her back," Dorothy Torrence recounted in *Sports Illustrated*. "When she'd get into fights with other girls, Willie would come rescue her." While Torrence was still young, the family moved out of the housing project to Decatur, a suburb of Atlanta.

TOO FAST. Torrence attended Columbia High School. She first caught the attention of track coach Ray Bonner while running away from a boy chasing after her. "The first time I saw Gwen run, a football player by the name of Fred Lane lit out after her on the track," Bonner recalled in *Sports Illustrated*. "Fred couldn't catch her. And he was fast."

Torrence has always been very shy. Her shyness affected her track career in high school. Bonner begged her to try out

Before breaking the tape, Torrence celebrates her win at the Indoor Track and Field Championships held in Atlanta, Georgia.

for the track team. "I told her that God gave her a gift, and if she didn't use it, he was going to be very upset," Bonner told *Sports Illustrated.* Torrence agreed to try out, but refused to wear shorts or running shoes because she was too embarrassed to show her legs. She then unofficially broke the state high school record in the 220-yard dash running in her dress shoes. "I felt [running shoes] were too hot for my skinny little legs," Torrence explained in the same magazine.

Torrence finally agreed to join the team, but only if she could practice after every one else went home. Coach Bonner picked her up and brought her to the track after her teammates had left. "From then on, it was the Gwen Torrence Show," Bonner recalled in *Sports Illustrated.*

ALL-AMERICAN. Torrence got over her shyness and excelled at Columbia High. Three times she won a Georgia state high school championship race, and she earned All-American honors her last two years in high school. At the Junior Olympics, held just after her senior year, Torrence won both the 100- and 200-meter dashes.

Many colleges throughout the country offered Torrence athletic scholarships. At first she turned them all down, claiming she wanted to work as a hairdresser. Coach Bonner convinced Torrence to change her mind and accept a scholarship at the University of Georgia. She had a hard time getting used to college schoolwork and started out in a special remedial learning program. "I had never written a paper," Torrence admitted in *Sports Illustrated.* "I thought I'd never get out of there." In 1986 Torrence made the dean's list for outstanding grades.

NCAA CHAMP. For four straight seasons at Georgia, Torrence qualified for the National Collegiate Athletic Association (NCAA) 100- and 200-meter and 55-meter indoor championships. From 1984 to 1987 she qualified for the NCAA 100-meter finals, finishing second twice (1985 and 1986) and winning the national title in 1987. She also won the 200-meters in 1987, accomplishing a double national championship.

The U.S. Olympic Committee had invited Torrence to compete in the 1984 U.S. Olympic Trials, but her shyness had forced her to decline. "She felt like she didn't belong there," Georgia women's track coach Lewis Gainey explained to

LIPS ARE LIPS

Torrence says that growing up in the South made her prejudiced against white people. An incident during her freshman year at Georgia, as she recalled in *Sports Illustrated,* changed her mind. "A white woman from Canada was drinking something and asked if I wanted some," Torrence recounted. "I said, 'Why? Are you really going to give it to me?' She gave me her drink. Then she drank after me without wiping it off, and I drank after her without wiping it off. I asked her about it, and she said, 'What's the difference? Lips are lips.' That opened my eyes."

Sports Illustrated. She did run at the U.S. Track and Field Championships in 1985 and 1986, although her best performance was fifth place in the 200-meters in 1985. Torrence achieved a great victory in 1986 when she defeated the great Evelyn Ashford in the 55-meter dash at the Milrose Games. "Before that I was running good times, but nobody noticed because I hadn't beat Evelyn," Torrence stated in *Sports Illustrated.*

MOVING UP. Torrence's breakthrough came in 1987. She won 16 straight races at 55 and 60 meters and won the NCAA titles at 100 and 200 meters. She qualified to represent the United States in the Pan-American Games in Indianapolis, Indiana, and won the gold medal in the 200-meters. At the World University Games, Torrence won the 100 and 200 and won another gold medal as part of the U.S. 400-meter relay team. She raced at the World Track and Field Championships for the first time in 1987, placing fifth in the 200-meters in Rome, Italy.

OLYMPICS I. In 1988 Torrence proved she was ready to take on the best in the world. In the spring she won 38 straight races during the indoor track season and tied the American record in the 60-meter dash (7.18 seconds). Torrence qualified for the U.S. Olympic track team set to compete at the 1988 Summer Olympics in Seoul, South Korea. She competed in both the 100- and 200-meters at the Olympics and missed medals by .12 of a second in the 100 and .22 second in the 200. Although Torrence did not win a medal, the Olympic experience was valuable.

BABY BREAK. Torrence took a brief time off from track in 1989 to have a child, her son, Manley Jr., with her husband and coach, Manley Waller. The pregnancy weakened her and Torrence had to work hard to get back into shape. "My determination was stronger," Torrence told *Women's Sports and Fitness* magazine. "You miss the sport, and you want to get back quickly, so you train hard." Torrence did not win a single race in 1990 and ran slow times. "I didn't let it get to me," Torrence revealed in the same magazine. "The potential and the desire were still there."

SO CLOSE. Torrence returned to form in 1991 and won her first national title at the U.S. Track and Field Championships. She won the 200-meter dash and added a second-place finish in the 100-meter dash. Again Torrence traveled to the World Track and Field Championships, and this time she earned medals, winning silvers in both the 100 and 200. Katrin Krabbe of East Germany won both gold medals. Krabbe tested positive for drugs the next year, and Torrence felt that maybe she had cheated to win the world championship races.

OLYMPICS II. The memory of losing to a possible cheater stuck with Torrence. She qualified for the 1992 U.S. Olympic team in both the 100- and 200-meter dashes. In the finals of the 100-meters, Torrence ran a personal best time of 10.86 but finished fourth. Frustrated, she accused some of the runners who finished ahead of her of using drugs. Torrence apologized the next day, but the damage was done. She had no proof of her charges, and the other runners, including gold medalist **Gail Devers** (see entry) of the United States, were hurt by what she said. Her comments made Torrence look like a sore loser.

The media pressure on Torrence distracted her, but she put her mistake behind her in the 200-meter final. She raced to a convincing win and a gold medal in the event, posting a time of 21:81. "It was a tribute to her focus that with reporters from all over the world besieging her, she won the 200 in her best time," her agent, Brad Hunt, told *Sports Illustrated.*

KEEPS RUNNING. Torrence further established herself as one of the world's best sprinters at the 1993 World Track and Field Championships in Stuttgart, Germany. She won a bronze medal in the 100-meter dash and a silver in the 200, losing to Merlene Ottey of Jamaica by .02 second. Torrence

FAST WOMEN

Since 1960 American women have dominated the competition to be the fastest woman at the Olympics. Wilma Rudolph won the women's 100-meter dash in 1960, and Wyomia Tyus kept the title for the United States in 1964 and 1968. The United States lost the title in 1972 and 1976, but American Evelyn Ashford brought back the gold in 1984. (The United States did not compete in the 1980 Summer Olympics.) Florence Griffith-Joyner (Flo-Jo) won the 100 in 1988, and Gail Devers took the title in 1992. Torrence says she hopes to keep the three-Olympic U.S. winning streak alive in 1996.

won an additional gold medal with the U.S. 1,600-meter relay team and a silver in the 400-meter relay.

Torrence had one of the best performances of her career at the USA/Mobil Indoor Track and Field Championships, held in Atlanta in 1994. In front of a hometown crowd, many of whom had not seen her compete since high school, Torrence won the 60-meter dash and twice broke her own American record in the 200-meter dash. She was named Female Athlete of the Meet.

Superstar

WORLD'S FASTEST. Torrence injured her right knee and hamstring before the 1995 U.S. Track and Field Championships. After one heat she broke down and cried from the pain. Her husband wanted her to quit, but Torrence refused. Despite the pain, she went on to win U.S. titles in both the 100- and 200-meter dashes.

At the 1995 World Track and Field Championships in Gothenburg, Sweden, Torrence crushed the field in the 100-meter dash, winning by almost a tenth of a second over Ottey. The win made Torrence the fastest woman in the world. "Gwen deserves it," fellow U.S. sprinter Carlette Guidry, who finished fourth in the 100-meters, told the *New York Times*. "She had a job to do and she did it." Torrence said in the same newspaper: "The 100 is every sprinter's favorite race. We all want to be the world's fastest woman."

Controversy followed Torrence again at the world championships. Before running in the 200-meter finals, she discovered that someone had stolen her running shoes. Wearing an old pair of shoes, she seemed to have her second gold medal wrapped up in the 200-meters, beating Ottey by 0.3 second. Her time was the fastest in the world in 1995, despite a stiff wind blowing in her face. Unfortunately, judges disqualified Torrence after they discovered that she stepped on the line dividing the lanes on the track. She did not realize she had made a mistake until she saw the result posted on the scoreboard while doing an interview. The news made her break out in tears. "I am not going to let this ruin my 100 gold," Torrence said after the judges' decision. "I had clearly beaten the others. I know that in my heart."

"If I stepped on the line, I didn't realize it," a disappointed Torrence explained to the *New York Times*. Experts agreed that the minor infraction did not give Torrence an advantage and that she would have won the race anyway. "Obviously, we're disappointed Gwen was not given a gold medal," U.S. women's track coach Teri Jordan told the same newspaper. "It's obvious she won the race by a decisive margin." The gold medal went to Ottey after the judges rejected Torrence's protest. "I don't believe anyone can really enjoy the medals, knowing they were not winning for real," Torrence said after the meet. Torrence finished 1995 as a finalist for the prestigious Jesse Owens Award, given annually to the best track-and-field athlete in the United States.

RUNNING HOME. Torrence says she looks forward to the 1996 Summer Olympics in Atlanta, her hometown. She is a favorite in both the 100- and 200-meter sprints. "My training is going very good, and things are looking very good if I can stay healthy," Torrence said recently. "I hope to get a medal, preferably the gold." Torrence has thought about running the 400-meters at the Olympics. "I'm just testing the waters to see what I might run in '96," Torrence explained in *Sports Illustrated*.

Many competitors still do not like Torrence because of her statements at the 1992 Olympics. "Gwen's a very honest person," her agent, Brad Hunt, told *Sports Illustrated*. "It's unfortunate that her comments sometimes draw more attention than her athletic ability." She tries not to let what other people think bother her. "If a person doesn't like me for no reason, that's a problem they have," she told the *New York Times*.

OFF THE TRACK. Torrence lives in Decatur with her husband and son. Sportscasters call her "the Pink Panther" because of the pink bodysuit she wears. Torrence hates pain and refused to have her ears pierced because she worried it would hurt too much. She graduated from the University of Georgia with a degree in early childhood education.

Torrence tries to go into each race with a good attitude. "God gave us a little more speed, but on the day of the finals, one of us will have to be faster than the rest," Torrence explained in *Sports Illustrated.* "I'm not into psyching. I just run."

Sources

New York Times, August 8, 1995; August 11, 1995; March 3, 1996.
Sports Illustrated, February 15, 1988; May 23, 1988; June 29, 1992; March 14, 1994.
Women's Sports and Fitness, July/August 1992.
Additional information provided by USA Track and Field.

WHERE TO WRITE:
C/O USA TRACK AND FIELD,
P.O. BOX 120,
INDIANAPOLIS, IN 46206.

Al Unser Jr.

1962—

Al Unser Jr. has a tremendous record of success as a race car driver. In both 1992 and 1994, he won the Indianapolis 500, the most famous automobile race in the world. Twice, in 1990 and 1994, Unser finished as the Championship Auto Racing Teams (CART) season points champion. With all of his championships, it might seem surprising that he is not the most successful race car driver in his family. The latest in a long line of champions, Unser is racing at a pace that might move him past his father and uncle and establish him as the greatest Indy-car driver of all time.

Growing Up

BORN TO RACE. Alfred Unser Jr. was born April 19, 1962, in Albuquerque, New Mexico. He was born into a racing family. Unser's grandfather, Jerry, moved to Albuquerque in 1936 and opened a garage on a stretch of the famous Route 66 now named Unser Boulevard. His father, Al Sr., won the Indi-

"Everything you do in life, you got to put your best effort towards."
—Al Unser Jr.

anapolis 500 four times (1970, 1971, 1978, and 1987), tied with A. J. Foyt for the most ever, and won the Indy-car driving championship three times. Unser's uncle, Bobby, won three times at Indianapolis and won the driving title twice. Al Sr.'s oldest brother, Jerry Jr., was the first member of the family to race at Indianapolis. He finished thirty-first in 1958 but died there in a crash the next year. His other brother, Louie, also raced until he developed multiple sclerosis. Now in a wheelchair, he builds racing engines.

Al Sr. and his wife, Wanda, divorced when their son was nine. Unser lived most of the year with his mother in Georgia, but when school got out for summer vacation he visited his father in Albuquerque. "I was just a regular person," Unser recalled in the *New York Times*. "I went to a public school. I was a regular student in school. I didn't have any pressure of my name being famous. I put my pants on one leg at a time like everybody."

FAMILY BUSINESS. Despite feeling like he had a normal upbringing, Unser always planned to be a race car driver. He began racing when he was nine in a go-cart. The cart had a souped-up chainsaw engine and could go faster than 100 miles per hour. Unser drove the go-cart while his father raced on the Indy-car circuit. "During the week dad would help me work on the [c]art," Unser recalled in the *New York Times*. "Then he'd go to his race and I'd go to mine. I almost never saw my dad drive because I was busy with my own racing."

Although he rarely saw his father, Unser tried to pattern his driving style after his dad's. "I've always taken after him [his father], and I hope I do have the style of my father," Unser stated in the *New York Times*. "I see my father's style so smooth and consistent but yet so aggressive and so safe. You just don't have that in a lot of other guys." Al Sr., however, has not given all his secrets to his son. "He's taught me everything I know, but he hasn't taught me everything he knows," Unser said.

HITS THE ROAD. When Unser was 16, he started to race dirt-track sprint cars against men much older than himself. He used this as a training ground, learning how to control the 600 horsepower cars on slippery dirt tracks. "The sprint cars taught me how to race aggressively, inches away from other guys," he recounted in the *New York Times*.

Unser was small, five feet six inches and only 85 pounds, and had to sit on two telephone books to see over the steering wheel. Soon he was racing at the Speedway Park track in Albuquerque, and he won for the first time in only his fifth race. By the time he was 18, Unser was already too good for the local competition. "I was too fast too soon," Unser said in *Sports Illustrated*. "Right away, I could drive a car at its limit and be totally under control. There was no learning curve at all. The bad thing about that is you do stupid things."

Unser learned about racing from Walter Judge, a mechanic with 35 years of racing experience. "Dad taught me a lot of lessons about racing, but Walter taught me about life,"

Leading the pack, Unser takes the turn on the way to victory at the Toyota Grand Prix.

Unser explained in *Sports Illustrated*. Judge and Unser traveled for two years on the dirt-track circuit in the southwestern United States. In 1980 the young driver won the Rookie of the Year title in the World of Outlaws Series. "Running the Outlaw circuit was like playing in a band," Unser recounted in *Sports Illustrated*. "We'd have our days off and perform at night, then move on to the next town. There were picnics, barn dances, state fairs. We didn't have any money, but those were happy days."

MOVING UP. In 1980 his father and uncle talked race team owner Rick Galles into giving Unser a ride in his Super Vee cars. (Super Vee cars are smaller versions of Indy cars and act as a training ground for the Indy-car circuit.) He won the second race he entered, and Galles signed him on for a full season. In 1981 Unser won the Bosch Super Vee Championship at age 19. He won three races, finished in the top three in eight of nine races, and earned Rookie of the Year honors.

In 1982 Galles moved Unser up to the Sports Car Club of America's Can-Am series for 550-horsepower-engine open-cockpit cars. He ran away with the championship. In the fall of 1982, Unser got his first taste of Indy-car racing. Galles rented an Indy car, and Unser raced in the California 500. Against the best competition in the sport, he placed fifth after running as high as third in the race. Unser beat many of his idols, including his father. "Next to my dad and Uncle Bobby, the drivers I always admired most were A. J. Foyt and Gordon Johncock," Unser explained. "But in that first race, I lapped A. J., I lapped Gordon, and I passed my dad. It was like I lost something. It was the day I knew I was one of them. I couldn't look at them the same way ever again." That race earned Unser the chance to race a full Indy-car season in 1983.

FIRST 500. Unser struggled in his first Indy car season, with mechanical problems keeping him out of the winner's circle. (He finished second twice.) He did finish seventh in the Indy-car season points championship, a title his father won. Unser and his father made history at the 1983 Indianapolis 500, becoming the first father-and-son combination to compete in the same race. "Ain't no way would I have tackled this place at 21," Al Sr. admitted in the *New York Times*. "It would have chewed me up and spit me out. I came here when I was 25, and I thought I was too young then." Unser was part of a controversy during the race when he tried to block Tom Sneva, the eventual champion, from passing his father, in first place at the time.

CHANGES TEAMS. The Galles team continued to struggle in 1984, finishing only eight races. Unser did win his first Indy-car race, however, at Portland International Raceway, and he wound up sixth in the overall point standings. To try to improve his chances, he quit the Galles team at the end of the 1984 season. "I think that it was just time for a change," he explained in the *New York Times*. He joined the Domino's Pizza team for the 1985 season.

LOSES TO DAD. Unser had his first real success in 1985, winning two straight races, the U.S. Grand Prix and the Cleveland Grand Prix. "I'm loving it," Unser told the *New York Times*. "These past few weeks have been like a fairy tale. It's good to feel all the hard work starting to pay off." His father, who was battling his son for the season points championship, was proud. "It makes me feel very good," Al Sr. confided in the same newspaper. "Now, regardless of whether he ever wins another race, he's a winner." Al Sr. edged his son by one point for the Indy-car championship after the final race of the season at Tamiami Park in Miami, Florida. The final result was the smallest margin ever to decide the championship.

SOLID STAR. Over the next four seasons, Unser established himself as a star on the CART circuit. In 1986 he finished fourth in the CART season points championship and had a series-leading 13 top-ten finishes. Unser also won the 24 Hours of Daytona and the International Race of Champions (IROC) overall title. (The IROC series features the best drivers from all forms of auto racing competing in identical cars.) He was the youngest IROC champion ever.

In 1988 Unser rejoined his first sponsor, Rick Galles, and became a member of the Galles Racing Team. He won four races that year and finished second in the CART season points championship behind Danny Sullivan. At Indianapolis, Unser was running second when a cracked suspension joint knocked him out of the race. He also captured his second IROC championship.

SO CLOSE. In 1989 Unser came as close as he had come to winning the Indianapolis 500. Emerson Fittipaldi, the former two-time Formula One champion, led for most of the race. With two laps left, however, Unser overtook him. As Fittipaldi tried to pass, his right front tire touched Unser's left rear wheel. The contact knocked Unser's car out of control and into the wall. Fittipaldi went on to easily win the race.

Instead of being angry about the accident, Unser applauded Fittipaldi after he got out of his wrecked car. He admired Fittipaldi for not backing off with a race on the line. "In racing there's a time you don't think about life, you don't think about money, you don't think about anything but winning," Unser explained to *Sports Illustrated*. "And winning means everything to me in life. This is the biggest race in the world, and this was its last couple of laps. I wasn't going to lift [back off]. Neither was he. There was only one car going to come out of it [the turn] and it was Emmo's [Fittipaldi's]. Fittipaldi's team deserved it. They led the whole way, and they did great. I congratulate Emmo and his whole crew."

Superstar

CART CHAMP. Unser won his first ever 500-mile race in 1990 at the Michigan 500 after his father hit the wall during practice and broke his leg, four ribs, and his collarbone. Fittipaldi led the race for 134 of the first 155 laps, but then his engine died. With Fittipaldi out of the race, Unser battled his teammate, Bobby Rahal, over the final 50 laps. Unser's winning average speed, 189.727, was the fastest ever for a 500-mile race. "I'm proud that it's an Unser who now holds it [the speed record]," Unser stated in *Sports Illustrated*.

Unser won six races in 1990, including four in a row, a record for the CART circuit. He edged another member of a famous racing family, Michael Andretti, for his first CART season point championship. CART named Unser Driver of the Year.

FOLLOWING IN FOOTSTEPS. Despite his success, Unser had not been able to add to the family's Indianapolis 500 trophy case. "This here's my favorite, you know, my favorite course," Unser revealed in *Road and Track.* "It's the smoothest course in the world and probably the simplest. And it can kill you that quick. But I have to tell you if I could just drive here and no place else, I would. The only reason I drive Indy cars is to drive here." He added in *Sports Illustrated:* "This race means the world to me. It's life to me."

Experts did not consider Unser a favorite in the 1992 Indianapolis 500. His car, powered by a Chevrolet engine, had been slow in practice. On race day, however, the weather was unusually cold, with a wind chill of only 39 degrees. The cold weather made it hard for the cars to get any traction. During the race 13 drivers were involved in crashes, and 60 of the first 109 laps were run under yellow caution flags. The slow pace of the race helped Unser, who would have been left behind in a fast race.

CLOSEST EVER. Only 12 cars finished the race. Unser and Scott Goodyear, who started the race in the thirty-third and last spot in the race, survived the crashes and were still running in the last few laps. With 13 laps to go, Unser passed Goodyear to move into second place. One lap later the car of the leader, Michael Andretti, who led for 163 of the first 189 laps, stopped on the edge of the track, the victim of a bad fuel pump. Andretti's misfortune put Unser in first place.

HARD ROAD

Despite being from a famous racing family, Unser's road to the top was not easy. His father made sure of that. "The drive and the will were always there, but they—Dad, Uncle Bobby, Walter—really worked on me to keep my head from getting too big," Unser explained in *Sports Illustrated.* Unser had to prove he had the desire to work hard and become the best driver he could.

Even with all his success, Unser has not achieved as much as either his father or uncle. "I've heard Al say that after he won the [1990 Indy car series points] championship, his dad and uncle told him, 'You ain't nothin' until you've won Indy,'" teammate Paul Tracy recalled in *Sports Illustrated.* "And then he won Indy two years ago, and they said, 'You still ain't much—we've won it seven times.' That's a lot to live up to." Unser, however, is proud of who he is. "I've always been proud of my father to the point that I'm really happy to be known as 'son of,'" Unser told the same magazine.

Heading into the last lap Unser led, but Goodyear was closing in fast. Around the track they raced, often side by side, at 223 miles per hour. "I thought, 'This is the infamous last lap that I've been trying to lead for so many years,'" Unser revealed in *Sports Illustrated*. "Coming off Turn 2, I started to get a little bit emotional, but I looked in my mirrors, and Scott was there. He gave me one heckuva scare that he was going to take it away then."

In the end, Unser won the race by .43 second, the closest victory in the history of the Indianapolis 500. "The closest call I had was at the checkered flag," Unser told the *Sporting News*. "I was very, very fortunate." Unser's average speed, 134.479 miles per hour, was the slowest in the race since the 1958 Indianapolis 500.

Al Sr., who finished third in the race, was proud of his son. "To love something as much as I love racing and to win at this place and then to have your son come along and win here is the greatest feeling there is," he confided in *Sports Illustrated*.

SECOND CHAMPIONSHIP. After the 1993 season, Unser signed on with the powerful team of Roger Penske. There he joined his old nemesis, Fittipaldi, and Paul Tracy as drivers. Penske, nicknamed "the Captain," is the winningest Indy car owner in history. Before the 1994 campaign got under way, he worked with Mercedes-Benz to develop a new, more powerful engine. While other racing teams claimed that the engine was illegal, racing officials ruled that it was within the rules.

The new engine allowed the Penske team to completely dominate the CART circuit in 1994. Penske cars won 12 times in 16 races, and the three team drivers finished one, two, and three in the points standings. Unser led the way, winning eight races during the year and the CART points championship. In fact, he so dominated during the season that he had wrapped up the championship with two races remaining. (Fittipaldi finished second and Tracy third.) ABC's *Wide World of Sports* named him Athlete of the Year.

SECOND 500. Two weeks before the 1994 Indianapolis 500, Al Sr. announced his retirement. For the first time in his career, Al Jr. would be the only Unser racing Indy cars. Having this extra motivation, Unser won his first pole at the big race, edging out Fittipaldi. Before the race began, Al Sr. took one last lap around the track in the car he had driven to his last Indy 500 victory in 1987.

The race quickly developed into a duel between Unser and Fittipaldi. With 12 laps remaining, Fittipaldi held a lead of almost one full lap. Unser realized time was running out and thought he would have to settle for second. "I had everything under control," Fittipaldi explained in *Sports Illustrated*. "The car was flying." Trying to finish Unser off, Fittipaldi moved to pass him in order to have a complete one-lap lead. In doing so, he lost control of his car, hit the wall, and knocked himself out of the race. With Fittipaldi out of the race, Unser cruised to the victory. Many experts commented that the win was revenge for the accident in 1989.

SHOCKER. The Penske team, so dominant in 1994, had problems at Indianapolis in 1995. They could not get their new cars to handle correctly, and when they tried to rent cars from other teams they could not get them up to speed either. In a major upset, after the first weekend of qualifying the Penske team did not have a car in the race.

In the final hour of qualifying, Fittipaldi temporarily made the field, only to have Stefan Johanson knock him out of the race. Unser failed to qualify, with his final attempt clocked at only 224.101 miles per hour. "I've got two of the greatest drivers in the world, and they gave it everything they had," Penske told *Sports Illustrated*. "I've got to take the responsibility for not getting a package here that would get us in the race." Unser became the first defending champion to not even qualify the next year. The race also marked the first time since 1962 that an Unser had not started the Indianapolis 500.

Despite his poor performance at Indianapolis, Unser did not give up on defending his CART season points championship. He won four races in 1995 (Long Beach, Portland, Mid-Ohio, and Vancouver), but not getting any points at Indianapolis hurt his chances. Unser finished second in the cham-

PASSING IT ON

Unser's son, called Mini Al, wants to follow in his father's footsteps and be a race driver. He races go-carts now, but when he was younger he was afraid of loud engines. Mini Al liked riding horses more than cars, but that changed when his father brought him into the winner's circle at the Indianapolis 500 in 1992. "One of my favorite things to do with my dad and grandpa is to go ride motorbikes or snowmobiles at our family's cabin in northern New Mexico," Mini Al told *Sports Illustrated for Kids.* "We got to go pretty fast."

Even though Mini Al is the heir to the Unser family business, his father says he does not pressure his son to race. "I've told him that it doesn't matter whether he plays soccer, races cars, or rides horses, as long as he tries his best," Unser confided to *Sports Illustrated for Kids.* "He doesn't have to go out and win all the time, just keep trying."

pionship race behind Jacques Villeneuve, the Indianapolis 500 champion, who won his first CART season points championship. At the end of the 1995 season Unser had won 31 of 204 Indy car events in which he raced, making him the winningest active driver on the CART circuit.

OFF THE TRACK. Unser lives with his wife, Shelley, and their three children, son Al and daughters Cody and Shannon, in Albuquerque. He likes to hunt and ride snowmobiles. The Unser family travels around the Indy-car circuit in a recreational vehicle. "I was a kid when my dad was traveling all the time, and I don't want my kids feeling what I did," Unser explained in *Sports Illustrated.* "Shelley's taught me a lot, especially about being open with my kids. I went through a steep learning curve in '87 after Cody was born. I didn't win any Indy Car races that year, and I thought it was because my family was distracting me. But it was the opposite: I had to learn to quit thinking racing all the time. You need to make yourself happy at home before you can be happy at work."

Unser told *Sports Illustrated* that the most important advice he ever got came from his father: "Everything you do in life, you got to put your best effort towards."

Sources

Car and Driver, January 1991.
New York Times, May 18, 1983; July 21, 1985.
Road and Track, September 1992; August 1994; October 1994.
Sport, October 1994.
Sporting News, June 1, 1992; June 5, 1995.
Sports Illustrated, May 29, 1989; June 5, 1989; April 30, 1990; August 13, 1990; June 1, 1992; June 6, 1994; May 29, 1995.
Sports Illustrated for Kids, May 1993.
Additional information provided by Championship Auto Racing Teams (CART).

WHERE TO WRITE:
C/O CHAMPIONSHIP AUTO RACING TEAMS (CART),
755 W. BIG BEAVER RD., SUITE 800,
TROY, MI 48084.

Mo Vaughn

1967—

Mo Vaughn, the big first baseman of the Boston Red Sox, scares many pitchers in the American League (AL). He stands six feet one inch tall and weighs 240 pounds. Vaughn wears gold chains and a scowl on his face that scares even the fiercest competitor. What really worries opposing pitchers, however, is Vaughn's powerful swing, a swing that sent 39 baseballs into orbit in 1995. Despite looking mean on the field Vaughn is one of baseball's nicest players. The 1995 AL Most Valuable Player (MVP) on the field, and a community leader in his private life, Vaughn has established himself as one of baseball's best players.

Growing Up

LEARNS FROM MOM. Maurice Samuel Vaughn was born December 15, 1967. He grew up in Norwalk, Connecticut. Vaughn's parents stressed education. His father, Leroy, is a high school principal, and his mother, Shirley, is an elementary school teacher.

Vaughn inherited his size from his father, who played for the Baltimore Colts in the National Football League. He first played baseball when he was three years old. Vaughn's mother taught him the game. "She stood me up there in the backyard and told me to hit that ball," Vaughn remembered in *Sports Illustrated*.

HIGH SCHOOL STAR. Vaughn was a four-year starter in baseball, basketball, and football at Trinity-Pawling High School in Pawling, New York. He led the basketball team to a league title as a senior and earned MVP honors. In football Vaughn was the team captain and MVP as a junior and senior. Vaughn also starred in baseball, winning team MVP honors as a sophomore, junior, and senior.

PIRATE POUNDER. Vaughn decided to attend Seton Hall University. In three college seasons he batted .417 for the Pirates and set school records for home runs (57) and runs batted in (RBI) (218). Vaughn also holds the school single-season records in home runs (28) and RBI (90) and hit an amazing .463 in his sophomore year (1988). In 1989 Vaughn played on the U.S. national team in a tournament in Taiwan. He led the team in hits (12) and RBI (10). The U.S. team won the silver medal, and Vaughn earned All-Tournament honors.

PLAYER OF THE DECADE. Vaughn earned All-American honors each season for the Pirates, and the Big East Conference named him their Player of the Decade for the 1980s. "This is a tremendous honor for Mo," Seton Hall athletic director Larry Keating said. "He was one of the most feared hitters we have had at Seton Hall and certainly he has caused a lot of trouble for our opponents."

His friends in the Omega Psi Phi fraternity gave him the nickname "Hit Dog." "I liked what my fraternity stood for: manhood, scholarship, perseverance, uplift," Vaughn related

Vaughn takes a swing.

in *Sports Illustrated*. He liked his fraternity so much that he tattooed the Omega Psi Phi symbol on his right arm with a heated coat hanger.

SOX SELECTION. In 1989 the Boston Red Sox selected Vaughn with the twenty-third pick in the first round of the major league draft. He moved quickly through the minor leagues. In 1990 Vaughn batted .295 with 22 home runs and 72 RBI for the Red Sox's top farm team in Pawtucket.

The Red Sox had a reputation around the major leagues for not treating African American players well. Boston players told this to Vaughn when he arrived as a rookie in 1991. He decided to ignore what other people said and find out about Boston for himself. "I just said, 'Maybe not everyone's going to like me, but they're going to respect me,'" Vaughn recalled in *Sports Illustrated*. "I have always tried to just do my job and be myself, and I've had no problems. When I was sent down [to the minors] it wasn't because of race. When I was cheered, they weren't cheering because of race. It's a tough place to play, but if you can make it here, it's the best place in the world." Vaughn wears number 42 in honor of the great Jackie Robinson, the player who broke the major league color line and cleared the way for African Americans to play in big league baseball.

GREAT EXPECTATIONS. Boston fans had high expectations for Vaughn. They thought he would be the next great Red Sox slugger—the next Jim Rice, Carl Yastrzemski, or Ted Williams. "Look, the Boston Red Sox will be good whether I make the team or not," Vaughn told *Sports Illustrated* during his first spring training with Boston. "The attention doesn't bother me. You only play this game for 10 years. To be a good man, a good person, that's what people remember."

Vaughn batted .260 with four home runs and 32 RBI during his rookie season (1991) and opened the 1992 season as the Red Sox's starting first baseman. He got off to a rocky start. Vaughn hit only .185 with two home runs in his first 23 games. The fans booed him. "Man, it hurt," Vaughn remembered in *Sports Illustrated*. "I was a pretty confident kid, but they really cut me down to size."

ROCKY ROAD. The Red Sox sent Vaughn back to their minor league team in Pawtucket. Before leaving, he met with his parents in a hotel room and cried all night. Vaughn thought about quitting baseball. "Lord knows I've had a lot of adversity," Vaughn revealed in *Sports Illustrated*. "A lot of things were said about me—like when I went down, that I'd never come back. It was like I was a bad person or something. I had to make sure that wasn't the case. See, in Boston they want success right away. You can't afford to have any problems."

It took six weeks for Vaughn to work his way back to the major leagues. He never went back to the minors. "Now I realize that it was the best thing that ever happened to me,"

BIGGEST HOME RUN

Vaughn hit the biggest home run of his career in 1993. Jason Leader, an 11-year-old cancer patient, wanted to talk to the Boston slugger on the phone for his birthday. Vaughn called him and promised to hit a home run that day. "He was just so positive and upbeat, that I said—'You know what, man? I'll try to hit a homer for you,'" Vaughn recalled in *Forbes*. "That night, in my third at bat, I hit the centerfield seats." When the ball landed in the centerfield seats, a legend was born. "It was crazy, because all I was doing was a little bit for a young man. I hope it gave him just a little more strength to push on, to keep going." Leader died in 1994, but his hero made a dream come true.

Vaughn admitted in *Sports Illustrated*. "When I'm feeling tired or sore now, I think back to those times when I got nailed pretty good, by the fans, the media, everyone." Vaughn finished 1992 with a .234 batting average, 23 home runs, and 57 RBI. He had established himself as a major leaguer.

IN BOSTON TO STAY. Vaughn broke out in the 1993 season. He batted .297, hit 29 home runs, and had 101 RBI. "This is the most fun I've ever had playing baseball," Vaughn told *Sports Illustrated* at mid-season. He gave a lot of the credit for his success to his batting coach, Mike "Hit Man" Easler. Easler taught Vaughn both hitting and confidence, filling the young slugger with the ability to get through the bad streaks that every major leaguer goes through. "This is not the Mo Vaughn story," Vaughn revealed in *Forbes*. "This is the Mo Vaughn and Mike Easler story. Mike will never know what he did for me." Vaughn added in *Sports Illustrated*, "The man saved my career."

FRIEND FIRED. Vaughn continued to put up great numbers in 1994 with a .310 average, 26 home runs, and 82 RBI in 111 games. His numbers would have been even better if the players' strike had not brought the season to a premature end in August. The strike also cost Vaughn his best friend on the team. Boston fired Easler in the spring of 1995 when he refused to work with players signed to replace the striking major leaguers. The firing of his friend hurt Vaughn, but he dedicated himself to making his coach proud. "I just wanted to let him know he's my hitting coach and always will be my hitting coach, that he taught me very, very well," Vaughn said in the *New York Times*. "Mike was the only one who believed that I could play. He also taught me feelings, taught me to understand what it is to go to war for nine innings, to focus completely every day."

Superstar

MO-MENTUM. Baseball experts did not expect Boston to contend in 1995. The Red Sox had finished with a losing record for three straight seasons, and most people picked them for fourth in the AL East in the new season. Their chances became even slimmer when standout pitcher Roger Clemens missed the first 31 games of the season with tendonitis in his shoulder and struggled when he returned. Jose Canseco, acquired to help protect Vaughn in the lineup so teams could not pitch around the big slugger, also missed 32 games with injuries.

Vaughn would not let his team slump. He put the Red Sox on his strong back and carried them through the hard times. With Canseco out, Vaughn batted .323 with eight homers and 24 RBI. Time after time Vaughn hit clutch home runs. "He doesn't hit them when we're eight runs up," Red Sox manager Kevin Kennedy explained in *Sports Illustrated*. "When Mo hits them, they usually mean something."

BAD NIGHT. The one bad moment in Vaughn's 1995 season occurred in July. He and his girlfriend went to a nightclub, and a man began to hassle them. Vaughn got into a fight, and the other man kicked him in the head. When he woke up, Vaughn discovered his eye was swollen shut. He missed two games and feared Boston fans would boo him when he returned. Instead, they gave him a standing ovation when he came to the plate. Vaughn stepped out of the batter's box, trying not to cry. "That was probably the highlight of my career," Vaughn told *Sports Illustrated*. "That was better than any home run I'd hit or game I'd won, because I didn't know if the people would stay behind me. I guess they felt like I was earning my pay."

HORSING AROUND. The Red Sox clinched the American League East Division title on September 20, 1995. The fans in Fenway Park stayed after the game chanting "Mo! Mo! Mo!" Vaughn came out of the dugout and, at the urging of his teammates, got on a policeman's horse. He had never ridden a

WHAT IS A ROLE MODEL?

Some people say Vaughn is not a good role model. They point out that he wears his baseball cap backwards, has his shirt open, and listens to rap music. Vaughn realizes, however, that the way he acts and dresses shows that he is just being himself and kids listen to him when they might not listen to someone else. "How should I wear my ball cap?" he asks the kids. "Backwards!" the kids reply. "My job," Vaughn told *Forbes,* "it's not just to hit home runs. It's to use the game and my love of the game to help the kids."

Vaughn makes regular appearances at an elementary school in Mattapan, Massachusetts. His message is clear—stay in school, stay off drugs, and believe in yourself. He also established the Mo Vaughn Youth Development Program, a counseling center for inner-city children. Vaughn sends get-well cards and organizes field trips for poor children.

horse before, but Vaughn waved to fans, thanking them for their support.

Vaughn put up big numbers during the season. He hit 39 home runs (tied for fourth in the American League), drove in 126 runs (tied for first in the American League), and batted .300.

"What has he meant to this team?" Red Sox shortstop John Valentin asked in *Sports Illustrated.* "One word: Everything." Another teammate, Tim Naehring, told the same magazine, "It's more than the RBI, it's more than the homers, it's more than anything you can see on the field. It's his presence. He brings a confidence and an attitude to this team that is hard to explain."

MVP. The only disappointment of Vaughn's season came in the play-offs. The Cleveland Indians, the AL Central Division champion, swept the Red Sox in three straight games. Reporters from around the AL recognized Vaughn's great season and leadership by voting him the AL Most Valuable Player. He edged **Albert Belle** (see entry) of the Indians in one of the closest votes ever. "Mo has been carrying this team consistently, day in and day out, and that to me is what makes an MVP," Canseco explained to *Sports Illustrated.* "Every time this team needed him, he was there with a clutch hit or a clutch home run."

OFF THE FIELD. Vaughn lives in Brookline, Massachusetts. He majored in physical education at Seton Hall. Many people think Vaughn is mean because he is always so intense on the field. Vaughn says that is just his image. "Yeah, I've got this face and these eyes of a killer," Vaughn admitted in *Sports Illustrated.* "But off the field I'm probably one of the most fun guys on this team. When I came here, I wanted to win, but I also wanted to have fun. I wanted to prove that it could be fun to play baseball here."

Vaughn has won over the hard-to-please Boston fans. "He's easily the Red Sox's most lovable player," Dan Shaughnessy of the *Boston Globe* explained in *Forbes*. "Kids love him. Fans love him. Older people love him. He's got a chance to own this town." Vaughn once served as the grand marshal of a Boston Christmas parade.

Vaughn's career ambitions are simple, as he told *Forbes:* "I want to be remembered as a person who played hard every day, and cared about winning, and helped kids and people who are not as fortunate as I am."

Sources

Forbes, March 14, 1994.
New York Times, August 14, 1995.
Sports Illustrated, April 7, 1991; June 7, 1993; August 2, 1993; October 2, 1995.
Additional information provided by Seton Hall University and the Boston Red Sox.

WHERE TO WRITE:
C/O BOSTON RED SOX,
FENWAY PARK,
BOSTON, MA 02215.

Chris Webber

1973—

Chris Webber has been a star basketball player since the eighth grade. That was when college recruiters began to take notice of his exceptional skills. His basketball career has taken him many different places. He was the main man of the "Fab Five" University of Michigan team, which reached the finals of the National Collegiate Athletic Association (NCAA) Basketball Tournament for two straight seasons. In 1993 Webber was the first player chosen in the National Basketball Association (NBA) Draft. Despite his success, many people only know him as the player who called a time-out his team did not have. Webber's career is a perfect example of how to deal with the ups and downs of being a celebrity and a professional athlete.

Growing Up

"THE BRADY BUNCH." Mayce Edward Christopher Webber III was born March 1, 1973, in Detroit, Michigan. His dad, Mayce, was a plant foreman for General Motors, and his mom, Doris, was a teacher working with retarded children in the Detroit school system. Webber was the oldest of five children and was a guardian for his three younger brothers and sister. His dad often worked double shifts at the plant. His mom worked to give her son a love of learning. In his book *Fab Five*, Mitch Albom writes: "People in their lower-middle-class Detroit neighborhood would tease the Webbers about their almost corny relationships, calling them 'the Waltons' and 'the Brady Bunch.' They would tease Chris about his clothes, which his mother often sewed herself."

Webber told the *Sporting News* that it was not always easy growing up and that he came from a tough neighborhood. His father recalled in the *Sporting News* that "it was a very poor environment. There were a lot of things Chris didn't have that some of the other children had. We kept repeating the same things to him—warning him about drugs, being with the wrong people, being out too long. We tried to give him a good environment."

SORRIEST GAME. Webber was always big, and doctors predicted from an early age that he would grow to be seven feet tall. Although he was tall, Webber was not immediately interested in basketball, but his parents urged him to try the sport. He played very little before sixth grade, when he joined a summer program to learn how to play. At the very first practice the other players laughed Webber off the court. "Young Chris showed up in a Hawaiian shirt and shorts because he hadn't played much basketball and had nothing more appropriate to wear," according to Mitch Albom in his book *Fab Five*. "The other players took one look at him and teased him mercilessly, especially because he was also a bit awkward and tentative [unsure of himself]. One of his tormentors, a bean pole of a kid named Jalen Rose, went up to him and said, 'You've got the sorriest game I've ever seen.'"

Webber was ready to quit after the second practice, but his parents found out and made him go back. "[My father] told me I was going back," Webber recalled in *Sports Illustrated*. "There wasn't a lot of discussion about it. He said a man doesn't run away from difficult situations, he stands firm and conquers them." Local coach Curtis Hervey saw potential in Webber and spent hours during the summer giving the young man private tutoring on basketball moves. Hervey also saw to it that other players helped the shy Webber become tougher. The hard work paid off. By the following year, Webber's Amateur Athletic Union (AAU) team, based in Detroit, was playing games all over the country against some of the premier talent in his age group.

DIFFERENT WORLDS. College recruiters began noticing Webber when he was in eighth grade. He received more than a dozen letters from college coaches when he was 13. Most experts expected Webber to play at one of Detroit's big, competitive public schools. His mother, however, insisted he attend Country Day School, a private academy in a suburb of Detroit. Country Day is a tough academic school not known for its athletic programs. It seemed like an unlikely destination for a teenager being recruited by major college basketball powerhouses. Webber was not comfortable, and even tried to flunk out. "We had to wear a suit to school every day," he told the *Sporting News*. "I didn't even have a suit. I got the chance to go to a private school on scholarship and saw kids get new cars on their 16th birthday. Then I would go home and eat beans for a week. I vividly [clearly] recall that. I was 16 years old, going to school with a kid whose father was the president of General Motors, and all we had to eat for a week was beans."

When Webber was a senior at Country Day, his basketball team won the Michigan Class B state championship. Webber and **Glenn Robinson** (see entry) of Gary, Indiana, were considered the best high school players in the nation. The pressure on Webber to decide where he would go to college was incredible. On the same night that his high school team celebrated their championship victory, Webber

announced his college choice. He announced that he would attend the University of Michigan.

"FAB FIVE." The 1991 freshman basketball recruiting class at the University of Michigan was one of the greatest of all time. Given the name "the Fab Five," the five players joining the University of Michigan Wolverines were all high school stars. In addition to Webber, the Fab Five included Jalen Rose (now with the Denver Nuggets), Juwan Howard (now Webber's

FITTING IN

Although Webber was great friends with the rest of the Fab Five, he did not always feel like he fit in completely. Studying at Country Day School exposed Webber to many areas and subjects that the average teenager never experiences. Sometimes at Michigan he would try to hide what he knew in order to be one of the guys. "It wasn't that I thought they [his teammates] would make fun of me," Webber admitted in the *Sporting News*. "They knew I knew. But I never wanted it to seem like, oh, Chris knows so much. Like I was different than they were. I had never really fit in any situation up to that point because I didn't have a normal life. Normal 18-year-olds where I come from don't read the stock pages and have an interest in all kinds of things. They just don't."

teammate with the Washington Bullets), Ray Jackson, and Jimmy King. Rose, who previously had not thought much of Webber's game, had become close friends with him through their many years of playing together on all-star teams. The two friends decided to attend Michigan and talked the other players into joining them.

The Fab Five became an instant sensation in Michigan and then throughout the country. It is rare that a freshman starts in the tough Big Ten Conference, but soon all of the Fab Five held starting spots. The members of the team were flashy, and even their uniforms were different, featuring knee-length shorts that soon became a fashion trend on basketball courts nationwide. Michigan's on-floor leader was Webber. He was the first freshman ever to lead the Big Ten in rebounding, and he averaged more than 15 points per game. Big Ten experts named Webber the Big Ten's Freshman of the Year.

FAB FINALISTS. Despite incredible confidence in their own abilities, the Fab Five struggled during the 1991-92 regular season. Michigan qualified for the NCAA Basketball Tournament, but no one expected them to go very far. Surprising everyone but themselves, the Wolverines beat four straight opponents to earn a spot in the NCAA Final Four in Minneapolis, Minnesota. Michigan then defeated Cincinnati in the semifinals and faced the defending champions, the Duke University Blue Devils in the finals. The Fab Five's dream season ended in disappointment; they lost 71-51 in the championship game. Despite the loss, the future looked bright for Michigan because the Fab Five would all return the following year.

The U.S. Olympic Committee honored Webber during the off-season by inviting him to be a member of the practice team working with the 1992 U.S. Olympic basketball "Dream Team." At age 19 he was competing against his heroes—Earvin "Magic" Johnson, Michael Jordan, Larry Bird, and Clyde Drexler. The experience proved to Webber that he could play in the NBA.

Webber had a sensational year as a Michigan sophomore (1992-93). He led his team in scoring (19.2 points per game), rebounding (10.1 per game), blocked shots (2.1 per game), and field goal percentage (.619). Webber also led the Big Ten in rebounding for the second straight year. He was a first-team All-Big Ten and All-American selection and was a finalist for two of college basketball's most prestigious awards, the Wooden and Naismith trophies.

FINALS FRUSTRATION. With Webber leading the way, Michigan advanced once more to the NCAA Final Four. In the semifinals the Wolverines faced the powerful Kentucky Wildcats. The game was a classic, going back and forth until the very end. In the end, Michigan survived in overtime, 81-78. Webber scored 27 points and had 13 rebounds in the victory. The Wolverines would play the University of North Carolina Tar Heels in the championship game, this time as the favorite.

Michigan played the championship game in April 1993 in New Orleans, Louisiana. The game was hard-fought throughout, and Webber was a force. He scored 23 points and grabbed 11 rebounds, but the event people remember him for occurred in the final few seconds. With Michigan down by two points and 11 seconds left on the clock, Webber had the ball in front of the Michigan bench. A basket would tie the game and force an overtime, and Webber called a time-out so that his team could set up a play. Unfortunately, Michigan had used all its time-outs, and the referee called Webber for a technical foul. The call awarded North Carolina two free throws and possession of the ball. The Tar Heels won the game and the national championship, 77-71.

The mistake crushed Webber. He took full blame for the loss at a postgame press conference and then began to cry in the arms of his father and brother. "I cost our team the game,"

Everyone makes mistakes, but few people make them in front of millions of people watching on television. Many people made fun of him, but Webber did not let it get him down. "I hear some of those things," Webber told *Sports Illustrated.* "I'm not going to tell you it doesn't bother me at all, but I don't get mad, because I know that they would all have given anything to play in a national championship game, and because anyone who takes that much pleasure in someone else's misfortune has a much bigger problem than I do." Webber added in the *Sporting News* that he found a good way to deal with his disappointment. "You can put me in a dark, dark cave, but I'll find a light somewhere. I won't stop searching until I find it."

he admitted in *Sports Illustrated.* The weeks after the game were difficult, but Webber dealt with his disappointment. "You not only find out who your friends are when something like this happens, you find out you have friends you didn't even know about," Webber revealed in *Sports Illustrated.* "I just have to deal with what happened. It's my responsibility." His teammates did not blame Webber, because they knew they would not have made it to the championship game without him. Later, President Bill Clinton sent him a letter of encouragement.

Superstar

TOP PICK. At first Webber said he would return to Michigan in 1993 to try to avenge the loss. He changed his mind, however, and decided to leave school early and enter the 1993 NBA Draft. "I didn't want him to leave, but he had to do what was best for Chris," said Michigan teammate Ray Jackson in the *Sporting News.* "It was time." It turned out to be a good decision, because Webber was the first player chosen, the pick of the Orlando Magic. Within minutes, however, Orlando traded Webber to the Golden State Warriors for **Anfernee Hardaway** (see entry) of Memphis State University and three number one picks in future drafts.

ROOKIE OF THE YEAR. Webber joined a Golden State team that was on the verge of becoming a very good squad. He wanted to start slowly, but injuries to other players soon forced Webber into the starting lineup. He made the most of his opportunity. Webber became the first rookie in NBA history to total more than 1,000 points, 500 rebounds, 250 assists, 150 blocks, and 75 steals in a season. He averaged 17.5

points, 9.1 rebounds, 3.6 assists, 2.2 blocks, and 1.2 steals per game. Webber led all rookies in rebounds, field goal percentage (.552), dunks (219), and blocks (169).

This performance was good enough to land Webber a spot on the NBA All-Rookie first team and unanimous selection as the NBA Rookie of the Year. "He's gone from being a rookie to being a veteran," his coach, Don Nelson, told the *Sporting News*. "I can't tell you when he arrived that I had the Rookie of the Year, but he's done his work." Webber was willing to improve. "I need to do the intangible things—set a better pick, things like that—for us to have a better chance," Webber admitted in the *Sporting News*.

During the off-season a feud between Webber and Nelson came into the open. Webber believed his coach was too tough on him and had frequently embarrassed the young star. "You have to respect people," Webber explained in the *Sporting News*. "You don't yell at them, 'Why did we draft you?' in front of little kids in the stands. I just don't know how he's going to act. I want to be treated like a man." Nelson claimed he was just trying to get Webber to reach his full potential. There was a clause in Webber's contract that allowed him to become a restricted free agent after one season. (Restricted free agents can sign a contract with another team. The player's original team then has the right to match the offer made by the other team.) Webber resigned with the Warriors, but the feud between him and Nelson made it impossible for the two to work together. The Warriors traded Webber to the Washington Bullets on November 17, 1994, for forward Tom Gugliotta and three first-round draft picks.

BULLET REUNION. Webber played only 54 games in his second season because of a dislocated shoulder. When he returned to the Bullets, he joined former Fab Five teammate Juwan Howard in a powerful 1-2 punch. Webber led the Bullets in scoring (20.1 points per game), rebounding (9.6 per game), steals (1.54 per game), and minutes (38.3 per game). The local media named Webber the Bullets' Player of the Year. Webber also made a prediction for the future. "This is definitely the team Juwan [Howard] and I will make a future with, and we'll turn it around." Unfortunately, Webber reinjured his shoulder before the 1995—96 season and missed the beginning of the year.

OFF THE COURT. Webber lives in the Detroit, Michigan, area, and tries to stay close to his old friends. One of the first things Webber did after signing his first professional contract was to buy his father a Cadillac. His father had built Cadillacs for many years but could never afford to buy one himself. Webber enjoys playing video games and endorses products for Nike. He works with charities helping abused and homeless children in the San Francisco, California, area, and with the Take Time Out Foundation in Detroit. The Foundation encourages needy children to stay in school. Webber has considered returning to Detroit after his basketball career is over and running for mayor.

Webber's main interest off the court is African American history. He collects letters and other papers signed by such famous African Americans as Martin Luther King Jr. and Frederick Douglass. Webber first got interested in African American history in junior high. "I didn't like to read until I got into black history," he told *Sports Illustrated for Kids.* "Then I got really curious." Someday Webber hopes to open an African American history museum.

Many people think Webber is mean because he is so intense during games. "People automatically assume that the way I am on the court, grimacing and talking trash and all that, is the way I am off the court," he told the *Sporting News.* Webber has come to realize a lot about himself. "Lately I've been starting to realize that it isn't necessarily important to fit in in every situation," he admitted to the *Sporting News.* "You see a lot of guys scared to admit that they know the answer in class, or that they do things that aren't necessarily popular, like read a lot. That's how I've been. But I'm beginning to see that when you hold part of yourself back like that, people get the wrong impression. Whatever opinion they do have isn't of the real you, and where's the value in that? If they're going to be jealous of me or hate me, that's OK, if they know what they're hating. I don't like the idea of someone having an opinion about me and not even knowing who I am."

Sources

Albom, Mitch, *Fab Five,* Warner Books, 1993.
Boys' Life, December 1994.
Sport, November 1993.
Sporting News, July 19, 1993; December 13, 1993; January 24, 1994; May 2, 1994; May 16, 1994; November 21, 1994; November 28, 1994; December 5, 1994; January 2, 1995; January 13, 1995.
Sports Illustrated, April 12, 1993; April 19, 1993; January 16, 1995; March 6, 1995.
Sports Illustrated for Kids, September 1995.
Additional information provided by Washington Bullets.

WHERE TO WRITE:
C/O WASHINGTON BULLETS, CAPITAL CENTRE,
ONE HARRY S TRUMAN DR.,
LANDOVER, MD 20785.

Venus Williams

1980—

Venus Williams is not your typical tennis star. While most professional tennis players come from high-priced tennis academies and country clubs, Williams learned how to play on the tough streets of Compton, California. Her father was her coach, and local gangs protected her from the violence that swirled all around her. Williams has come a long way from her hometown and now stands on the verge of becoming one of the best female tennis players in the world.

Growing Up

CINDERELLA OF THE GHETTO. Venus Ebonistarr Williams was born June 17, 1980, in Lynwood, California. Her father, Richard, owns a private security company. Her mom, Oracene, is a nurse. South Central Los Angeles is one of the poorest and most dangerous neighborhoods in the United States. Gangs and drugs rule the streets, and graffiti often covered the small house in which Williams grew up. While the violence was going on outside, Williams dreamed of playing at the legendary Wimbledon tournament in far-away England. She also dreamed of one day jumping into a spaceship and traveling to Jupiter.

Williams took up tennis at an early age. Her father, Richard, was her coach. He had taught himself the game and decided his girls would play tennis. Williams's three older sisters had not liked the game, but Venus and her younger sister, Serena, were different. Mr. Williams began taking Williams to the courts when she was only four. While most tennis stars learn the game at fancy tennis clubs, Williams learned on the public courts in Compton. The surrounding neighborhood sometimes interfered with their practices. "We've been shot at on the tennis court," Mr. Williams told *Sports Illustrated*. "But now gang members know us and protect us when the shooting starts." Mr. Williams calls his daughter "the Cinderella of the Ghetto."

Before she began concentrating solely on tennis, Williams was undefeated in 19 track meets as both a sprinter and middle-distance runner. Her long legs helped her run fast. Mr. Williams wanted Venus to continue to run track, but her mom said that tennis and track were too much for a young girl.

VENUS RISING. Williams first made headlines when tennis greats John McEnroe and Pete Sampras noticed her when she was only seven years old. At age 10 Williams already had the speed and size to mark her as a future champion. She was ranked the number one player in the very competitive southern California area in the under-12 division. When Williams grew too old for this division, her sister Serena became the number one player.

Being a star so young was an overwhelming experience. Older ball boys and girls asked Williams for her autograph. She could not write in cursive script yet, so she printed her

SCOREBOARD

BEGAN PLAYING TENNIS AT AGE FOUR.

RANKED NUMBER-ONE PLAYER UNDER 12 YEARS OF AGE IN SOUTHERN CALIFORNIA.

WON FIRST PROFESSIONAL MATCH AT AGE 14.

WILLIAMS'S GOAL IS TO GO FROM THE PLAYGROUNDS TO BE A FORCE ON THE WOMEN'S PROFESSIONAL TOUR.

Williams returns a shot during the Acura Classic in California.

name. Coaches from all over the country wanted Williams to come to their camps. Sporting goods manufacturers gave her free rackets, shoes, and clothes. Agents were fighting each other for the right to represent the young star. "She is from California and she is from a minority background, and both of those facts mean she is going to get attention," Seena Hamilton, a tournament director, explained in *Sports Illustrated*. Williams had to change elementary schools three times to keep the reporters away.

TOO YOUNG? Some people thought Williams was too young to have to deal with the pressure. "She's 10 years old and agents are talking to her?" said former player Dennis Ralston. "What's happened to our sport? How's that kid [Williams] going to enjoy anything that a 10-year-old should enjoy?" Her parents agreed and decided to give their daughter a break from tennis. "It's time to back off a little from tennis," her dad admitted in *Sports Illustrated*. "I'd like for the racket to stay out of her hand for a while. Venus is still young. We want her to be a little girl while she is a little girl. I'm not going to let Venus pass up her childhood. Long after tennis is over, I want her to know who she is."

Superstar

FLORIDA BOUND. Eventually, Mr. Williams decided to send Venus and Serena to Ric Macci's tennis academy in Delray Beach, Florida. Macci had trained two other famous teenage players, Jennifer Capriati and **Mary Pierce** (see entry). Mr. Williams decided in 1991 that his daughters would not play in any junior tennis tournaments. He claimed he did not want them to face the pressures of constant competition. Williams did not play any tournaments for three years. Because she did not face any competition, experts did not really know how good Williams was. In 1993 Mr. Williams pulled his daughters out of school and began to teach them at home.

TURNS PRO. Under the rules of the Women's Tennis Association (WTA), Williams could not turn pro until the year of her fourteenth birthday, or 1994. The WTA decided to change the rule, making the minimum age 15, starting in 1995. Williams had to make a decision about turning pro before the rule changed. Her father wanted her to wait. "If I have my way, Venus won't turn pro until she is 18 or 19, maybe 20," Mr. Williams told *Ebony*. It was Williams herself who made the final decision to become a professional, although she had to get good grades on her report card first.

Williams made her professional debut in 1994 at the Bank of the West Classic in Oakland, California. She defeated her first professional opponent, Shaun Stafford, 6-3, 6-4. Stafford was the fifty-ninth-ranked player in the world at the time. She then faced top-seeded Arantxa Sanchez Vicario. Williams won nine of the first 11 games and seemed on the verge of a shocking upset. Sanchez Vicario, however, used her superior experience to wear down her younger opponent. The top-seed won the match in three sets. "I'm not satisfied," Williams told *Newsweek* after the match. "I didn't come here to lose."

MEDIA STAR. Williams liked the attention she received from reporters. "I like answering questions," Williams revealed in *People* magazine. "I think it's fun." She told the same magazine that missing out on kids' stuff did not bother her. "I never really had a lot of friends, so I don't miss out on not having them. I don't plan to be in tennis long. Maybe when I'm 25, I'll go to college and become a paleontologist or an archaeologist. I like digging into the past. Maybe because I wasn't there. But I need to catch up on biology first." Williams entered just three tournaments in 1995, finishing with a 2-3 record.

Williams, unlike a lot of young players, likes to play with an aggressive style on the court. "If you give me a short shot, I will attack you," Williams told *Sports Illustrated*. "I'm not a baseliner who rallies. I try to get the point over with." Williams has confidence in her ability. "I think I can change the game," Williams told *Sports Illustrated*.

OFF THE COURT. Williams lives in Pompano Beach, Florida. She likes playing soccer, tag, and hide-and-seek with her four sisters. Williams also enjoys in-line skating and swimming. She likes to read and go to movies, arcades, and water parks. Her favorite movie is *Ace Ventura: Pet Detective*. Williams has two dogs, a beagle and a Labrador.

Williams currently is under contract to promote equipment made by Reebok. If she does not make it as a tennis player, Williams would like to be an archaeologist or an astronaut. Williams practices four or five hours a day. She likes giving speeches at inner-city schools. "I know I should go back there, because that's where I'm from," Williams explained in *Sports Illustrated*. "It's my roots." Serena Williams says she plans to follow her sister onto the professional tennis circuit.

The only program Williams likes to watch on television is tennis. "I look at the grips they [other players] use and their technique," Williams explained in *Sports Illustrated*. "I try to see if they're playing smart and concentrating, and playing to their opponents' weaknesses. That's what I try to do when I play." Williams knows what she has to do to succeed, as she explained to *Sports Illustrated:* "I think you have to believe in yourself and never give up and one day you'll make it."

Sources

Ebony, May 1995.
Newsweek, December 26, 1994.
People, November 21, 1994.
Sports Illustrated, June 10, 1991; October 17, 1994; November 14, 1994.
Sports Illustrated for Kids, August 1994; January 1995.
Tennis, August 1994.
Additional information provided by Women's Tennis Association.

WHERE TO WRITE:
C/O WOMEN'S TENNIS ASSOCIATION,
133 FIRST ST. NE,
ST. PETERSBURG, FL 33701.

Eldrick "Tiger" Woods

1975—

"I want to be the Michael Jordan of golf. I'd like to be the best ever."
—Eldrick "Tiger" Woods

Eldrick "Tiger" Woods began playing golf almost from the time he could walk. His father wanted to give his son the opportunities denied him as a child. Woods has taken advantage of those opportunities and has already, at age 20, surpassed his father's wildest hopes. He is the youngest golfer and only African American to ever win the U.S. Junior Amateur (unpaid) title and the only player to win the title three times. In 1994 Woods became the youngest golfer and the only African American to ever win the U.S. Amateur title, and in 1995 he successfully defended his crown. In his young career, Woods has already shattered most amateur golfing records. Although he is a reluctant role model, golf experts have called Woods "potentially the most important player to enter the game in 50 years."

Growing Up

LIKE FATHER, LIKE SON. Eldrick Woods was born December

30, 1975, in Long Beach, California. His father, Earl, is African American, and his mother, Kultida, is from the Asian country of Thailand. His dad is a former Army lieutenant colonel and met Woods's mother while stationed in Thailand.

Woods's nickname, "Tiger," came from a South Vietnamese soldier, Nguyen Phong, who saved his father's life. Mr. Woods says he hopes that some day his old friend will see the names "Tiger" and "Woods" together and recognize his son. Woods received his athletic ability from his dad, who was a baseball catcher and the first African American to play at Kansas State University.

Woods's father is an excellent golfer. He took up golf at age 42, too late to become a professional. "I was a black kid, and golf was played at the country club—end of story," Mr. Woods revealed in *Sports Illustrated*. "But I told myself that somehow my son would get a chance to play golf early in life." Mr. Woods began teaching golf to his son when Woods was only ten months old. "I wanted to give Tiger a game for a lifetime," Woods's father explained to *Sports Illustrated*. Woods would watch his father hit golf balls into a net set up on their garage. His dad shortened a putter for him, and Woods carried it everywhere. His dad also taught him the proper way to swing a golf club, and Woods practiced what his dad showed him.

TIGER CUB. Woods shot a respectable 48 for nine holes (par is usually 36) when he was three years old. He entered his first golf tournament when he was only four. Woods appeared on the *Mike Douglas Show,* winning a putting contest against comedian Bob Hope, and *That's Incredible* before he was five. He was signing autographs when he was five years old. (He could not write yet, so he printed his name.) Woods was undefeated in more than 30 southern California junior tournaments by age 11.

ROBO-GOLFER? Woods's father strove to make his son the best player he could be. He "debriefed" his son after every round, talking about what he did right and wrong. Woods listened to "subliminal" tapes, designed to make him learn when he slept. When Woods was 13 years old, a doctor hypnotized him to help him concentrate and block out distractions on the course. His dad would do his best to make noises and distract his son when he was swinging and would outright cheat, just to make Woods concentrate. "I wanted to make sure he'd never run into anybody who was tougher mentally than he was," Woods's father explained in *Sports Illustrated*. "I'd get angry sometimes," Woods admitted in the same magazine. "But I knew it was for the betterment of me. That's what learning is all about, right?"

Despite this high-tech training, Woods claims he had a normal childhood. "I did the same things every kid did," Woods recalled in *Sports Illustrated*. "I studied and went to the mall. I was addicted to TV wrestling, rap music and *The Simpsons*. I got into trouble and got out of it. I loved my parents and obeyed what they told me. The only difference is I can sometimes hit a little ball into a hole in less strokes than some other people."

YOUNGEST EVER. When Woods was eight years old, he won the ten-and-under division of the Junior World Golf Championship. When he was only 15, Woods became the youngest player ever to win the U.S. Junior Amateur championship. Woods was also the first African American champion. "I said to him, 'Son, you have done something no black person in the United States has ever done, and you will forever be a part of history,'" his dad proudly told *Sports Illustrated* after Woods's historic victory. Woods went on to win the championship two more times, becoming the first person to win the U.S. Junior Amateur title three times. Woods came from behind to win in each of these victories, developing a reputation as a great clutch performer.

Woods won his age group at the Junior World Golf Championship six times, more than any junior golfer in history. He played with golfing greats like Jack Nicklaus, **Greg Norman** (see entry), and Sam Snead. In 1990 Woods played against touring pros at the Insurance Golf Classic, a tournament for amateurs and professionals in Fort Worth, Texas. He shot a round of 69, beating 18 of the 21 pros entered in the event. "I wish I could have played like that at 14," one pro said after the tournament. "Heck, I wish I could play like that at 27."

PLAYS WITH PROS. Woods got his first taste of the big time when he was a sophomore at Western High School. In February 1992, when he was 16 years old, Woods played in his first Professional Golfers' Association (PGA) tournament, the Nissan Los Angeles Open. He was one of the youngest players to ever participate in a PGA event. Woods failed to make the cut (qualify for the last two rounds of the tournament), but he still impressed the older pros.

Superstar

ANOTHER RECORD. The U.S. Amateur Golf Championship is the oldest golf tournament in the United States. Before 1994 no African American had ever won the tournament. Woods became the first. He was also the youngest champion ever at only 18 years old, one year younger than the great Jack Nicklaus when the legendary golfer won the same title. Woods defeated 156 of the best male amateur golfers in the country. He won the final round of the tournament with a birdie on the second-to-last hole after being six strokes behind at one point. "Coming back from that far back is the best thing about winning," Woods said after his victory. With the victory, Woods became the first person to win both the U.S. Junior Amateur and U.S. Amateur titles.

Later in 1994 Woods and his teammates defeated the combined Britain-Ireland team to win the World Amateur golf title, ending a streak of five consecutive second-place finishes for the United States. Woods was the star of the tournament, held in France. The French papers gave him the nickname "Tiger La Terreur" (Tiger the Terror).

CARDINAL CHIPPER. Many colleges and universities recruited Woods to play golf. He eventually settled on Stanford University. "I'm not a celebrity at Stanford," Woods revealed in *Sports Illustrated.* "Everybody's special. You have to be to get in here. So then nobody is. That's why I love the place." Woods won two tournaments for Stanford in 1995 and finished second three times. He also set the Stanford record for lowest season-long scoring average. Golf experts named Woods to the All-American team. He ended the season ranked as the number one collegiate player.

Woods claims he will stay at Stanford for four years, but most experts do not believe him. His mom says the pro tour can wait. "What he need money for?" she asked *Sports Illustrated.* "If you turn him pro, you take his youth away from him." Woods, not surprisingly, agrees with his mom. "Money can't make me happy," he told the same magazine. "If I turned pro, I'd be giving up something I wanted to accomplish. And if I did turn pro, that would only put more pressure on me to play well, because I would have nothing to fall back on. I would rather spend four years here at Stanford and improve myself."

MOVING UP. Woods continued to set records in 1995. He successfully defended his U.S. Amateur title, becoming the first player in 12 years to accomplish that feat. His win at the U.S. Amateur tournament qualified Woods to play at the prestigious Masters tournament at the Augusta (Georgia) National Golf Club. He became only the fourth African American to play in the tournament. "Can I do well?" Woods said, repeating a reporter's question before the tournament. "Doing well is winning. To walk where [legendary golfer Bobby] Jones and Nicklaus walked, that will be daunting [frightening]. But I'm not afraid of the Mas-

ROLE MODEL

Although his race should not matter, Woods receives a lot of attention because he is African American. Actually, Woods is part Thai, part Chinese, part Indian, and part African American. His father admitted in *Sports Illustrated* that he raised his son differently. "Before, black kids grew up with basketball or football or baseball from the time they could walk," Mr. Woods explained. "The game became part of them from the beginning. But they always learned golf too late. Not Tiger. Tiger knew how to swing a golf club before he could walk." Woods learned about discrimination early in his life. White students tied him to a tree and taunted him his first day of kindergarten. Woods has received death threats before appearing in tournaments. In his first season at Stanford University, Woods won a tournament at a country club that until shortly before that time had not allowed African American members. All this pressure has made Woods uncomfortable with the role given him as an African American in a sport dominated by white people. "I'm only a role model because other people make me one," Woods told *Sports Illustrated.* "I don't want to be the best black golfer. I want to be the best golfer, period."

ters. I've never been afraid of anything. I'm going down there to win." His dad was his caddy at the Masters.

Woods finished forty-first in the Masters but was the only amateur to make the cut. He played at the U.S. Open for the first time, but an injury forced him to withdraw in the second round. Woods also made his first appearance in the legendary British Open, finishing in a tie for sixty-seventh. In February 1995 Woods was one of ten finalists for the Sullivan Award, given to the top amateur athlete in any and all sports. *GQ* magazine named Woods one of their "Top 50 Most Influential People in the Next 10 Years."

Woods is a mostly an A student and his favorite subject is math. He has said he would be an accountant if he could not be a golfer. Woods admits, however, that his mind is not always on his books. "I daydream a lot about golf," he told *Sports Illustrated for Kids*. "I work on my swing in my mind." His swing enables the six-foot-tall Woods to drive the ball 280 yards. He also has a soft touch, enabling him to make the difficult short shots near the green. Woods's biggest strengths are his ability to block out distractions and a competitive streak that makes him hard to beat. "I wouldn't bet against Tiger doing anything, any time," his dad stated in *Sports Illustrated*. Woods has won more than 100 tournaments in his career and is looking forward to many more victories in the future.

OFF THE COURSE. Woods collects coins and likes music. He also lifts weights to give his swing added strength. Woods's father acts as his manager, and his mom monitors his schoolwork. With all he has accomplished, Woods still sets his goals high. "I want to be the Michael Jordan of golf," he told *Boys' Life*. "I'd like to be the best ever."

Sources

Boys' Life, September 1992.
Ebony, May 1995.
Jet, August 30, 1993; September 12, 1994; November 14, 1994.
Newsweek, April 10, 1995.
Sports Illustrated, September 24, 1990; March 25, 1991; August 9, 1993;
    September 5, 1994; March 27, 1995.

Sports Illustrated for Kids, June 1992; November 1994.
Time, September 12, 1994.
Additional information provided by Stanford University.

WHERE TO WRITE:
C/O MEDIA RELATIONS OFFICE,
STANFORD UNIVERSITY,
STANFORD, CA 94305.

Rod Woodson

1965—

A cornerback is the loneliest player on the football field. One mistake, one slip, and a speedy wide receiver will run by and catch a touchdown pass. Rod Woodson loves the challenge of facing the game's greatest wide receivers. The Pittsburgh Steelers star is considered one of the most versatile players in the National Football League (NFL). A six-time selection to the Pro Bowl game and a member of the NFL's 75th Anniversary Team, Woodson is a player quarterbacks hate to see and try to avoid.

Growing Up

NEVER BE AFRAID. Roderick Kevin Woodson was born March 10, 1965, in Fort Wayne, Indiana. He is the youngest of three boys. His father, James, was a factory worker by day and worked as a custodian at night. His mother, Linda Jo, worked several part-time jobs, but her children were always first.

536

Since he was young, Woodson has known he is different. His father is African American and his mother is white. Kids used to tease him about his parents. "I was taught to never back down," Woodson recalled in *Sports Illustrated*. "When you're mixed, you have three options; stay in the middle, pick a side or stand on your own. My parents let me know I didn't have to pick a side, because I always had a friend in my family. I learned to stand up for myself and to never be afraid."

White and black racists terrorized Woodson's family. Members of the Black Muslims once pushed and knocked down Woodson's mom. The Ku Klux Klan made harassing phone calls and once sent a threatening package through the mail. "I never knew who my true friends were, so I had to stick with my own," Woodson told *Sports Illustrated*. "The only people I knew who were mixed, like me, were my brothers, and that made us a very close and protective family. No threats could intimidate [scare] our family." His parents taught him to be proud of his heritage and use humor against racists. The Woodson brothers would make fun of racists who called on the phone and then hang up on them.

FAMILY AFFAIR. Woodson was always close to his brothers. "I started playing football because I wanted to play with them," Woodson revealed in *Sports Illustrated for Kids*. "All we did was play sports all day." Woodson credits sports with keeping him out of trouble. "There's nothing good in the streets for a young kid," Woodson admitted in *Sports Illustrated for Kids*.

HIGH SCHOOL STAR. Woodson was a three sport star at Snyder High School. He played football and basketball and ran track. Woodson's football career almost ended in the tenth grade when he quit the team for a short time. "The coaches were yelling at me," Woodson recalled in *Sports Illustrated for Kids*. "My dad doesn't yell at me this much. I don't need

SCOREBOARD

ALL-AMERICAN AT PURDUE UNIVERSITY.

MEMBER OF THE NFL'S 75TH ANNIVERSARY TEAM.

SIX-TIME SELECTION TO PRO BOWL GAME.

WOODSON USES HIS SPEED, TOUGHNESS, AND BRAINS TO CONTAIN THE BEST WIDE RECEIVERS IN THE NFL.

Woodson (left) chases Chicago Bears' quarterback Jim Harbaugh.

that stuff." His track coach talked him into going back, telling him not to be a quitter.

ALL-AMERICAN. During his senior season *Parade* magazine named Woodson an All-American as both a cornerback and running back. He also made the all-conference team in basketball and won the track state championship in the low and high hurdles two times. College football coaches heavily recruited Woodson out of high school, and he chose nearby Purdue University. Woodson went on to be a four-year starter for the Boilermakers and played 44 consecutive games. During his career at Purdue he set 13 team records, including solo tackles (320) and interceptions (11).

SPEED DEMON. Woodson developed his great speed by running track as a hurdler and sprinter. While at Purdue Woodson won the Big Ten indoor 55-meter hurdles four times and twice won the 60-meter dash. He never developed good technique in hurdling, however, and often tried to run through the hurdles, not over them. "At practice, blood was always streaming down his legs," his track coach at Purdue, Mike Poehlein remembered in *Sports Illustrated*. "He had scars all over his knees. Most hurdlers would call for medical attention, but Rod wouldn't stop until practice was over." Woodson qualified for the 1984 Olympic trials in the 100-meter hurdles in 1984 and twice earned All-American honors in track.

MR. VERSATILE. Woodson was so good at so many positions in football that his coaches had a hard time settling on one. He was switched from position to position, and he did not become an expert at any one of them. In his final game at Purdue Woodson played tailback and cornerback, returned kickoffs and punts, and covered kicks as part of the special team units. He rushed for 97 yards, caught three passes for 67 yards, made 10 tackles, forced a fumble, and returned two kickoffs for 46 yards and three punts for 30 yards. Purdue won the game, 17-15, over intrastate rival Indiana. Woodson earned All-American honors his senior season and finished second in the voting for the Jim Thorpe Award, given annually to the nation's best collegiate defensive back.

STEELERS' STAR. The Pittsburgh Steelers drafted Woodson with the tenth overall pick in the 1987 NFL Draft. When Woodson joined the Steelers he had to stick to one position, cornerback, for the first time. "I was a nervous wreck," Woodson admitted in *Sports Illustrated*. "I'd relied too long on my speed and physical talents, and I didn't understand the game."

In 1989 Woodson fell in love with Nickie Theede, a white woman. The loving relationship of his parents gave him the courage to ignore the problems this relationship might cause him. Woodson decided his children would understand about their heritage. "I'll let Marikah [his first daughter] know that there are choices you make in life, with friends and in dating, and I'll tell her that when people find out she's one-quarter black, they'll probably still consider her black," Woodson explained in *Sports Illustrated*. "She too will find out who her true friends are, but that's a valuable lesson to learn. My parents never allowed me to get to that stage every kid of any color goes through: Who am I? Where do I fit in? Marikah will always know she's special and that she's an important person."

He learned quickly. "I had to make myself play well," Woodson confessed in the *Sporting News*. "It might sound funny, but I did."

The Steelers used Woodson in a limited role in 1987. He played as a backup on defense and returned kicks. Woodson started at cornerback in 1988 and also returned kicks. In 1989 he led the NFL in kick returns with a 27.3-yard average and his fellow players named him to his first Pro Bowl game, as a kick return specialist. Woodson did not lose any of his speed in the NFL. In 1988 he finished second to Darrell Green of the Washington Redskins in the NFL Fastest Man Contest. (He finished third in 1990.)

DAD DIES Woodson suffered a great loss in May 1992, when his father died after having brain surgery. After their father's death, Woodson's brother Jamie admitted that he was jealous of how their father and other people treated Woodson. "It was the first time Jamie ever told me how he felt about others treating me different from him," Woodson told *Sports Illustrated*. "All my life I've known what it's like to be accepted not for what I am inside, but for what I look like or, later in life, for being a successful athlete. I told Jamie that I'm still the same person I was in diapers, and that I'd be his brother when football's over. Nothing can ever come between us."

Superstar

CHALLENGED. In 1993 Coach Bill Cowher of the Steelers challenged Woodson to be an even better player. "He kind of thrives on that and has taken his game to another level," Cowher told the *Sporting News*. "You have to try to get him around the football as much as you can. If you leave him in one spot, they can scheme away from [avoid] him. We want him involved."

Woodson knew he would have to work harder to live up to his new responsibilities. "This year, I said I am going to concentrate for 16 games," Woodson explained in the *Sporting News*. "And let's see what happens. It is so much easier to play that way. If I had known it would be so much easier, I would have done it earlier. But maybe it's because of maturity, experience, all of the above. I'm just trying to play more from the shoulders up this year and let my ability take over. I am trying to think about what I am doing. That's the key. In the past, I'd have two or three great games and two or three bad ones. I've eliminated those lapses."

The hard work paid off. Woodson intercepted a career-high eight passes in 1993, and the NFL voted him the Defensive Player of the Year. The Steelers squeaked into the play-offs as a wild-card team, but their stay was a short one. Joe Montana and the Kansas City Chiefs eliminated the Steelers in the first round.

"BLITZBURG." The Steelers' "Blitzburg" defense dominated opponents in 1994. Pittsburgh's defensive linemen and linebackers put intense pressure on quarterbacks. The added pressure put on the quarterback helped Woodson, who continued to blanket receivers. The Steelers defense finished second in the NFL, and Pittsburgh won the American Football Conference (AFC) Central Division title with a 12-4 record. Woodson had 83 tackles, three sacks, four interceptions, and 23 pass defenses. He won the AFC Defensive Back of the Year award.

Pittsburgh's record earned home-field advantage throughout the play-offs. The Steelers had a chance to make history. If Pittsburgh went all the way in the play-offs, the team would become the first franchise in NFL history to win five Super Bowls. They defeated their bitter division rival the Cleveland Browns, 29-9, in their first play-off game. The Steelers next faced the San Diego Chargers in the AFC Championship Game.

Football experts believed that Pittsburgh would bury the Chargers, and unfortunately the Steelers believed them. Pittsburgh players predicted a shutout and began work on a Super Bowl rap video. The Steelers' talk and action angered San

Diego players, especially All-Pro linebacker **Junior Seau** (see entry). The Chargers took their anger out on Pittsburgh, defeating them 17-13 in the AFC Championship Game. "They only made two plays on us all day," Woodson grumbled in the *Sporting News,* referring to two long San Diego touchdown passes that proved to be the difference in the game. Woodson recorded six tackles and one interception in the defeat.

SUPER COMEBACK. Woodson's 1995 season ended almost before it began. He seriously injured his knee in the Steelers' first game trying to tackle Barry Sanders of the Detroit Lions. Doctors told Woodson that it might be one year before he could play football again. Woodson underwent surgery to repair his anterior cruciate ligament and then began the long process of rehabilitating his knee.

The Steelers struggled early in the season, going 3-4 in their first seven games. Pittsburgh's defense missed Woodson and the team's other starting cornerback, Deion Figures, who was injured in a shooting accident during the off-season. Just when it seemed that the Steelers would miss the play-offs, the team turned their fortunes around. Pittsburgh won eight games in a row to win the AFC Central Division title with an 11-5 record. All-Pro safety Carnell Lake moved to cornerback to fill in for Woodson and the defense finished the season as one of the best in the NFL.

RETURNS TO LINEUP. Missing the entire season was hard on Woodson, but he did not give up hope of returning during the play-offs. The Steelers defeated the Buffalo Bills and the Indianapolis Colts to reach the Super Bowl for the fifth time in team history. Prior to the big game, Cowher announced that Woodson would play against the Dallas Cowboys. Experts considered Woodson's return remarkable. "All I did was go out there and rehab," Woodson told the *Orlando Sentinel.* "God blessed me with some good talent, but with some good recovery period, too, and healing powers or whatever you want to call it to come back from this. I did all the rehab our doctors and trainers said to do."

SUPER BOWL. The Cowboys opened up an early 13-0 lead in Super Bowl XXX in Tempe, Arizona. The Steelers defense had a hard time stopping the Cowboys offense, especially All-Pro wide receiver **Michael Irvin** (see entry). Pittsburgh scored a touchdown just before halftime and trailed 13-7. Woodson played sparingly during the first half, but his knee held up under the pressure and game conditions.

At halftime the Steelers made a big decision. They decided to use Woodson more, and even let him cover Irvin man-to-man. The strategy worked and Irvin did not catch a pass in the second half. In the fourth quarter, Woodson knocked away a pass intended for Irvin, ending a Dallas drive. The Steelers' defense shut-down the Cowboys attack in the second half, but two interceptions by Dallas cornerback Larry Brown led to the Cowboys' scoring 14 points. Pittsburgh could not overcome these mistakes and lost the game, 27-17. Dallas became the first team to win three Super Bowls in four years. (The Cowboys also won the Super Bowls following the 1992 and 1993 seasons.)

BEST OF ALL-TIME

Woodson received a great honor when the NFL named him to its all-time team during the league's 75th anniversary celebration in 1994. Only four other active players received this honor—Ronnie Lott, Joe Montana, Jerry Rice, and Reggie White. "He's one of those fantastic athletes that everyone would like on their team," San Diego General Manager Bobby Beathard told the *Sporting News*. "He can cover and he can tackle and he can blitz and he has so much speed and quickness and size. And he is a dangerous return man, too. You don't find many great corners anymore. If you have a great one, it allows you to do so much more stuff with your defense." Woodson is also the Steelers, all-time leading punt- and kickoff-return specialist.

WHY SO GOOD? Woodson is one of the toughest players in the game. The only protection he wears during a game is shoulder pads. This makes him be lighter on his feet and lets him run with speedy wide receivers. Woodson believes that cornerbacks have to be the best athletes on the field. "You're all by yourself against a wide receiver," Woodson explained in *Sports Illustrated*. "You have to run backward, which isn't natural, then turn and sprint as soon as the receiver makes his break, matching him stride for stride at top speed." Woodson has proved his worth, being elected to the Pro Bowl game six times.

Woodson realizes that no matter how well he plays, he can always be beaten. He always covers the other team's best wide receiver, players like Jerry Rice of the San Francisco 49ers and Michael Irvin of the Dallas Cowboys. Any mistake by Woodson can lead to a touchdown for the other team. "You've got to resign yourself to the fact that you can't stop the perfect pass," Woodson confessed in *Sports Illustrated*. "Let the receiver catch the ball but then tell him, 'I'll be here all day. I'm not going anywhere. Next time you're going to have to pay.' You've got to respect wide receivers but never fear them. If you fear them, you'll lose."

Woodson can have a great game without ever touching the ball. "They've stopped throwing much my way and it can get boring after a while," Woodson told the *Sporting News*. This means that teams do not throw to their best receivers. It also means that Woodson does not get as many interceptions as some other cornerbacks. Statistics, however, do not matter to him. "What you learn in this league is that as long as you win, interceptions don't matter a bit."

OFF THE FIELD. Woodson lives with his wife and two children, Marikah and Demitrius, in Wexford, a suburb of Pittsburgh. He enjoys golf, swimming, and music. Woodson's favorite food is Mexican. He earned his degree in criminal justice at Purdue. Woodson serves on the board of directors of the Leukemia Society.

Woodson has advice for all of us. "We all have obstacles that we have to overcome," Woodson related in *Sports Illustrated for Kids*. "You have to figure out a way to outsmart the obstacles. Go around them. Go under them. Go through them."

Sources

Boys' Life, December 1994.
Chicago Tribune, January 11, 1996.
Orlando Sentinel, January 24, 1996.
Sporting News, November 29, 1993; January 17, 1994; January 16, 1995; January 23, 1995; January 15, 1996; January 22, 1996; February 5, 1996.
Sports Illustrated, September 7, 1992; January 16, 1995; January 23, 1995; September 11, 1995; January 19, 1996.

Sports Illustrated for Kids, September 1995.
Additional information provided by Pittsburgh Steelers.

WHERE TO WRITE:
C/O PITTSBURGH STEELERS,
300 STADIUM CIRCLE,
PITTSBURGH, PA 15212.

Index

Italic indicates series number; **boldface** indicates main entries and their page numbers.

H

Habetz, Alyson *2:* 40
Habitat for Humanity
    King, Betsy *2:* 237
Hall of Fame, LPGA
    Lopez, Nancy *1:* 343
Hamill, Dorothy *1:* 575-576, 579
Hamm, Mia *2:* **141-145**
Hanshin Tigers
    Fielder, Cecil *1:* 150
Harbaugh, Jim *2:* 93-94, 104
Hardaway, Anfernee *2:* **148-156,**
    313, 518
Hardaway, Tim *2:* 408
Harding, Tonya *1:* 41; *2:* 29, 218-
    219, 221-225, 246-248, 251
A Hard Road to Glory *1:* 35
Hargrave, Bubbles *2:* 376
Harmon, Butch *2:* 355
Harper, Alvin *2:* 171
Hart, Clyde *2:* 183
Hart Memorial Trophy
    Fedorov, Sergei *2:* 107-108,
      111
    Gretzky, Wayne *1:* 185, 320
    Hull, Brett *1:* 215
    Jagr, Jaromir *2:* 175
    Lemieux, Mario *1:* 323
    Messier, Mark *1:* 378, 380
Haynie, Sandra *2:* 240
Heavyweight championship
    Bowe, Riddick *1:* 87
    Foreman, George *1:* 164,
      167-168
    Holyfield, Evander *1:* 209-
      210
Heiden, Eric *1:* 60
Heisman Trophy
    Detmer, Ty *1:* 583
    Faulk, Marshall *2:* 91
    Jackson, Bo *1:* 226
    Rozier, Mike *1:* 582
    Sanders, Barry *1:* 497
    Staubach, Roger *1:* 463
    Testaverde, Vinny *1:* 583
    Torretta, Gino *1:* 583
    Walker, Herschel *1:* 122
    Ware, Andre *1:* 517
Henderson, Rickey *1:* 152

Hendrick, Rick *2:* 127
Henie, Sonja *1:* 40, 572-573; *2:* 30
Henry P. Iba Citizen Athlete
    Award
    Dawes, Dominique *2:* 54
Hermann Award
    Akers, Michelle *2:* 2
    Hamm, Mia *2:* 142-143
    Lalas, Alexi *2:* 282
Hershiser, Orel *2:* 14, 136
High School Player of the Year,
    basketball
    Hardaway, Anfernee *2:* 149
    Kidd, Jason *2:* 228
Hill, Brian *2:* 151
Hill, Calvin *2:* 155
Hill, Graham *1:* 159
Hill, Grant *2:* **155-162,** 230-231,
    410-411
Hit Man (See Easler, Mike)
Hodgkin's Disease *1:* 322
    Lemieux, Mario *2:* 179
Holman, Brian *2:* 192
Holmes, Larry *1:* 209
Holmgren, Mike *2:* 101
Holyfield, Evander *1:* 87-88,
    167, **204-211**
Honda-Broderick Cup
    Hamm, Mia *2:* 143
Hope, Bob *2:* 39, 529
Hornsby, Rogers *1:* 491; *2:* 139
Hostetler, Jeff *2:* 438
House, Tom *2:* 194
Houston Astros *1:* 117; *2:* 153
    Ryan, Nolan *1:* 470
Houston Gamblers
    Kelly, Jim *1:* 271
Houston Oilers
    Moon, Warren *1:* 407
Houston Rockets *1:* 53, 55, 242
    Olajuwon, Hakeem *1:* 358,
      422
Howard, Juwan *2:* 515, 519
Howe, Gordie *1:* 184, 187-188,
    216; *2:* 111
Howe, Mark *2:* 111
Howe, Steve *2:* 375
Hrdina, Jiri *2:* 177
Hull, Bobby *1:* 188, 212, 216
Hull, Brett *1:* **212-217;** *2:* 116

R

Rahal, Bobby *2:* 498

Raines, Tim *2:* 192

Randy Johnson Rule *2:* 192

Rawls, Betsy *2:* 240

Reagan, Ronald *2:* 175

Recchi, Mark *2:* 177

Reebok *1:* 91, 174, 431, 532

Reese, Wayne *2:* 89

Reeves, Dan *1:* 123, 125

Retton, Mary Lou *1:* 384-385; *2:* 52, 316, 320-321

Rexford, Bill *2:* 130

Reynolds, Butch *2:* 186

Rheaume, Manon *2:* **398-405**

Rice, Glen *2:* 329

Rice, Jerry *1:* 400, **446-452**; *2:* 169, 543-544

Rice, Jim *2:* 507

Riley, Dawn *2:* 299, 301

Riley, Pat *1:* 138, 241, 243; *2:* 329

Ripken, Cal, Jr. *1:* 153, **453-459**

Ripken, Cal, Sr. *1:* 453, 456

Roberts, Robin *2:* 119

Robinson, David *1:* 430, **460-466,** 499

Robinson, Frank *1:* 195, 457, 532

Robinson, Glenn *2:* 160, 230, **406-412,** 514

Robinson, Jackie *1:* 32; *2:* 507

Robitaille, Luc *2:* 116

Rod Carew on Hitting *1:* 116

Rodriguez, Ivan *1:* 169

Rookie of the Year, Baseball
Alomar, Sandy, Jr. *1:* 26
Nomo, Hideo *2:* 340-341, 346
Piazza, Mike *2:* 370, 375
Ripken, Cal, Jr. *1:* 455

Rookie of the Year, LPGA
Lopez, Nancy *1:* 340

Rookie of the Year, NASCAR
Earnhardt, Dale *2:* 72, 74
Gordon, Jeff *2:* 127

Rookie of the Year, NBA
Bird, Larry *1:* 53
Ewing, Patrick *1:* 137
Hardaway, Anfernee *2:* 151

Hill, Grant *2:* 155-156, 161, 231
Johnson, Larry *1:* 251
Jordan, Michael *1:* 256
Kidd, Jason *2:* 227-228, 231
Mourning, Alonzo *2:* 327
O'Neal, Shaquille *1:* 431
Robinson, David *1:* 464
Webber, Chris *2:* 513, 519

Rookie of the Year, NFL
Marino, Dan *1:* 370
Sanders, Barry *1:* 498
Smith, Emmitt *1:* 517
White, Reggie *1:* 558

Rookie of the Year, NHL
Lemieux, Mario *1:* 319

Rose, Jalen *2:* 157, 513, 515

Rose, Pete *1:* 192; *2:* 135

Ross, Bobby *2:* 428-429

Round Mound of Rebound (See Barkley, Charles)

Roy, Patrick *2:* **413-421**

Rudolph, Wilma *1:* 202; *2:* 489

Russell, Bill *1:* 55, 424, 426; *2:* 327

Rutgers University
Lalas, Alexi *2:* 282

Ruth, Babe *1:* 100, 152-153, 531; *2:* 14

Ryan, Buddy *1:* 559-560

Ryan Express (See Ryan, Nolan)

Ryan, Nolan *1:* 2, 24, 97, 116, 345, **467- 473;** *2:* 189, 194, 196

Ryder Cup
Faldo, Nick *1:* 142, 144

S

Sabatini, Gabriella *1:* 178-180; *2:* 384

Safe Passage Foundation *1:* 35

Sampras, Pete *1:* 11, 90, 107, **474-479;** *2:* 523

Sampson, Ralph *1:* 111, 422, 423

Samuelsson, Ulf *2:* 334

San Antonio Spurs
Robinson, David *1:* 463

Sanchez Vicario, Arantxa *1:* 93, 179, **480- 486,** 511; *2:* 379, 386-387, 526